GANDHI AND THE STOICS

Mahatma Gandhi on his visit to the London Round Table Conference.
Reprinted from Kusoom Vadgama, *An Indian Portia* (Delhi: Zubaan Books, 2011).

GANDHI AND THE STOICS

Modern Experiments on Ancient Values

RICHARD SORABJI

THE UNIVERSITY OF CHICAGO PRESS
CHICAGO

TO WOLFSON COLLEGE, OXFORD,
WITH ITS INTERNATIONAL, FAMILY,
AND RESEARCH VALUES

RICHARD SORABJI is Honorary Fellow of Wolfson College at Oxford University and fellow and professor emeritus at King's College, London. He is the editor of over one hundred books and author of twelve, including *Aristotle on Memory; Necessity, Cause, and Blame*; and *Self*, all published by the University of Chicago Press.

The University of Chicago Press, Chicago 60637
Oxford University Press, Oxford OX2 6DP

Printed in the United States of America

21 20 19 18 17 16 15 14 13 12   1 2 3 4 5

ISBN-13: 978-0-226-76882-3 (cloth)
ISBN-10: 0-226-76882-1 (cloth)

Library of Congress Cataloging-in-Publication Data

Sorabji, Richard, author.
Gandhi and the Stoics : modern experiments on ancient values / Richard Sorabji.
pages cm
Includes bibliographical references and index.
ISBN-13: 978-0-226-76882-3 (cloth : alkaline paper)
ISBN-10: 0-226-76882-1 (cloth : alkaline paper) 1. Gandhi, Mahatma, 1869–1948.
2. Stoics. 3. Philosophy, Comparative. I. Title.
DS481.G3S582 2012
188—dc23

2012010014

⊗ This paper meets the requirements of ANSI/NISO Z39.48-1992 (Permanence of Paper).

CONTENTS

ILLUSTRATIONS

ACKNOWLEDGMENTS

I am grateful to a large number of people. Vinit Haksar first alerted me to the philosophical interest of Gandhi. Phillip Mitsis encouraged me to present my thoughts on Gandhi in a seminar on the Stoics at New York University in a chair founded by another group whom I thank, the community of Cyprus, birthplace of the founder of Stoicism. Suparna Gooptu, Priyambardar Sarkar, Nirmalya Chakrabarti in Kolkata, and Vijay Tankha in Delhi invited me to try out some of my early thoughts. I benefited in Kolkata from Gopalkrishna Gandhi's gift of his book, *The Oxford India Gandhi: Essential Writings.* Mohamed Mehdi and I were each pleased to find that the other had thought of comparing Gandhi and Stoicism in different respects, he in a McGill Ph.D. dissertation. I learned a great deal when he and Akeel Bilgrami joined me in a conference at Fordham University, New York, and he, Uday Mehta, and Faisal Devji at a conference in Oxford. I have learned especially from a large number of conversations with Faisal Devji. I learned further from trying out the material at a conference on nonviolence at New Jersey City University, and in a seminar at the Graduate Center of the City University, New York. I acknowledge below the contributions to the seminar by Kyle Ferguson, Jordan Backstrom, and Cosim Sayid. I am grateful to Mohamed Mehdi as referee for extensive and perceptive comments, and to two additional anonymous referees. I am very grateful to Bhikhu Parekh for reading the manuscript and offering me the benefit of his knowledge of Gandhi's thought.

Finally, I have pleasure in dedicating the book to my college, Wolfson College, Oxford, which shares Gandhi's international values, but combines them with the family values that he downgraded (chapters 1 and 4).

ABBREVIATIONS

Autobiography	M. K. Gandhi, *An Autobiography*, or *The Story of My Experiments with Truth,* translated from 2 vols. of Gujarati by Mahadev Desai, Navajivan Publishing, Ahmedabad 1927 and 1929, Penguin edition, Harmondsworth 1982.
Chatterjee, *Religious Thought*	Margaret Chatterjee, *Gandhi's Religious Thought*, Notre Dame 1983.
CW	*Collected Works of Mahatma Gandhi*, 100 vols., Navajivan Publishing, Ahmedabad, 1955. A new edition is expected soon. Note that between *CW* and *eCW* there are disputed differences of content, and different volume and page numbers.
Day to Day	Mahadev Desai, *Day to Day with Gandhi*, 2nd ed., 9 vols., Varanasi 1968-73. The diary of Mahadev Desai, Gandhi's secretary from 1917 to 1942, translated from the Gujarati, with Gandhi's words in English.
eCW	*Collected Works of Mahatma Gandhi*, electronic edition on CD ROM, accessible online at http://www.gandhiserve.org/cwmg/cwmg.html. Note that between *CW* and *eCW* are disputed differences of content, and different volume and page numbers.
Gopalkrishna Gandhi, *Essential Writings*	Gopalkrishna Gandhi, ed., *The Oxford India Gandhi: Essential Writings*, New Delhi 2008.

Hind Swaraj	M. K. Gandhi, *Hind Swaraj*, published in Gujarati in Gandhi's newspaper, *Indian Opinion*, 1909, translated by Gandhi as *Indian Home Rule*, Phoenix, Natal, 1910 (citations from English version edited by Anthony J. Parel, in *M. K. Gandhi: Hind Swaraj and Other Writings*, Cambridge 1997).
Iyer, *Essential Writings*	R. Iyer, ed., *The Essential Writings of Mahatma Gandhi*, Ahmedabad 1990, Delhi 1993.
Iyer, *Thought*	R. Iyer, *The Moral and Political Thought of Mahatma Gandhi*, Delhi 1973 (citations from the paperback edition of 2000).
Iyer, *Writings*	R. Iyer, ed., *The Moral and Political Writings of Mahatma Gandhi*, 3 vols., Oxford 1986-87.
Parekh, *Political Philosophy*	Bhikhu Parekh, *Gandhi's Political Philosophy*, Notre Dame 1989.
PG	*Patrologia Graeca*, ed. J.-P. Migne, 166 volumes of the Greek Church Fathers, Paris 1857-1866.
Stobaeus	Stobaeus, *Eclogae*, vols. 1-2 ed. C. Wachsmuth, vols. 3-5 ed. O. Hense, Weidmann, 1884.
SVF	Hans von Arnim, *Stoicorum Veterum Fragmenta*, 3 vols, Stuttgart 1903-5, vol. 4, indexes by M. Adler, 1924.
Tolstoy, *Kingdom*	Leo Tolstoy, *The Kingdom of God Is Within You*, 1893, translated by Constance Garnett, New York 1894 (citations from the Dover Books reprint of 2006), and by Aylmer Maude, Oxford University Press, London, 1935.

INTRODUCTION

Gandhi's use of Platonic, Christian, and Stoic values: reinterpretation, experimentation, and mere convergence

GANDHI AS PHILOSOPHER

Was Gandhi a philosopher? Yes. He was forever seeking a consistent rationale for all that he did, and, more than any philosophers I have encountered, he subjected his views to relentless criticism, sometimes his own, but more often that of other people, which he published voluminously in his weekly newspapers. He wrote daily letters and sought to answer criticisms and explain his ideas in relation to new situations. Moreover, he thought himself obliged to *live* by what he taught. Philosophy as a way of *life* was the main tradition of ancient and of much subsequent philosophy, and went hand in hand with the *thinking* to which philosophy has sometimes more recently been confined. Gandhi was indeed a thinker, and he offered philosophical *reasons* for what he thought. His plea, for example, which we shall meet shortly, that we can learn from religions other than our own, a Hindu from Christ's Sermon on the Mount, has a profound philosophical basis concerning the nature of God and humanity. It should become clearer as we go along why I regard Gandhi as a philosopher, and I shall return to the question in chapter 11, both to confirm Gandhi's philosophical credentials and to draw a further conclusion about the unusual character of his philosophical method.

Was Gandhi influenced by the Stoics? No. He felt that some of his views chimed with those of the Stoics, when he read about them. But the Western thought that directly influenced him was rather Plato's account of Socrates and St. Matthew's of Christ, along with writing in those traditions. So Platonic and Christian influences will certainly need discussing. But whereas those influences are well known, few have noticed the much more indirect relation to the Stoics. Moreover, I hope that the comparison with the Stoics

Fig. I.1. Cynic Diogenes defied convention by wearing a coarse cloak, which he doubled up, in order to sleep in it. Here, living in his wine jar, he refuses a gift from Alexander the Great. Credit: *Alexander and Diogenes*, 1818 (oil on canvas) by Nicolas Andre Monsiau (1754–1837). Musee des Beaux-Arts, Rouen, France/ Peter Willi/ The Bridgeman Art Library.

will throw light not only on Gandhi, but also on the Stoics, or sometimes just on the ideas themselves.

CONVERGENCE OF STOIC VALUES AND GANDHI'S EXPERIMENTATION

Stoic values overlapped with Gandhi's to some extent. For different reasons, they both sought to practice emotional detachment. Yet, despite the detachment, they both believed in extending *love* to all humans, and both sought to engage in *politics*. The emotional detachment gave to both a certain kind of *freedom*. The concern for all humans took each of them in the direction of human duties, not of human rights. In deciding on duties, each had a conception of being true to your own individual persona. Each was correspondingly suspicious of universal rules of human conduct. Each was ready to accept poverty, though in different ways. Each sought in different ways to square ideals of perfection with imperfect people. Gandhi made a merit of unattainable ideals as a counsel of perfection.

It was particularly hard to realize the Stoic ideals of feeling kinship with all human beings and of detachment from most natural objectives. It was hard to combine detachment with love, whether of family or of all human beings, and again to combine it with the urgency of political objectives. Yet the emotional detachment had to be rigorous if it was to confer the kind of freedom they sought. It was at least rare to fulfill the ideals of being true to your own persona—although the Stoics had a favorite example in the Stoic Cato—and of exercising Stoic freedom—where they had to seek examples outside Stoicism in Socrates and Diogenes the Cynic.

The Stoics tended to admit that probably no Stoic had succeeded in putting all their ideals into practice. But Gandhi sought to practice most of these pursuits, and he did so in a wealth of instances and with almost daily commentary, discussion, explanation, and answers to criticism, all within living memory and preserved in writing for posterity. Insofar therefore as his ideals overlapped, albeit only in part, with those of the Stoics, he was showing how their ideals might fare if they actually were put into practice. I do not say that Gandhi always lived up to his ideals, but, given their difficulty, I think that the extent to which he did was remarkable. And in chapter 11, while recapitulating some of his lapses, I shall also offer a reason why I think not so much can be made of the lapses as is sometimes thought.

Gandhi has often been thought of as a politician who made up inconsistent rationales as he went along. I have already said that in fact he sought consistency. Stoicism can reveal how close he was in certain ways to an ethical system that was exceptionally self-consistent, and how little he would have had to change in order to achieve a higher measure of consistency himself.

Gandhi knew the Stoics at most only through a book on three major Stoics that he records having read between 1922 and 1924 in Yeravada jail and which he specially picked out from his huge volume of reading as "an inspiring book."[1] In addition, it was noticed by Gandhi's learned secretary, Mahadev Desai, that his ideals were sometimes remarkably similar to theirs.

1. Frederic William Farrar, *Seekers After God*, recorded by Gandhi in "My jail experiences XI," *Young India* 4 Sep 1924, in *CW*, vol. 25, p. 85. I thank Syed Mohamed Mehdi for the reference, which I draw with his permission from his McGill Ph.D. dissertation of 2007, "The Political Dimension of the Contemplative Life: Engagement and Disengagement in Plato, Seneca and Gandhi."

In translating into English and commenting on Gandhi's Gujarati translation of the *Gita*, we shall see that in two places Desai compares statements by the Stoics Epictetus and Marcus Aurelius. The comparison between Gandhi and the Stoics is not based on his having read them as he read some of Plato and of Christian thought. But even though the overlap of values was a mere convergence, and not the result of influence, Gandhi's devotion to experiment—the term he used in the title of his autobiography—throws light on the Stoics. The point is that both Gandhi and the Stoics were accused of having impractical and bizarre ethical ideals. If the Stoics did not succeed in achieving their ideals, whereas, I believe, Gandhi to a surprising extent did succeed, this is enough in some cases to throw light in both directions. With the Stoics we can see how some of their ideals might have worked out in practice, and on what scale, if any, they might have been practical, and whether it would have been for good or ill. With Gandhi, we can see how close he came to a much more consistent ethical system than he actually managed to formulate, and we can see where he deviated from consistency. The Stoics could have made him more the consistent philosopher. He could have shown the Stoics how far and in what ways some of their ideals would look practical and attractive, when realized.

Stoicism was founded in Athens by Zeno from Citium in Cyprus around 300 BCE. Zeno studied with philosophers of several schools in Athens, including Crates, a major representative of the shockingly eccentric Cynic individualism. Zeno managed to create out of these origins a respectable and lasting philosophy that became a model for many ordinary Greek citizens and eventually for Roman aristocrats and even for the emperor of the Roman world, Marcus Aurelius.

In later Stoicism from the late second century BCE, the Stoics seem to have responded to the criticism that the ideal Stoic sage had never been realized.[2] They turned their attention instead to the possibility of *progressing* in the direction of the ideal, and in the absence of the elusive ideal sage they turned to the ordinary person with ordinary problems and imperfections. This gave Stoic ethics an unparalleled ability to reach out across the millennia and tap us on the shoulder. It also inspired the continuous prose in the next three centuries of Cicero's expositions, and of the Stoics, Seneca, Epictetus, and Marcus Aurelius, which is much easier to read than the early Stoic fragments, although it presupposes that early Stoic thought.

2. The Stoic Panaetius represents the new approach at Cicero, *On Duties* 1.46.

The stress in this later Stoicism is on the *individual,* and I will focus on that aspect of Stoicism in chapters six to eight below. But the idea that different individuals have different duties will already have permeated the discussion of Gandhi's nonviolence in chapter 4. I shall also give a central place in Chapters One to Three and Nine to Ten to another feature of Stoicism that was introduced by its founder, Zeno. This is the idea that most of our ordinary objectives are *indifferent,* and we should therefore not be attached to them, but yet that some of them are naturally *preferred,* and with these it may be our *duty* at least in normal circumstances to prefer them, in a way that avoids attachment.

THE INFLUENCE OF PLATO'S SOCRATES, CHRIST, AND CHRISTIAN WRITERS RUSKIN AND TOLSTOY

It would not be satisfactory, or even possible, to compare such a multifaceted thinker as Gandhi with just one strand of thought. Inevitably, I shall refer to the Socratic and Christian strands, as well as others. It might be thought that since Gandhi knew these strands and was influenced by them, the comparison in these cases would be closer. That is not necessarily so. Where he was actually influenced, he still reinterpreted almost everything he read. The result is that ideas inspired by Western influence may finish up looking rather unlike the originals, whereas ideas that have merely *converged* with the Western ones may be less altered.

DIFFERENT FRUITS OF STUDYING INFLUENCE AND CONVERGENCE

Where there is mere convergence, mutual light can be thrown, as indicated, with the Stoics offering a consistent and justified ethical system, and Gandhi revealing how such a system might work out in practice. Where the attitudes of Gandhi and the Stoics are further apart, as for example with restrictions on property, the differences can throw light on the ideas themselves, showing how many different ways there are of accepting restrictions on property. Where Gandhi has been actually influenced, his reinterpretations of the influences bring out what matters particularly to him, as with Ruskin, and what new he has to contribute, as with Tolstoy. Moreover, with Gandhi undertaking such extensive reinterpretation, it helps more than usual for clarifying the resulting thought to see what the original influences were.

In chapter 11 I shall recapitulate some of the *Indian* influences on Gandhi, but more briefly because they have been more discussed, and require special Indianist knowledge.

GANDHI'S REINTERPRETATIONS

Gandhi read both Western and Indian ideas, and transformed both. What struck me first was his borrowings from the Christian and Platonic traditions and his similarities to Stoics and to some Platonists. What struck me next was his differences from any of them. Both are there, but the borrowings and similarities can be illuminating so long and only so long as the differences are recognized. I shall take a series of examples in which there were borrowings or at least similarities, but in most of them, there were reinterpretations as well.

RUSKIN

Ruskin's *Unto this Last* of 1862 impressed Gandhi enormously, and in 1908 he wrote an abbreviated paraphrase for Indian readers,[3] but he changed the original very considerably. Ruskin's title referred to Christ's parable about the worker who arrived *last* in the vineyard, and to whom the same wage was nonetheless given (unto this *last*) as the prompter workers received. Ruskin's was a devastating critique of economic science as he interpreted it in John Stuart Mill. He saw it as a science that omitted all moral terms, and treated humans as if they were machines that had no other interest than gaining economic advantage at the expense of other humans. Even in their own terms, he thought, they were failing to maximize their own wealth by ignoring such motives as affection and loyalty.

Gandhi omitted for his readers all Ruskin's redefinitions of key economic terms such as "just wage," "value," "wealth," "price," "production," and "capital." He also drew the conclusion that Indians should live in villages, not in cities, which he saw as designed to promote industry for the purpose of selective increase in individual wealth. Ruskin by contrast wanted to preserve factories, although he wanted them run by government in a beneficial way. He protested that he was not against private enterprise and private trade. At most he thought that there was an inevitable limit to the spread of factories, because humans need farming for food, trees for pure

3. Gandhi, *Sarvodaya* (Advancement of all), nine articles in *Indian Opinion*, 16 April–18 July 1908, repr. Iyer, *Writings*, vol. 3, pp. 410–32.

air, slopes for shade and running streams, and the beauty of nature for felicity. Gandhi omitted also Ruskin's insistence that equality among humans is impossible, because some men are superior and they should be leaders.

TOLSTOY

An even greater influence on Gandhi was Tolstoy, especially his book of 1894, *The Kingdom of God Is Within You*,[4] which again takes its title from Christ's sayings. Even better known is Christ's teaching that if someone strikes you on one cheek, you should offer the other cheek also.[5] Gandhi said that he had never been impressed by the conceptions of nonviolence he learned in India. He thought that they omitted compassion for suffering in animals and substituted a ritual of outward behavior that was satisfied without regard to suffering so long as killing was avoided. From Tolstoy by contrast he learned that nonviolence meant an inner attitude, an ocean of compassion and good will, and he borrowed Tolstoy's expression, "the law of love."

Gandhi reinterpreted violence again in that, as we shall see in chapter 4, he did not forbid all physical violence, although he sought unpersuasively to rule it out against Hitler. What he did forbid was hatred, not hatred of what some people did, but hatred of the people. Hatred is different from anger, and even though he deplored his own anger, anger is surely sometimes appropriate. Gandhi's rejection of hatred, however, is one of his most attractive ideals.

There are, I shall argue,[6] ways in which Gandhi's understanding of nonviolence went far beyond Tolstoy's. To take only the most important, Tolstoy says very little in *The Kingdom* to prepare people for the personal cost of civil disobedience, or noncooperation. As a result it could never become a mass movement. Gandhi, by contrast, insisted that only those with the ability to withstand the cost and remain nonviolent should attempt it.[7] Moreover, for true nonviolence he advocated various ascetic renunciations as prerequisite for acquiring the right emotional detachment.[8] Further, he made the sacrifice of nonviolent suffering of punishment not merely a price to be borne, but an actual weapon for breaking down the resolve of the colonial power. And this was not the only weapon he added to Tolstoy's armory.

4. For what follows, see chapter 4.
5. New Testament, Gospels of Matthew 5:39, Luke 6:29.
6. In chapter 4.
7. See chapter 6.
8. See chapter 1.

There was to be a "constructive" social program, of which spinning one's own clothes without relying on the British textile industry was merely the centerpiece. The constructive program, sufficiently pursued, could lead to complete independence in every sense, including the ousting of foreign domination.[9]

CHRIST'S SERMON ON THE MOUNT

Tolstoy's pleas for nonviolence followed the message of Christ's "Sermon on the Mount," a sermon for which Gandhi repeatedly expressed his admiration. In 1926 from July 24 to November 20, he gave a series of lectures to students of the Gujarat National College on what he saw as the centerpiece of the Christian Bible, the first six chapters of Matthew.[10] He called Christ's Sermon on the Mount "the pivot of the New Testament,"[11] and he started by praising Christ's message, "if anyone strikes you on the right cheek, turn to him the other also." He acclaimed as the quintessence of the New Testament the principle that it is only weakness if we beat the man who beats us.[12] Both the affirmation "blessed are the merciful" and the injunction to turn the other cheek he regarded as statements of *ahimsa*—nonviolence, which he called the highest duty.[13] The immediately following injunction, "and if anyone would sue you and take your coat, let him have your cloak as well," Gandhi understood as requiring nonpossession. He added that one should even be ready to give away one's own body, and he fitted in his qualification that if one had riches, one should hold them only as trustee for the poor.

It was not only this part of Christ's story and teaching that Gandhi admired. He was pleased that at the outset of his mission Christ had fasted in the desert for forty days and nights and he later called for fasting to be undertaken with a cheerful countenance, and carried out in private to avoid ostentation. He was pleased that Christ underwent and surmounted temptations in the desert, including the temptation of hunger that fasting con-

9. See again chapter 4.

10. *Day to Day*, vol. 8, pp. 226–328. Matthew's Gospel is also extensively quoted in Gandhi's Speech at Muir College Economic Society, Allahabad, 22 Dec 1916, in *Collected Works*, vol. 13, pp. 310–17, repr. from *The Leader* 25 Dec 1916. The Bible consists of the Jewish books, called the Old Testament, which Christ claimed to be fulfilling with his life and teaching. That life and teaching came to be recorded in the New Testament, principally in the Gospels of four disciples, Matthew, Mark, Luke, and John.

11. *Day to Day*, vol. 8, p. 265.

12. *Day to Day*, pp. 228–29.

13. *Day to Day*, pp. 285, 304–9.

fronts,[14] and he approved Christ's teaching of the Lord's Prayer. He took prayer to be necessary for enabling Christians to follow the preceding teaching.[15] Many Christians thought that Gandhi might easily be converted. But in fact he was once again reading selectively to create his own very different view.

He said that his reading of the Gospel had confirmed him in his own ideas, that the story of such divine life and action was possible among all countries and peoples, that nobody could claim the monopoly of inspired thoughts, that the Sermon on the Mount was very like the Hindu Bhagavadgita and was confirmed in the Muslim Koran, and that the ideas of the Lord's Prayer could be reproduced in the language of every religion, and had been expressed in a few letters in the ancient Vedic Gayatri Mantra.[16] The ideas of Christ's Sermon on the Mount belonged equally in other religions, not only in Christianity. Christ belongs not solely to Christianity, but to the whole world.[17] Gandhi's admiration for Christ's Sermon on the Mount looks different when it is seen in a context that disagrees with much else in Christianity, and he himself stressed how far it left him from being a Christian.[18] For example, he says elsewhere that he would value Christ's Sermon on the Mount even if Christ had never existed, just as he valued Krishna and Rama even though Krishna's conversation with Arjuna was imaginary.[19] It was against reason to suppose that God could beget, and he did not believe that Christ or anyone else was an incarnation of God, although any human might come close to God.[20] Nor could Christ's sacrifice redeem other people,[21] although Gandhi himself fasted "many times" in the ashrams to atone for other members when he felt *responsible* for their actions, or to draw their

14. *Day to Day*, pp. 259–60.

15. *Day to Day*, pp. 324–26.

16. *Day to Day*, pp. 227, 232, 265–66, 326.

17. *Harijan* 30 Jan 1937, 26 Jan 1947, p. 517; "What Jesus means to me," *Modern Review* Oct 1941, repr. Iyer, *Writings*, vol. 1, pp. 518–19.

18. On Gandhi's religious belief, I have learned particularly in what follows from Chatterjee, *Religious Thought*, and Parekh, *Political Philosophy*, ch. 3.

19. *Day to Day*, vol. 7, p. 135, Gandhi to missionaries in Calcutta, ibid., vol. 1, pp. 105–7, repr. Iyer, *Writings*, vol. 2, pp. 173–75; letter to P. Gandhi, 18 Apr 1932; "Who and where is God?" *Harijan* 22 June 1947. Compare interview to Dr. Crane, 25 Feb 1937, repr. *Harijan* 6 March 1937, pp. 25–28, and in *CW*, vol. 64, pp. 397–402.

20. Discussed by Anthony J. Parel, *Gandhi's Philosophy and the Quest for Harmony*, Cambridge 2006, pp. 186–87. See interview to Dr. Crane, 25 Feb 1937, repr. *Harijan* 6 March 1937, pp. 25–28, and in *CW*, vol. 64, pp. 397–402; "What Jesus means to me," *Modern Review* Oct 1941, repr. Iyer, *Writings*, vol. 1, pp. 518–19; "Who and where is God?," *Harijan* 22 June 1947.

21. "My jail experiences XI," *Young India* 4 Sep 1924, in *CW*, vol. 25, p. 85.

attention to the wrongness of what they did.[22] Christian conceptions could claim no monopoly. There is no such thing as one true religion.[23] Every religion and every individual that describes God attempts the impossible, because God is actually indescribable.[24] Moreover, Gandhi repeatedly said that he accepted the Jain view that only partial perspectives on the truth are available to any one person.[25] These two ideas, to which I will return shortly, were here used to support tolerance as between religions. His own religion was a synthesis of all religions, so he could not compare religions or advise what religion to prefer. He would call his synthesis Hinduism. A Christian attracted by Hinduism should call his synthesis "Christianity." There should be no conversion.[26] This was not a bland plea, "let us be nice to other religions." It was a philosophically thought-out rationale.

PARAPHRASE OF PLATO'S *APOLOGY*: SOCRATES AS A SOLDIER OF *TRUTH*

Gandhi admired not only Christ, but also Socrates, as Plato presents him, and accordingly he published a summary in 1908 of Plato's *Apology*. This was not an apology in our sense, but Plato's reconstruction of Socrates' very unapologetic defense when on trial for his life. Gandhi started in his preface by emphasizing Socrates' fearless acceptance of *death*, which made him an immortal exemplar. Readiness to accept death, we shall see,[27] was part of what Gandhi's nonviolence required. But death should be accepted only in the right cause. Gandhi saw Socrates as sharing his own cause of telling the *truth* and he called his paraphrase "Story of a satyagrahi" (translated as "soldier of truth"). Socrates told the truth to his compatriots about their own defects. He was Gandhi's model here in a way the Stoics could not have been, with their readiness to make exceptions to the ban on lying.

22. *Autobiography*, part 4, ch. 36; Usha Thakkar and Jayshree Mehta, eds., *Understanding Gandhi: Gandhians in Conversation with Fred J. Blum*, Delhi, 2011, p. 515.

23. *Autobiography*, part 2, ch. 15; "What Jesus means to me," *Modern Review*, Oct 1941, repr. Iyer, *Writings*, vol. 1, pp. 518–19; interview to Dr. Crane, repr. *Harijan* 6 March 1937, *CW*, vol. 64, p. 397; Shrirampur diary, *Harijan* 26 Jan 1947.

24. See introduction below.

25. Letter to Devdas Gandhi, 5 March 1922, *eCW*, vol. 26, p. 287; letter to Mathuradas Trikumji 6 March 1922, *eCW*, vol. 26, p. 288; "Three vital questions," *Young India* 21 Jan 1926, *eCW*, vol. 33, pp. 408–11; letter to D. B. Kalelkar, 2 July 1926, *eCW*, vol. 35, pp. 454–56; discussion with Dharmadev, *eCW*, vol. 59, pp. 494–97.

26. Interview to Dr. Crane, 25 Feb 1937, repr. *Harijan* 6 March 1937, pp. 25–28, and in *CW*, vol. 64, pp. 397–402; letter to Santoji Maharaj, 22 July 1927, *CW*, vol. 34, pp. 89–95; "What Jesus means to me," *Modern Review* Oct 1941, repr. Iyer, *Writings*, vol. 1, pp. 518–19.

27. Chapter 4 below.

Satyagraha was a term that Gandhi coined himself in 1908 as a name for his kind of nonviolent resistance. *Satya* means truth in Sanskrit, and *agraha*, as applied to truth, was glossed by Gandhi as firmness, a relentless search and determination to reach (truth) and a holding onto (truth).[28] Bhikhu Parekh explains that in Gandhi's Gujarati, as opposed to Sanskrit, *agraha* means insisting on something without becoming obstinate or uncompromising.[29] It was an insistence on truth in oneself and in one's interlocutor. In *Satyagraha in South Africa*, Gandhi added that the firmness *engenders* force, evidently the force used in nonviolent resistance, and he inferred (surprisingly) that it therefore becomes a *synonym* for such force. It turns out that he means that it is the force "born of" (the insistence on) truth, which he called "truth-force" or "soul-force." The text went on to say that the force is "born of" love as well as of truth, and it works through love and suffering without causing anyone else to suffer.

Gandhi's summary of Plato's *Apology* was much closer to the original than was the abbreviated paraphrase of Ruskin. But the interest in *truth* led to at least two reinterpretations. First, Gandhi substituted reference to the man of *truth* for Plato's reference to the *good* man (*agathos*) as always happy. Second, Gandhi summarized the account ascribed to Socrates of his practice, which brought in truth in a different way, since Socrates always sought for *consistency* in himself and his interlocutors. But Gandhi once again differed from his source, as he did from Tolstoy's treatment of civil disobedience, by adding the emotional considerations that the source—this time Plato—had omitted. In the case of Socrates, Plato shows how badly Socrates' interlocutors often reacted to being shown that they were inconsistent. Similarly in the *Apology*, Plato presented Socrates as unwilling to compromise not only with his accusers, but even with the jury. Although Gandhi presented Plato's Socrates in 1908 as a practitioner of *satyagraha*, by 1909 in *Hind Swaraj* he had analyzed his own practice further, and recognized soul-force as imposing the constraint of hurting no one else.[30] Increasingly, he went on to stress good will and love as an integral part of *satyagraha*, and love was used, as Bhikhu Parekh has emphasized,[31] to "open the ears" of his interlocutors and to help them change their minds and reach a common agreement. Socrates, in Plato's account, was a soldier of truth

28. Gandhi, *Satyagraha in South Africa*, Ahmedabad 1928, pp. 102–6 in the 1950 edition; *Autobiography* 1927 and 1929, part 4, ch. 26; *Young India* March 1921 and March 1925, cited by Iyer, *Thought*, pp. 269–73.

29. Parekh, *Political Philosophy*, ch. 6, p. 143.

30. *Hind Swaraj*, pp. 90–92.

31. Parekh, *Political Philosophy*, pp. 143–44. See below, chapter 4.

in a straightforward sense. But as Gandhi reflected on his own practice, he reinterpreted his concept of *satyagraha* in the direction of amity that moved beyond the model of Socrates.

A PLACE FOR ENERGY, INTENSITY, AND EVEN EMOTION IN GANDHI AND THE STOICS

Although I have spoken of Gandhi and the Stoics as being emotionally *detached*, Gandhi opened other people's ears by appealing, through his own love and suffering, to their *emotions*. Was this concern with emotions un-Stoic? No; for one thing, I shall explain in chapter 1 that Gandhi's love was like Stoic true love in involving a certain detachment. The same was true of his suffering. It would be better to speak of his acceptance of austerities and punishment, because he showed very little sign of emotional suffering when imprisoned. I shall also explain in chapter 1 that the Stoics allowed a place for energy, intensity, and even for certain types of emotion—provided they involved no misconceptions. There was one group on which Gandhi seemed to bestow warm family love, and that was the circle of his closest workers, and they did not feel this as compromised by his also imposing what they recognized as harsh discipline.

MORAL CONSCIENCE

Gandhi made very extensive appeal to a concept that the Christian St. Paul had adapted to Christian uses from Graeco-Roman thought—the concept of *conscience*. Gandhi preferred following one's conscience to following law or scripture. But he diverged from St. Paul, and from the main Christian tradition, in treating his own conscience, for example over the need to fast, as often indubitable.[32] This was despite his acceptance as a general rule of his human fallibility. His reinterpretation of the inner voice as infallible will have attracted him to Socrates' treatment of the divine voice, when he summarized Plato's *Apology*. Socrates, in Plato's representation, regards the divine voice as indubitable. Some ancient Platonists equated that voice with conscience, and in his summary of Plato's *Apology* Gandhi included one of the passages referring to the divine voice. His belief in the

32. See chapter 8. On faith in his inner voice: letter to Rajagopalachari, 15 Sep 1924, repr. Iyer, *Writings*, vol. 2, pp. 128–29; "All about the fast," *Harijan* 8 July 1933, repr. Iyer, *Writings*, vol. 2, p. 132; letter to Bhuskute, 25 May 1932, repr. Iyer, *Writings*, vol. 2, p. 130.

voice's indubitability will have been connected with his attitude to faith as opposed to reason.

FAITH

The importance of faith was a Christian motif, but Gandhi reinterpreted it again by treating reason as fallible, faith as infallible. The claim of infallibility was made in response to an Englishman who asked Gandhi to help him believe in God. He replied that when the felt presence of God rules the heart and conduct, not merely the intellect, that is when faith is infallible.[33] The realization of God is then definite and immovable, whereas reason is easily upset by superior logic.[34] But how does one reach the realization of God's presence? Gandhi tells his English agnostic inquirer that he feels heaven to God, the purer he tries to become.[35] Elsewhere he says that he engages in his fasts in the hope of gaining a glimpse of God.[36] We shall see in chapter 8 his descriptions of training yourself to listen for the inner voice of God. Most often he says that he sees Rama, or sees God in the face of the starving millions or the suffering workers and in serving the oppressed Dalits and others.[37]

On the other hand, faith is not infallible outside its own sphere. Intellect and faith must each be given its own province. Faith in the divine origin of Jesus may be set aside, because it goes against intellect, and that encourages delusions.[38] But Gandhi still offered a striking defense of faith by drawing attention to its ubiquity in the heart of medical science. To a doctor who wrote to him that faith is believing unreasonably he replied that he would need faith in order to accept the doctor's medicines.[39] The same was true in general in ordinary matters of life. Without it "the world would come to naught in a moment." Proponents of rationalism themselves relied on it.[40]

It is not clear, however, that faith in a doctor's prescriptions, important as it is, is quite the same as the religious faith of which Gandhi was

33. "God is," *Young India* 11 Oct 1928, p. 368.

34. Speech at Congress Workers' Conference, *Harijan* 31 March 1946, *CW*, vol. 82, p. 368.

35. "God is," *Young India* 11 Oct 1928, p. 341.

36. Letter to Santoji Maharaj, 2 July 1927, repr. Iyer, *Writings*, vol. 1, p. 89, and *CW*, vol. 34, p. 94.

37. *Young India* 24 Sep 1925; 24 March 1927; *Autobiography*, part 5, ch. 14, p. 373; *Day to Day*, vol. 7, p. 135.

38. *Day to Day*, vol. 8, p. 230.

39. "Faith v reason," *Young India* 14 Apr 1927.

40. "Tyranny of words," *Young India* 14 Oct 1926.

speaking.[41] Science is particularly dependent on faith in the more ordinary sense. It has been pointed out that it depends on faith in testimony, because science seeks to advance on the basis of earlier discoveries and does not want each scientist to repeat centuries of earlier experiment before making any new advance. To suppose that the earlier experimental results are believed by beginning scientists merely on the basis of inference about their probability would be to confine belief to the narrow sphere of the beginner's experience.[42] But there is a difference between Gandhi's religious faith and faith in the scientific record. Faith in the scientific record can be rational, as has been argued in defense of the Nyaya school of Indian philosophy, which viewed faith in testimony as rational. Gandhi preferred to speak of religious faith as *distinct* from reason.

HOW ARE DUTIES CONNECTED WITH RIGHTS?

We may seem to be on familiar Western ground when Gandhi says that there are no rights without duties. This claim has been advanced in modern Western thought in order to add precision to the concept of rights. A person has a right to something when *others* have a duty to allow him access to it. The connection that Gandhi makes is characteristically and startlingly different. It is only if I first perform my duties that *I—the self-same person*—can acquire any rights for myself.

NONVIOLENCE, *AHIMSA*

It was not only Western sources that Gandhi reinterpreted. We have already seen the example of his rejecting the Indian conception of nonviolence as he knew it, as rules about nonkilling, in favor of the idea of compassion. He reinterpreted the treatment of violence also in the Bhagavadgita (or Gita), where the Lord Krishna told the warrior Arjuna to overcome his reluctance to fight in the battle that led to such comprehensive carnage. According to Gandhi, Krishna was in no way accepting violence. The subject of violence was not even raised, because it never occurred to Arjuna not to engage in killing. What beset him was merely a squeamishness about killing his *relatives*, and it is a theme of the Bhagavadgita that one should not privi-

41. I am grateful to Akeel Bilgrami for the point.

42. See Arindam Chakrabarti's survey of the subject in his introduction to Bimal Matilal and Arindam Chakrabarti, eds., *Knowing from Words*, Dordrecht, 1994, 1–21.

lege one's relatives.[43] But even if Gandhi's understanding of the Gita can be taken as right so far, it needs to be added that his discussion of the Gita seems to reinterpret it again when he says that one should kill one's relatives *first*.[44] Gandhi was impressed as a child by a play about the truthful Harishchandra, and was prepared to change the story as he knew it. When Harishchandra, in fidelity to a vow, raised his hand to behead his wife, he was not violent. For attitude is all-important, and "his heart was filled with compassion. The poet says that he had hardened his heart, but in truth he had hardened only his hand."[45]

SPIRITUAL LIBERATION, *MOKSHA*

Scholars of Indian thought have brought out how Gandhi also changed the concept of *moksha*, spiritual liberation.[46] It is normally seen as escape from rebirth and some kind of unification with the supreme God, Brahman. Gandhi may have thought of it as involving a vision of God. But it has been pointed out that Gandhi used a prayer in his ashram (resident community) that, so far from seeking escape from rebirth, renounced escape from rebirth, and desired only release from misery of those suffering.[47] I do not think, however, that he went quite as far as this in his explicit statements. He hoped in 1908 that after one more life following his present path he would escape rebirth.[48] In 1921 he said:[49] "I do want to attain *moksha*. I do not want to be reborn. But if I have to be reborn, I should be born as an untouchable, so that I may share their sorrows, sufferings, and the affronts levelled at them, in order that I may endeavour to free myself and them from that miserable condition. I therefore prayed that if I should be born again, I should do so not as a Brahmin, Kshatriya, Vaisya, or Sudra, but as an *Atishudra* [Shudra of Shudras]." That was still his view in 1925, when he said that

43. Gandhi, *Discourse* 8 *on the Gita*, ch. 2, 4 March 1926, *CW*, vol. 32, p. 103; "Meaning of the Gita," *Navajivan* 11 Oct 1925, repr. Iyer, *Writings*, vol. 1, p. 82; Letter to Santoji Maharaj, 2 July 1927, CW, vol. 34, p. 90, repr. Iyer, *Writings*, vol. 1, p. 85; Gandhi, "The law of our being," *Harijan* 26 Sep 1936, repr. Iyer, *Writings*, vol. 2, pp. 324–27.

44. I thank Faisal Devji for alerting me to this tendency in Gandhi. See chapter 1.

45. I thank Cosim Sayid for pointing out the reinterpretation involved here.

46. Chatterjee, *Religious Thought*, ch. 9; Parekh, *Political Philosophy*, pp. 100–107; Anthony J. Parel, *Gandhi's Philosophy and the Quest for Harmony*.

47. Chandrakant Kaji, ed., *Prayer*, Ahmedabad, Apr 1977, appendix 1, quoted by Chatterjee, *Religious Thought*, p. 27.

48. Letter to Maganlal Gandhi, 21 May 1908, *eCW*, vol. 8, p. 332.

49. Speech at suppressed classes conference, Ahmedabad, 13 Apr 1921, printed in *Young India* 27 Apr, 4 May 1921, in *eCW*, vol. 23, p. 45; repeated in interview with Adi-Hindu deputation, 4 Feb 1932, *eCW*, vol. 63, p. 109.

if he was reborn, he would like to be a perfect person (*purnapurusha*), but in an Antyaja family.[50] What was unusual was the route to *moksha* through helping the oppressed, rather than through retreat from the world, and the idea that this route could already allow a glimpse of God, anticipating the hoped-for vision in *moksha*. As we saw in connection with his concept of faith, he claimed to see Rama in the starving millions of India and to be face to face with God in meeting the suffering indigo workers and in serving the suffering. In general he felt the presence of God at the painful sights he saw in the world.[51]

Gandhi took over the Indian traditions in which *moksha* and unification with God, Brahman, are approached not only through intellectual meditation, but through spiritual exercises that discipline the body and the senses. But whereas traditionally the spiritual preparation required solitary retreat, it has been pointed out that Gandhi's spiritual exercises were of a very different sort. Basic ones included serving Dalits (then called Untouchables), spinning,[52] and the cleaning of ashram latrines.

MULTIPLE PARTIAL TRUTHS, *ANEKÂNTAVÂDA*

We have seen Gandhi claiming to follow the Jain view that each person knows only partial truths, *anekântavâda*. He describes this most fully by giving the Jain analogy of seven blind men trying to describe an elephant. One feels only its trunk, one its ear, one its leg, one its back, one its tusk, and so on.[53] The idea of partial perspectives was used by the Jains, as it was later used by John Stuart Mill,[54] to support religious tolerance. But Gandhi used it not only for this purpose, but also to draw a surprising conclusion going far beyond Jainism, which I shall describe at the end of the book in chapter 11.

FURTHER AFFINITIES WITH PLATONISM AND CHRISTIANITY

I have so far been talking of Gandhi's reinterpretations of what he read or knew about. But there are affinities with strands in Platonism or Chris-

50. Speech at Virsad, 12 Feb 1925, *eCW*, vol. 30, p. 254

51. Gandhi, *Young India* 24 Sep 1925, 24 March 1927; *Autobiography*, part 4, ch. 14, p. 373; *Day to Day*, vol 7, p. 135; *Harijan* 29 Aug 1926.

52. *Young India* 24 Sep 1925; *Day to Day*, vol. 2, letter of 19 May 1919; *Harijan* 20 Apr 1935; speech at Gandhi Seva Sangh, 22 Feb 1940, repr. Iyer, *Writings*, vol. 1, p. 427.

53. "Three vital questions," *Young India* 21 Jan 1926, *eCW*, vol. 33, pp. 408–11.

54. J. S. Mill, *On Liberty*, ch. 2.

tianity even in cases where it is not clear how much, if anything, he knew about them.

GOD'S INDESCRIBABILITY, *NIRGUNA*

We saw above the idea that God is indescribable, *nirguna* not *saguna*, and that this was used to support tolerance as between religions. Gandhi thought of God not as a person, but as a force or law and a pure consciousness.[55] The Upanishads, the early philosophical scriptures, could say only what God was not: "not this, not this." Gandhi gives examples of opposite attributes that we are tempted to ascribe. God is creative and noncreative, one and many, large and small. Reason cannot grasp God, and faith is needed instead. Even the Jains, who deny that God creates, find that they need images of him. Saraswati, the goddess of wisdom, and Ganesh, the elephant god, are names of the indescribable God. We need falsely to imagine something that has no form or attributes.[56] And yet even "nirguna," the indescribable, is a misdescription. Gandhi's favorite description, "God is truth," or "Truth is God," is imperfect, although it helps us avoid some pitfalls.[57]

In calling God indescribable, Gandhi was following a strand in Hinduism, and I doubt if he will have known how close it was to some aspects of Platonism. Already Plato set out the conflicting conclusions that would follow if there existed such a thing as the One.[58] Even early Platonists treated God as indescribable and later the Neoplatonists construed Plato's One as the supreme and indescribable God. Their founder, Plotinus, shared a common source of influence with Gandhi, since he had tried to find out all he could about the Indian thought of his time in the third century CE. The last head of the Athenian Neoplatonist school in the sixth century, Damascius, added, like Gandhi, that we cannot even say what God is not. And all this influenced one strand in Christianity, since it was imitated by pseudo-Dionysius, who passed off his Neoplatonizing "negative theology"

55. *Young India* 11 Oct 1928; "Question box," *Harijan* 28 July 1946, "Who and where is God?," *Harijan* 22 June 1947.

56. *Young India* 21 Jan 1926; letter to P. Gandhi, 18 Apr 1932, repr. Iyer, *Writings*, vol. 2, pp. 173–75; "History of the Satyagraha ashram," 1932, *CW*, vol. 50, pp. 200–201, first published Ahmedabad 1955.

57. Letter to Santoji Maharaj, 2 July 1927, *CW*, vol 34, pp. 93–94, repr. Iyer, *Writings*, vol. 1, pp. 88–89; letters to boys and girls, 21 March 1932, and to P. Gandhi, 18 Apr 1932, repr. Iyer, *Writings*, vol. 2, pp. 172–75.

58. Plato, *Parmenides*.

as a Christian work.[59] But any closeness of Gandhi to Platonists and Christians here may owe something to a common Indian influence, but owes nothing, I believe, to a Western influence on Gandhi.

REINCARNATION

Of course it was only Platonists, not Christians, who shared Gandhi's belief in reincarnation. And even on the prospect of escape from rebirth Gandhi and Plato had somewhat different expectations, Plato hoping for at least temporary escape from rebirth after one, or elsewhere three, incarnations as a philosopher.[60] Gandhi hoped for permanent escape from rebirth, we saw, after one more incarnation. Plato was unlike Gandhi insofar as he suggested the possibility of *choosing* your next life, with a choice free precisely to avoid the errors of the last one.[61] Gandhi emphasized *karma*, the influence of your previous lives on the next one, and concluded that reform could not be achieved by many people at the same time, because of the weight of influence from past lives.[62]

BRAHMACHARYA, CELIBACY, AND SELF-PURIFICATION

Gandhi was drawn to celibacy by the Indian tradition of *brahmacharya*, not by the Western religious traditions. But he spoke of it and of the difficulties of practicing it in terms drawn from Christianity, even alluding to original sin, the dysfunctionality inherited, according to the tradition of St. Augustine, from the first human being. Gandhi's renunciation of sexual relations leaves him looking close to the ascetic traditions of Christianity. For the male Fathers in the desert, sexual abstinence was a prominent concern; I shall point out in chapter 1 that their recorded experiences were often close to Gandhi's own.

Whether or not Gandhi read Plato's *Phaedo* in its entirety, he is likely to have known that Plato depicted Socrates as having turned away all his life from bodily concerns to prepare himself for the soul's separation at death from the body. Socrates' asceticism is described vividly in another work of

59. For a survey, see my *The Philosophy of the Commentators* 200–600 *AD: A Sourcebook*, London and Ithaca, N.Y. 2005, vol. 1, ch. 16.

60. Plato, *Phaedo* 80C–82D; *Phaedrus* 248E–249D.

61. Plato, *Republic* 617E3 ff.

62. See chapter 4 below.

Plato's that Gandhi is thought to have read, the *Symposium*.[63] There Plato makes Alcibiades describe Socrates' imperviousness to cold and to his own homosexual advances. Gandhi likes to use a metaphor from Plato, that the body is a prison for the soul, and he uses it in expounding the Gita, in passages where the Gita does not use it.[64] Plotinus was later to describe Socratic purification from bodily concerns as the first step in the process of seeking union with God.

SELF-SACRIFICE

Gandhi inherited from India a rich tradition of stories that he admired about self-sacrifice and sacrifice of one's dearest. The Jewish, Christian, and Platonist traditions are not quite so rich. But this will have increased the appeal to Gandhi of the stories of the death of Socrates, the death of Christ, and the readiness of Abraham to slay his only son at God's command.

LOOKING AT GANDHI'S PHILOSOPHY TO ASSESS HIS CONSISTENCY

To return to my characterization of Gandhi as a philosopher, I think we need to look at his *philosophy*, before we can assess the *consistency* of his statements and what he stood for, and therefore of his life as a whole. These all appear more consistent when we recognize the underlying philosophy with its reinterpretations and subtleties. To take three examples, the complex criteria, to be discussed in chapter 4, for what can count as nonviolent need to be understood, if we are to avoid a misleading appearance of inconsistency. Again, if different people have special duties of their own—a different *svadharma*—then different advice to them need be no sign of inconsistency. Third, the revised concept of *moksha* helps to show how Gandhi could consistently combine being a spiritual leader with being a politician, although that will become clearer again, when we discuss the dominance for Gandhi of spirituality over politics.[65] Of course, Gandhi changed his mind in the light of growing experience, and quite rightly so. But even then, the changes

63. At the Mani Bhavan, where Gandhi once lived in Mumbai, his reading of the *Symposium* is represented by a later translation in the bookshelves.

64. Gandhi is likely to have got the idea from Plato, *Phaedo* 62B, or expositions of it, rather than from Plato, *Cratylus* 400C. Gandhi, letter to P. Gandhi, 18 Apr 1932, repr. Iyer, *Writings*, vol. 2, pp. 173–75; *Discourses on the Gita*, 34 on 2.59, 3 Apr, and 64 on 4.9, 8 May 1926, *CW*, vol. 32, p. 137; *eCW*, vol. 37, p. 174.

65. In chapter 2 below.

did not always involve retraction, so much as addition to what he had said before. An example will be encountered again in chapter 4, where Gandhi added extra criteria that would have to be met if a killing was to qualify as nonviolent. But in this case he did not withdraw the criteria he had used before, but rather added an extra criterion, in order to deal with newly encountered situations.

THE STOICS—AGAIN

One idea in Stoicism that is hard to understand is that even in trivial activities, like walking about, the virtuous person performs them in an inimitably virtuous way. Descriptions of Gandhi give a hint of something comparable in the meticulousness that he exercised and expected of others in his circle, in apparently trivial details. His placing his clothes and his little cup in the right place, to avoid wasting time in looking for them, went along with his strictness in teaching, his requiring of his followers great precision and meticulous care. It also connected with his insistence on truth and his rejection of half-measures. He gave advice to his sons and daughters-in-law about such small details as threading the oil lamp, reusing match sticks, keeping vegetable skins for the cow, stitching clothes and keeping them clean, viewing these as matters of character building. In his letters he was brief, neat, and careful to avoid the need for rewriting, preferring reused paper and dispensing, if possible, with envelopes. He insisted that his handwriting to them would improve if theirs did to him.[66]

In the chapters that follow, I shall on the whole be discussing Gandhi and the Stoics together, usually addressing very similar ideas. Even where their views, as on poverty, are further apart, as with their restrictions on property, this still reveals the wide range of approaches available to those ready to accept poverty and where Gandhi and the Stoics fit into the range. But in addition to the Stoics, Plato's Socrates and Christianity will inevitably enter the story, and in the chapters on conscience, on nonviolence, and on property restrictions, one or other of them will provide the main comparison with Gandhi. Chapter 10 will concentrate on the Stoics and chapter 11 on Gandhi.

66. Sucheta Kripalani, in Usha Thakkar and Jayshree Mehta, eds., *Understanding Gandhi: Gandhians in Conversation with Fred J. Blum*, 2011, p. 464; Nilam Parikh, ed., *Gandhi Wrote to His Sons and Daughters-in-Law "Be Fragrant Wherever You Go,"* Delhi 2008, pp. xxviii–xxxiii, xiv.

Fig. I.2. The Stoic Chrysippus, scantily dressed as impervious to cold, but intent on teaching. Reprinted from Paul Zanker, *The Mask of Socrates: The Image of the Intellectual in Antiquity*, translated by Alan Shapiro (Berkeley: University of California Press, 1995).

The pictures in the book show an idealized Cynic, a Stoic (Chrysippus), and Gandhi. In each case, as has been brilliantly brought out for the Greeks by Paul Zanker,[67] there is something symbolic about their attire. There is also something in common. The Cynic Diogenes defied convention by wearing a coarse cloak doubled up so that he could also sleep in it. Here, living in his wine jar, he refuses any gift from Alexander the Great, other than "standing out of his light." The lack of any undervest in the Stoic shows his indifference to cold, while at the same time he is intent on his teaching.

67. Paul Zanker, *The Mask of Socrates*, Berkeley and Los Angeles 1995.

Gandhi shortened his costume, to avoid wasteful cost, and insisted on its being made of homespun cloth, as against refined cloth made by machines. Diogenes and Gandhi alike created profound shock, in Gandhi's case on some of the British, including, notoriously, the eventual Prime Minister, Winston Churchill.

CHAPTER ONE

Emotional detachment: how to square it with love of family and all humans in the Stoics and Gandhi[1]

The ancient Greek and Roman Stoics did not influence Gandhi, but some of their values were very similar. On the subject of emotional detachment more than anywhere, I think that Gandhi and the Stoics throw light on each other. I have indicated how in the introduction. The Stoics tended to acknowledge that no Stoic had been able to achieve their ideals in practice.[2] Gandhi tried to put into practice all his ideals and discussed the results, publishing criticisms of the results and his own replies. So he helps us to see to what extent similar Stoic ideals would have been practical and to what extent their outcome would have been good or bad. Conversely, Gandhi has been seen as inconsistent, more politician than philosopher. The logically structured philosophy of the Stoics could have provided Gandhi with a consistent rationale for some of his attitudes. We can see how close he came to agreeing with such a rationale, and where he deviated from it.

We shall see in chapter 4 that Gandhi believed in an attitude of love for all. That is what he meant by nonviolence. Love for all humans was also desiderated by the Stoics, on the model of family love. That raises the first of two questions I want to ask about emotional detachment. How can Gandhi or the Stoics square emotional detachment with family love or universal love, for is not love an emotion? In the next chapter I shall raise a second question: how can either party square emotional detachment with political activity, which both believed in, for can political activity be emotionally detached?

1. This chapter updates a paper first delivered in January 2009 for publication by Dr. Suparna Gooptu at the Gandhian Studies Centre, Department of History, University of Calcutta, and due to be published in *Philosophy as Samvada and Svaraja,* ed. Shail Mayaram et al.

2. Seneca, however, suggested that Cato the Younger might even have exceeded them. *On the Constancy of the Wise* 7.1.

THE STOICS AND FAMILY LOVE FOR ALL HUMANS

On the first question, how emotional detachment can be squared with love, Bhikhu Parekh has said that Gandhi had no successful answer. Partly, he failed to live up to the idea of emotional detachment since politics often made him despondent or angry. Partly, he argued his case by weakening love from an emotion to mere good will.[3] Against this I shall present below the case made by one of the late Stoics, Epictetus, for saying that what looks like mere good will can be a truer form of love.

Already in the third century BC, the Stoics said something unprecedented in Western philosophy: that a certain kind of love, like that found among the closest family members, should be extended to all human beings, even to foreigners who spoke no Greek and to slaves. Such an extension would be natural. That is not to say that it would be easy, but it would be in accordance with nature.[4] This novel view was to have a benign effect at intervals in European history. Over 1800 years later, in the sixteenth century CE, a version of it was used to oppose the conquest of the American Indians in Latin America.[5]

THE STOICS AND EMOTIONAL DETACHMENT

Family love is a strong emotion. So how could the Stoics square setting up family love as a model with another recommendation of theirs. They thought (and this is an aspect of Stoicism with which I do not agree) that we should get rid of many, I think most, of our emotions. Their principal objection to most emotions was that they involve *mistaken* evaluations. To follow an account of Stoic emotion that I have sought to substantiate elsewhere,[6] the Stoics thought that one of the very few things that matters in and of itself was good or bad character. But we get emotional about a host of other things: wealth, pleasure, health, and life itself. These things have

3. Parekh, *Political Philosophy*, ch. 4, pp. 97–99.

4. The view is described by Cicero, *On Ends* 3. 62–68, and by Hierocles, *Elements of Ethics*, as excerpted by Stobaeus, vol. 4, pp. 671.7–673.11. It is sketched in my *Animal Minds and Human Morals*, London 1993, ch. 10.

5. In *The Ethics of War: Shared Problems in Different Traditions*, ed. Richard Sorabji and David Rodin, Aldershot 2006, pp. 13–29, I cited at p. 18 three sixteenth-century Spanish defenses of the American Indians in: Francisco de Vitoria, *On Civil Power*; *On the Indians*, question 3, articles 1–3; Bartolomé de Las Casas, *Apologetic History of the Indians*.

6. Richard Sorabji, *Emotion and Peace of Mind*, Oxford 2000, chs. 2, 11, 13, 15–16, with further support in "Did the Stoics value emotion and feeling?" *Philosophical Quarterly* 59, 2009, pp. 150–62.

a certain limited value (*axia*).[7] They are, or are connected with, objectives that we are naturally constituted to pursue, and the Stoics believed that we should follow nature.[8] Moreover, these objectives acquire a derivative value from the fact that good character, the objective that really matters, consists in a readiness to pursue the other natural objectives for ourselves and others.[9] So it is our duty to pursue these objectives energetically. But what if through no fault of our own we fail to secure them for ourselves or others? Then what matters is whether we exercised good character by pursuing them in the right way, and whether the intended recipients exercise good character in face of their failure to get them. The objectives do not in themselves matter in the same way as good character. In Stoic terminology, these objectives are *indifferent*, although they are indifferents that it is normally natural and right to pursue. They are called *preferred* indifferents.[10] I shall return repeatedly to the idea of preferred indifferents in the following chapters, and will attempt to describe it a little more fully each time. Belief in preferred indifferents allows room for, and even requires, energetic action and sometimes intensity. Energy is required in pursuing indifferent natural objectives for oneself and others, so long as they are seen for what they are: natural, but in the end indifferent. Some objectives, like good character, are not indifferent, and so a certain *intensity* is called for in trying to educate people in the right direction. But here too one must avoid mistakes, such as distress if education proves impossible. One accepted kind of education is called erotic. The Stoic sage, if male, is allowed to be in *love* with a young man, provided that his erotic love (*erôs*) is not an emotion, but an *epibolê*. An *epibolê* is defined as a two-stage impulse, and I have conjectured that the idea is an impulse to make friends for the further purpose, not of sex, but of educating a promising young man towards good character.[11]

This acceptable type of *erôs* is not classified as emotion, but some emotions are accepted. The Stoic is free, for example, to feel joy at God's good governance of the universe, because that involves no mistaken evaluations.

7. Diogenes Laertius, *Lives of Eminent Philosophers*, 7.105; Stobaeus vol. 2, pp. 84.18–85.11; Cicero, *On Ends* 3.20

8. Cicero, *On Ends* 3.20.

9. Cicero, *On Ends* 3.22; Plutarch, *On Common Conceptions* 1071B–C.

10. Diogenes Laertius, *Lives of Eminent Philosophers*, 7.104–6; Stobaeus vol. 2, pp. 84.18–85.11.

11. I cite in *Emotion and Peace of Mind*, pp. 280–83, for the definition, Stobaeus, vol. 2, pp. 87.18, and for its application to permissible erotic love, Diogenes Laertius, *Lives* 7.113, 7.130; Stobaeus vol. 2, pp. 66.11–13, 91.15–16, 115.1–2; Cicero, *Tusculan Disputations* 4.72; Sextus, *Against the Experts* 7.239; Pseudo-Andronicus, *On Emotions* 4 (in *SVF* 3.397); Alexander, *Commentary on Aristotle's Topics* (*Commentaria in Aristotelem Graeca*, vol. 2) 139.21.

These mistake-free emotions, available only to the Stoic sage, are called "good emotions" (*eupatheiai*).[12] The Stoics also allow temporary exceptions for pedagogic purposes, to help people to progress in the direction of good character. The Stoic Epictetus in the first century CE says that it is the mark of a good lecture on morality that the students should feel *agony* at their lack of good character.[13] But agony is not what the perfected Stoic should feel

The Stoics help us to get rid of unwanted emotions, and this is where I believe they are really helpful; because we all have emotions we would rather be rid of, even if we do not agree that most emotions are such. To get rid of emotions, we must understand the three different phases in the development of an emotion. First, by a daring generalization which I think is nearly true, they claim that every emotion is preceded by an appearance that benefit or harm is at hand and that it is appropriate to react accordingly. This appearance is not yet the emotion, but it is enough to cause what they call a "first movement" or "pre-passion." By this they mean a shock that may be a physical one in the body, like crying, or a psychological sensation. That too is not yet the emotion. According to the fullest Stoic account,[14] the emotion occurs when we give the assent of our reason to the appearance that harm or benefit is at hand and that it is appropriate to react accordingly. Most people do not even realize that this is a distinct phase, because no sooner do they have the appearance than they give their assent to it. But Stoicism teaches you to stand back and say to yourself, "That is the appearance, but should reason assent to it?'

The Stoics have much advice on how to withhold assent. Is it really harm at hand, or merely the shock of something unexpected, which, however, is no harder to cope with than what you were expecting? Is the apparent harm any different from what everyone experiences? And is it really appropriate to react, or did you not yourself treat someone only the other day the way you have been treated?

The Stoics further help us to withhold assent by distinguishing the first movement, the shock, from the question of harm. That helps to prevent the William James effect. William James once said: "We do not cry because we are sad. We are sad because we cry." That is an exaggeration, but there is some truth in it. People often think, "Look, I am crying. I *must* have been

12. Pseudo-Andronicus, *On Emotions* 6 (in *SVF*, 3.432); cf. Diogenes Laertius, *Lives* 7.116; Cicero, *Tusculan Disputations* 4.12–13.

13. See Epictetus, *Discourses* book 3, chapter 23, sections 30 and 37; 3.19.1, 4.9.10, 4.10.3.

14. Seneca, *On Anger* 2.4.1–4. More generally, impulsion to action (*hormân*) requires assent, as reported by Plutarch, *On Stoic Self-contradictions* 1057A.

maltreated." But of course that does not follow. The crying is merely the shock, but it leaves the important question unanswered: have you really suffered harm? What the Stoics invented was *cognitive* therapy—a therapy that calms the emotions by altering one's *thoughts* about the situation.

Another aid that the Stoics give us is getting us to qualify our desires and expectations with a reservation, "if God wills," a recommendation with parallels in Islam and Christianity. Understanding of Stoic "reservation" has recently been much advanced.[15]

Stoic love for all humans should, then, be unemotional. As to how it can be love if it is unemotional, I shall come before long to the explanation offered by the Stoic Epictetus. But first I will turn to Gandhi's form of unemotional love for all.

GANDHI AND TOLSTOY'S NONVIOLENT LOVE FOR ALL HUMANS

Gandhi described Tolstoy as having converted him to the acceptance of nonviolence. He learned from Tolstoy that true nonviolence is an inner state of mind, an ocean of compassion free from any trace of ill will for anyone. It is not an outward practice of refraining from killing animals. That practice of certain Indian groups seemed to Gandhi to be indifferent to actual suffering in the animals.[16] In the work which most influenced Gandhi,[17] Tolstoy derived his idea ultimately from Christ's Sermon on the Mount, in which Christ, speaking of humans, not animals, taught that if you are struck on the cheek, you should turn the other cheek to your assailant.[18]

But what was this love like that extended to all humans? Gandhi was often felt as warm by his foes, harsh yet loving by his immediate circle of workers, and simply as harsh by one of his relatives. Books and a film have been produced about Gandhi's bad relations with one of his sons, Harilal.[19]

15. By Tad Brennan, "Reservation in Stoic ethics," *Archiv für Geschichte der Philosophie* 82, 149–77; Jacques Brunschwig, "Sur deux notions de l'éthique stoïcienne: de la 'réserve' au 'renversement,'" in G. Rhomeyer-Dherbey and J.-B. Gourinet, *Les Stoïciens*, Paris 2005, 357–80. I draw some conclusions from their findings in "Stoic Reservation: a footnote," in Katerina Ierodiakonou and Ben Morison, eds., *Epistêmê, etc.*, Oxford, 2011.

16. Gandhi, speech for the anniversary of Tolstoy's birth, 10 Sep 1928, repr. Iyer, *Writings*, vol. 1, no. 59.

17. Tolstoy, *The Kingdom of God Is Within You*, translated into English by Aylmer Maude and by Constance Garnett.

18. Matthew 5:38–40; Luke 6:29.

19. Candulal Bhagubhai Dalal, *Harilal Gandhi*, translated into English by Tridip Suhrud, Hyderabad 2007; *Gandhi, My Father*, written and directed by Feroz Abbas Khan, 2007.

But his relation to his other sons and to their wives was different. Even so, his love for all seems to have been somewhat detached, except for the warmth he showed to his closest workers. If Gandhi tells us that he learned about nonviolence as *love* from Tolstoy, he learnt about *detachment* from a quite different source, neither Tolstoy nor the Stoics

GANDHI AND EMOTIONAL DETACHMENT: THE BHAGAVADGITA

Gandhi learnt about emotional detachment from the Bhagavadgita, although his reading of the Gita, as he calls it for short, was no doubt influenced by the man he names[20] as the foremost influence on his life ahead of Tolstoy, the ascetic Jain—Rajchandra. Gandhi translated the Gita into Gujarati, having read, and perhaps relying on, the Victorian English translation of Arnold in 1908 and a Gujarati version of a translation by Tilak in 1922–24.[21] Gandhi's lieutenant Mahadev Desai in turn translated Gandhi's Gujarati into English in such a way as to bring out Gandhi's interpretation. I shall use Mahadev Desai's rendering.

> *The Gita repeatedly tells us to avoid attachment especially to the fruit of action.*
> 2.47 Action alone is thy province, never the fruits thereof; let not thy motive be the fruit of action, nor shouldst thou desire to avoid action.
> 2.48 Act thou, O Dhananjaya, without attachment, steadfast in *Yoga*, even-minded in success and failure. Even-mindedness is *Yoga*.
> 3.25 Just as, with attachment, the unenlightened perform all actions, O Bharata, even so, but unattached, should the enlightened man act, with a desire for the welfare of humanity.
> 4.20 He who has renounced attachment to the fruit of action, who is ever content, and free from all dependence,—he, though immersed in action, acts not.
> 5.12 A man of *yoga* obtains everlasting peace by abandoning the fruit of action; the man ignorant of *yoga* selfishly attached to fruit, remains bound.
> 18.2 Abandonment of the fruit of action is called *tyaga* by the wise.

20. Gandhi, speech on Tolstoy's anniversary, 10 Sep 1928, repr. Iyer, *Writings*, vol. 1, p. 115.

21. *Autobiography*, part 1, ch. 20, pp. 76–77; "My jail experiences XI," *Young India* 4 Sep 1924, in *CW*, vol. 25, p. 84.

18.6 But even these actions should be performed abandoning all attachment and fruit; such, O Partha, is my best and considered opinion.
18.9 But when an allotted task is performed from a sense of duty and with abandonment of attachment and fruit, O Arjuna, that abandonment is deemed to be *sattvika*.
18.11 For the embodied one cannot completely abandon action; but he who abandons the fruit of action is called a *tyagi*.
18.26 That doer is called *sattvika* who has shed all attachment, all thought of 'I', who is filled with firmness and zeal, and who recks neither success nor failure.

The Gita further advocates avoidance of emotion.

2.40 Here no effort undertaken is lost, no disaster befalls. Even a little of this righteous course delivers one from great fear.
2.55 When a man puts away, O Partha, all the cravings that arise in the mind and finds comfort for himself only from *Atman*,[22] then he is called the man of secure understanding.
2.56 Whose mind is troubled in sorrows and longeth not for joys, who is free from passion, fear and wrath—he is called the ascetic of secure understanding.
2.57 Who owns attachment nowhere, who feels neither joy nor resentment whether good or bad comes his way—that man's understanding is secure.
2.62 In a man brooding on objects of the senses, attachment to them springs up; attachment begets craving and craving begets wrath.
2.70 He in whom all longings subside, even as the waters subside in the ocean, which, though ever being filled by them, never overflows—that man finds peace; not he who cherishes longing.
2.71 The man who sheds all longing and moves without concern, free from the sense of 'I' and 'Mine'—he attains peace.
12.17 Who rejoices not, neither frets nor grieves, who covets not, who abandons both good and ill—that devotee of Mine is dear to Me.

The Gita urges impartiality towards whatever one encounters.

5.18 The men of Self-realisation look with an equal eye on a brahmana possessed of learning and humility, a cow, a dog and even a dog-eater.
14.24 He who holds pleasure and pain alike, who is sedate, who regards as same earth, stone and gold, who is wise and weighs in equal scale things pleasant and unpleasant, who is even-minded in praise and blame.

22. The true self.

The Gita applies the need for impartiality to friend and foe, to children, wife, home and family. Indeed, it finds dear the one who (like the Greek Cynics) has no home.

14.25 Who holds alike respect and disrespect, who is the same to friend and foe, who indulges in no undertakings—That man is called *gunatita*.

12.18 Who is same to foe and friend, who regards alike respect and disrespect, cold and heat, pleasure and pain, who is free from attachment;

12.19 Who weighs in equal scale blame and praise, who is silent, content with whatever his lot, who owns no home, who is of steady mind,—that devotee of Mine is dear to Me.

13.9 Absence of attachment, refusal to be wrapped up in one's children, wife, home and family, even-mindedness whether good or ill befall.

Mahadev Desai supplies comments; he notes comparisons with the Christian Gospel. Christ demanded that disciples abandon their families (Luke 14.26) "If any man come to me and hate not his father, mother, wife and children and brethren and sisters, yea and his own life also, he cannot be my disciple." He taught (Matthew 5.44) "Love your enemies, bless them that curse you." Regarding the fruit of action, Mahadev Desai compares Tolstoy's *What I Believe*: "The belief in a remuneration of work [. . .] rests on the assumption that we have a claim to something; but man has no rights and can have none. He is ever in debt for the welfare given him." Elsewhere, when the Gita talks of one's own personal duty (compare Stoic *prosôpon, persona* in chapter 6 below) at 3.35 and 18.27, the learned Desai compares these texts with two Stoic passages from Epictetus and Marcus Aurelius. But he does not do so for the texts just cited. That comparison was left to Edwyn Bevan in a passage within a set of Oxford lectures published in 1913,[23] but Bevan's insight was not taken up.

Gandhi not only translated the Gita; he also gave a set of discourses on it in his ashram at Ahmedabad in 1926. It may seem very strange that a man who so believed in nonviolence should base himself on the Gita, in which the Lord Krishna tells the warrior Arjuna that it is his duty to fight in a long and destructive war that left almost all the participants dead. But in his *Discourses on the Gita*, Gandhi interprets the point as being that Arjuna's reluctance to fight was not based on any inkling of the idea of nonviolence, but on a squeamishness about killing his relatives. He was perfectly pre-

23. Edwyn Bevan, *Stoics and Sceptics*, Oxford 1913, who drew attention to most of the passages cited. I thank Vishwa Adluri for drawing my attention to four further passages.

pared to kill others. It is that attachment to relatives, on Gandhi's interpretation, that the Gita is attacking.[24]

GANDHI ON THE DETACHMENT NEEDED FOR A NONVIOLENT MIND

Gandhi wrote in *Hind Swaraj* in 1909 (translated by him as *Indian Home Rule*,1910) that four things are needed to become a passive, or nonviolent, resister: chastity, truthfulness, fearlessness, and poverty.[25] *Chastity* is needed because it is the greatest discipline. Many of the early male Christian ascetics in the desert agreed that it was the hardest discipline to keep, but Gandhi had the added belief, shared by some ancient Greek and Roman thinkers and by some of Gandhi's European contemporaries whom he cites,[26] that sexual activity emasculates. He further held that sufficient chastity in thought gives spiritual strength and ability to change the world by nonphysical means, an ability that would be lost by indulgence. He thought, for example, that his imperfect success in inculcating nonviolence was due to an insufficient level of chastity.[27]

Fearlessness is not only about possessions, false honor, the government, bodily injury and death, but also about relatives. There were different versions of the rules for Gandhi's ashram founded in Ahmedabad in 1915, but the version displayed on my visit required fearlessness with regard to parents and readiness to disobey them.

24. Gandhi, *Discourses on the Gita*, *CW*, vol. 32, pp. 103–4. Similarly Gandhi, introduction to his Gujarati translation of the Gita, translated in Iyer, *Essential Writings*, pp. 69–70, and "Meaning of the *Gita*," 11 Oct 1925, and letter to Santoji Maharaj, 2 July 1927, repr. Iyer, *Writings*, vol. 1, pp. 77–89.

25. *Hind Swaraj*, Cambridge 1997, pp. 96–98. For truthfulness, see Introduction and chapters 4, 7 and 11.

26. R. B. Onians, *The Origins of European Thought*, Cambridge 1954, pp. 109–10 n 4, 118, 149–50; Bhikhu Parekh, "Sex, energy and politics," ch. 6 of *Colonialism, Tradition and Reform*, New Delhi, rev. ed. 1999, p. 193, citing Gandhi, *Self-Restraint versus Self-Indulgence*, Ahmedabad 1933.

27. Examples are cited by Bhikhu Parekh, *Colonialism, Tradition and Reform*, p. 217, and Judith Brown, *Prisoner of Hope*, New Haven, Conn. 1989, p. 285. Gandhi expressed worry in 1938 that his failure to develop nonviolence further was due to his own impurity: letter to Amrit Kaur, 24 Oct 1938, *CW*, vol. 62, pp. 211–12. The same year he made a particularly full statement in *Harijan* 23 July 1938, pp. 195–96 (compare *Harijanbandhu*, 22 Oct 1939, pp. 287–89): sexual purity even in thought husbands "creative energy of the highest order," "power of the highest potency." "Such power is impossible in one who dissipates his energy in any way whatsoever, even as steam kept in a leaky pipe yields no power." Gandhi again expressed anxiety in 1946 that inability to stop intercommunal riots at Noakhali might be due to his insufficient chastity. *CW*, vol. 87, p. 14.

With *poverty*, you do not have to throw money away, but you must be indifferent about losing it. Gandhi uses the word "indifferent" to describe an attitude of mind, rather than in the way the Stoics used it to characterize an objective. He recognizes property as a "cause of quarrels," better given up,[28] even though in another mood he complains that it is only through inertia that we suppose that lawful possession must attract violence rather than respect.[29] Clearly the original acquisition of wealth has sometimes involved physical violence, and competition for wealth can encourage the violent attitude of mind that Gandhi deplored. Gandhi may have recognized elsewhere[30] that the very idea of private property involves readiness to defend it with violence from unwanted trespassers, if it is to be private. If a spouse is considered private property, the same would apply there. He could also have added that those who have given up private property and sex have less to lose, and so are freer to act with neither fear nor hatred towards an oppressor.

NON-STOIC ANALOGUES FOR THE ASCETIC SIDE OF GANDHI'S EMOTIONAL DETACHMENT

The Stoics did not have to be ascetics, because they were required, with due reservation, to seek Zeno's naturally preferred objectives. The ascetic side of Gandhi's emotional detachment was especially encouraged by his Jain friend Rajchandra. Analogues in the West to Gandhi's ascetic detachment, and especially to his concern with chastity, can be found in the ascetic strand of Christianity, rather than in the Stoics.

A Christian of the 3rd century CE turned the Stoic theory of how to avoid emotion into a theory of how to avoid sin. This was not a Stoic perspective. The Christian, Origen, took the idea of a Stoic first movement or pre-passion, and instead of regarding it as a mere shock, devoid of thought, described it as a *bad thought*,[31] very nearly the phrase used also by Gandhi, as we shall see. A bad thought for Origen is only a first movement; it is a temptation, but not yet a sin, because you have not yet given your assent or consent to anything. But it would be a sin if you consented to prolonging the bad thought or enjoying it, much more so if you consented to acting on it. This was made clear in the next century, the fourth century CE, by the

28. Letter to G. D. Birla, 22 March 1925, *CW*, vol. 26, p. 364 = *eCW*, vol. 31, p. 9.

29. "The eternal problem," *Harijan* 22 Feb 1942.

30. *Ashram Observances in Action*, Ahmedabad 1955, from ms. of 1932, repr. Iyer, *Writings*, vol. 2, p. 581.

31. Origen, *On First Principles* 3.2.2, 3.2.4.

Christian monk Evagrius, a semi-hermit in the Egyptian desert, who developed the idea of bad thoughts.

Evagrius distinguished eight bad thoughts that assailed him in the six days of solitude he accepted each week in the heat of the Egyptian desert, before joining his fellow-monks on Sundays. I have described elsewhere Evagrius' positively Trollopean descriptions of his bad thoughts.[32] They included a kind of bored depression (*akêdia*), and thoughts of avarice, gluttony, lust, anger, distress, love of reputation (vainglory), and false belief in self-sufficiency (pride). Evagrius, unlike Gandhi, worked out a whole technique for forestalling bad thoughts by noticing at what time of day different ones attack, or in what sequence. The beginner can get rid of one bad thought by stirring up an opposite one, although he should learn how to pass beyond that imperfect remedy. But if he is assailed by thoughts of lust, he can get rid of them by stirring up thoughts of vanity: what would the head of the monastery think of him? Conversely, if he is assailed by thoughts of vanity, he can expel them in an instant by stirring up thoughts of lust.

It is again Christians, not Stoics, who provide parallels for Gandhi's concern with celibacy in particular. The Christian bishop St. Augustine at the end of the century around 400 CE, like Gandhi, favored celibacy in marriage after producing children, although he insisted that it should be only by mutual agreement of husband and wife.[33] He was also worried by sexual dreams as a sign of failure in chastity,[34] as were many Christian males by sexual discharges after they had become desert ascetics. Dreams were worrying, because in dreams one may give one's assent or consent. The similarities to Gandhi, however, were, in this case not due to any Christian influence. For one thing, Gandhi was following the Indian tradition of *brahmacharya*. For another, the difficulties he experienced in practicing celibacy seem to be common to males of different cultures just because of biological human nature.

The similarities across cultures mean that Gandhi's interest in testing his moral progress would have been familiar not only to the Christian Augustine, but also to the pagan Greek philosophers. The Platonist, Plutarch, wrote a treatise on how to test moral progress.[35] And two Stoics, the founder Zeno and Epictetus, both regarded sexual dreams as an area for

32. Richard Sorabji, *Emotion and Peace of Mind*, Oxford 2000, ch. 23.

33. In *Emotion and Peace of Mind*, p. 276, I cite: Augustine, *New Sermons* (Mainz) 41 and 42; *Sermon on the Good of Marriage*, ed. Dolbau, *Rev. bénédictine*, 102, 1992, 275ff = *De bono nuptiarum*.

34. Sorabji, *Emotion and Peace of Mind*, ch. 26, citing e.g. Augustine, *Confessions* 10.30.

35. *How to Recognise One's Progress in Virtue*, in Plutarch, *Moralia* 75A–86A.

testing it.[36] Gandhi, who tested his chastity by sleeping beside some of his closest women supporters, could have drawn support from Plato's *Symposium*, which it is believed he read, where Socrates is presented as paying not the slightest attention all night when the young Alcibiades crept under his cloak and made sexual advances.[37]

In his autobiography, first published in 1927–29, Gandhi describes the *process* of detachment, especially in connection with his vow of chastity. He speaks like the early Christians of having "undesirable thoughts."[38] He says, in the same breath and elsewhere, like Evagrius and Augustine, that without surrender to God's *grace*, one cannot master one's thoughts, and he ascribes this view to the Bhagavadgita.[39] He even says that he accepts the theory, which Augustine made prominent in Christianity, of "original sin" inherited from the sin of the first human.[40] The part he accepts, presumably, is that no human can avoid sinning. When Bajaj asked him how to keep the mind free from lustful thoughts, he not only repeated the need for God's grace, but said that although we must not allow thought to rule action, we need not fret about evil thoughts themselves.[41] This is like Evagrius' idea that a bad thought is not itself a sin, although Evagrius would add that even before action, prolonging the thought can be a sin. Gandhi's omission of this point connects with his not having worked out, as Evagrius did, a technology for combating bad thoughts, apart from the one remedy that diet is vital. Diet is what Gandhi recommends to Bajaj and repeatedly, for example, in his autobiography.[42] Evagrius would have agreed on diet as one measure among others. In his view, lustful thoughts are not too difficult a temptation, provided thoughts of gluttony have been brought under control.[43]

36. Zeno, according to Plutarch, *Recognise Progress* 82F; Epictetus, *Discourses* 1.18.23, 3.2.5, cited in Sorabji, *Emotion and Peace of Mind*, p. 413.

37. Plato, *Symposium* 218E–219B. The Mani Bhavan's record of Gandhi having read the *Symposium* is mentioned in the introduction above. The parallel was mentioned to me by Tarik Warel and K. P. Shankaran. Gandhi paraphrased Plato's *Apology* in *Indian Opinion* in 1908, with a preface repr. *CW*, vol. 8, p. 246. He later says that he read *Dialogues of Plato* in Yeravada jail in 1922–24: "My jail experiences XI," *Young India* 4 Sep 1924, *CW*, vol. 25, p. 85.

38. *Autobiography*, part 4, ch. 25, p. 291.

39. The need for grace is affirmed in *Autobiography*, part 4, chs. 25 and 30, pp. 291, 301; and *Harijan* 29 Feb 1936, *CW*, vol. 62, pp. 211–12 (ascribed to the Bhagavadgita); *Harijan* 23 July 1938, *CW*, vol. 67, p. 196; *Harijan* 22 Feb 1942.

40. *Autobiography*, part 3, ch. 18, p. 220.

41. Letter to Jamnalal Bajaj, 5 Oct 1922, *CW*, vol. 23, pp. 140–41.

42. *Autobiography*, part 3, ch. 8, pp. 198–99.

43. Pseudo-Nilus = Evagrius, *On Eight Spirits of Wickedness*, ch. 1, *PG*, vol. 79, col. 1145A; cf. Pseudo-Nilus = Evagrius, *Sentences to the Virgin*, *PG*, vol. 40, 1284A, cited in Sorabji, *Emotion and Peace of Mind*, p. 365.

THE FAMILY: THE STOICS ON WHY *TRUE* FAMILY LOVE NEEDS TO BE DETACHED

I must now turn to emotional detachment within the family, because this above all makes acute the first of my two questions: How can the Stoics offer family love as a model of how you should approach all your fellow humans, if family love is emotional, and they want you to rid yourself of most emotions? The answer emerges, as so often, I think, from the later Stoic Epictetus in the first century CE. He suggests that the true Stoic will transcend *ordinary* family love. Of course, it is the wise Stoic's duty to pursue life and health for his family with all his ability. But notoriously, Epictetus recommends that when you kiss your wife or child, you should say to yourself, "I am kissing a mortal."[44] That will prepare you for the possibility of bereavement, although it will surely also make you a little detached. Epictetus goes further. Ordinary family love can turn into hate in an instant.[45] A husband and wife have loved each other for twenty years. Suddenly the bribe of a necklace comes between them and love turns into hate. The two brothers look so charming as they play together. How they love each other! But the father's throne comes between them and suddenly hate replaces love. Or a woman estranges the devoted guest and host. Only the Stoic's love is true family love, because only the Stoic's love could never turn into hate. Why not? Because the true Stoic never attached the same value to an inheritance, or to sexual satisfaction. Such things never had the same value as his or her own character. Epictetus admires the school of philosophers called Cynics who were even more individualistic than the Stoics. The true Cynic, unlike the Stoic, does not have a family at all. For the Cynic a family would be a tyranny: he would not be free if he was worried about whether their lives were secure.[46] Epictetus reveals how one might defend the idea of the founder of Stoicism, Zeno, when he said 350 years earlier that only *good* people are family.[47] Epictetus is saying that it is people with the right values, people who value character above an inheritance, who are true family. And the Stoics think (too optimistically to my mind) that if you have the right values, you will be good.[48] For Epictetus, then, the family love that one should extend to all humans is presumably this rather detached family love.

44. Epictetus, *Handbook* 3; *Discourses* 3.24.84–88; cf. 4.111.

45. Epictetus, *Discourses* 2.22.

46. Epictetus, *Discourses* 4.1.67 and 87.

47. So the founder, Zeno of Citium, is reported by Diogenes Laertius, *Lives of Eminent Philosophers* 7.32.

48. Sorabji, *Emotion and Peace of Mind*, ch.20, pp. 305–15.

It is a love that values the family's life more than a Cynic would, but that does not value their life as highly as their character.

Epictetus' account of extending family love was in some ways opposite to that of the younger Stoic Hierocles, who emphasized the strength of attachment to what was closest—one's own body and then one's closest relatives. Hierocles, so far from disowning the body like Epictetus, urged one to extend outward to the rest of mankind something of the *strength* of attachment that one feels for one's own body. He explicitly denied that the feeling for distant humans could be equally strong: distance would remove some affection. But he recommended counteracting this through the *behavioral* therapy of calling cousins "brothers," and aunts "mothers." Even Epictetus thinks that there is a special duty to relatives, but he seems to give to his detachment the strength that Hierocles reserves for attachment. At least he comes closer than Hierocles to the idea of impartial good will to all.

The idea of detachment had been extended by Cato the Younger to friendships in the century before Epictetus. It is reported that Cato would not entertain or even receive his biographer Munatius, when he reached Cyprus, because he was doing business with someone else, and merely rebuked Munatius, saying that the expectations of excessive friendship often led to hatred.[49]

For the problem of this chapter—how love, in particular love of all humans, could be emotionally detached—I have offered Epictetus' Stoicism as a model. We have seen Epictetus arguing that his detached attitude could be seen not as mere good will, but as a truer type of love. Gandhi does not offer any such rationale, and this is one of the points at which Stoicism might have helped him. But he does provide an actual example of the kind of detached love for all humans that Epictetus was advocating. In fact, Gandhi's refusal to privilege relatives went a little further than the Stoics would approve.

THE FAMILY: GANDHI'S NONATTACHMENT TO RELATIVES

The Gita, as quoted above, provided Gandhi with a scriptural basis for maintaining a certain equidistance from friend and foe, kin and non-kin. Let us see how Gandhi applied the idea of nonattachment to relatives. The film *Gandhi, My Father*, focuses on an unhappy case, that of his eldest son, Harilal. Gandhi decided in 1909 not to give to any of his sons a scholarship

49. Plutarch, *Life of Cato the Younger* 37.

even though a scholarship had been offered him for any one of the sons old enough to train as a barrister. Instead, Gandhi freed himself to give it to someone else who proved a failure and then to someone else again. In 1903, Harilal had gone to jail in the service of one of Gandhi's South African campaigns, and Gandhi wrote, "I want every Indian to do what Harilal has done."[50] But by May 1906, Gandhi had already written to his brother about Harilal's marriage, of which he disapproved. "For the present at any rate I have ceased to think of him as a son," naming someone else as "dearer to me than one who is a son because so born."[51] Harilal wrote bitterly to his father in 1915 about the earlier denial of educational funding. "For a year I cried. I was bewildered. You did not lend me your ears. [. . .] I am married [. . .] with four children. I cannot [. . .] become a recluse. Therefore I have separated from you with your permission."[52] In 1920, in the course of explaining "love, the active state of *ahimsa*," Gandhi wrote, "if my son lives a life of shame, I may not help him to do so by continuing to support him; on the contrary, my love for him requires me to withdraw all support from him although it may mean even his death."[53] As the film presents it, Harilal's alcoholism, debt, and temporary conversion to Islam were partly caused by his father's nonattachment. That is what one could have expected, and it constitutes a warning also to the Stoics, to the extent that their family love also involves a certain detachment.

Nonetheless, Gandhi's relation to his other three sons and their wives was different. All four sons supported his campaigns and were imprisoned at one time or another. His letters to all the sons and their wives have been collected by a granddaughter of Harilal.[54] He wrote to them as a mentor, instructing them in numerous details, including on health. The letters are always demanding, occasionally laudatory, sometimes critical and stern and felt as such, with many remarks on and hopes for their character, always attentive. The second son, Manilal, only went as far as saying that the strictness and sternness were never *intolerable*.[55] But the letters do not

50. Gandhi in *Indian Opinion* 20 Aug 1903, quoted in Gopalkrishna Gandhi, *Essential Writings*, p. 103.

51. *CW*, vol. 5, pp. 334–35, quoted in Gopalkrishna Gandhi, *Essential Writings*, p. 108.

52. Quoted from an earlier source by Rajmohan Gandhi, *Mohandas: A True Story of a Man, His People and an Empire*, Penguin Viking, Delhi 2006, p. 197.

53. Gandhi, *Young India* 25 Aug 1920, Mahatma Gandhi, *Non-Violent Resistance (Satyagraha)*, Schocken Books, New York 1961, p. 161.

54. Nilam Parikh, ed., *Gandhi Wrote to His Sons and Daughters-in-Law "Be Fragrant Wherever You Be,"* Delhi, 2008. I thank Makarand Paranjape for telling me of this book.

55. Nilam Parikh, *Gandhi Wrote*, p. 24.

reflect Gandhi's ability at playing with grandchildren, nor the warmth that he was able to show by personal contact with his closest workers. The love was there, but detached, and with an emphasis on character building that the Stoics would have approved—not that his stress on *dharma*, duty, is the same as the Stoic stress on virtue.[56] In fact, Gandhi was able to raise character to greater heights among those to whom his love was warmer, as might be expected in moral education.

Relations with his older brother were strained after Gandhi refused to pay him back by taking over the financial support of both families, which his brother had supplied while Gandhi was training. He expected his brother to understand that in adopting a life of poverty, which precluded paying back, he was supporting a *wider* human family.[57]

With his wife Kasturbai, Gandhi spoke to her of his vow of *brahmacharya*, celibacy, only on the day he took the vow.[58] Augustine would not have considered this consultation. Gandhi raised as a question, without answering it, what a wife's rights were in the matter.[59] It might be said on Gandhi's behalf that the Hindu tradition of *brahmacharya* had allowed its followers to practice celibacy at one or another of the four stages of life or *âsramas*. At the final stage, after being a householder with a family, the practitioner would normally leave his wife and practice celibacy in solitude. Gandhi might, then, be seen as less hard on his wife than that, in that he kept her with him. However, he says that the dominant factor in turning him to *brahmacharya* was not Hinduism, but his Jain friend Rajchandra; and the Jain tradition of sexual restraint was different.[60]

He insisted that his wife give up a costly gold necklace and later other ornaments, saying that she could refuse, but could not then live in the ashram community with him. It was a poor country and as a member of the ashram, she was being trained for a life of service. The members are like soldiers, and soldiers cannot wear what they like. Moreover, traveling everywhere in their campaigns, she should not draw the attention of men.[61] Gandhi had a

56. For the Stoic differentiation of virtue from duty, see chapter 7.

57. *Autobiography*, part 4, ch. 5.

58. *Autobiography*, part 3, ch. 8, p. 197.

59. Gandhi, *Hind Swaraj*, ch. 17, p. 97.

60. *Autobiography*, part 3, ch. 7. See Carl Olsen, ed., *Celibacy and Religious Traditions*, Oxford, 2008, esp. ch. 8 by Patrick Olivelle, "Celibacy in classical Hinduism," and ch. 10 by Paul Dundas, "Sthulabhandra's lodgings: sexual restraint in Jainism."

61. *Autobiography* part 3, ch. 12, supplemented by Raihana Tyabji, in Usha Thakkar and Jayshree Mehta, eds., *Understanding Gandhi: Gandhians in Conversation with Fred Blum*, Delhi 2011, pp. 190–91. I thank Bhikhu Parekh for drawing my attention to this illuminating collection

habit of rebuking her in public, in one case because she was slower to notice an ashramite's illness than she would have been with her son.[62] Once Gandhi rebuked Mahadev Desai's wife and Kasturbai at the same time, because they had both entered a temple that had not been opened to Dalits. Desai, who was very upset, had the good humor to write in *Harijan*, "To live with the saints in heaven is a bliss and a glory. But to live with a saint on earth is a different story."[63]

Gandhi thought that a votary of self-reliance (*swadeshi*) would be his family's truest friend, if he caused his family to die of plague by enlisting their help with plague victims in their own village.[64] He urged a trusted helper, who volunteered to join Gandhi in trying to calm religious riots in the most dangerous spot in Bengal at Noakhali, to bring along her daughter under two years of age, in order to secure the confidence of the villagers.[65] He discussed circumstances in which he would put to death a daughter, if he had one.[66] He particularly admired Harishchandra as a beacon of truth, when, in the story, he reluctantly prepared to behead his wife, in order to be true to a vow to God.[67] Westerners may compare the Judaic story of Abraham being ready to sacrifice his son Isaac simply because God had commanded it.

Among the many demands made on those closest to Gandhi, another that has worried people is his testing of his progress in chastity by having his closest women attendants, one a relative, sleep beside him.

I shall return in chapter 5 to the difference between Gandhi's treatment of nationalism and of family love. Nationalism he considered compatible with the love of all nations.

Gandhi's mentor Gokhale put to him that he had a strain of cruelty and put far too heavy burdens on people.[68] He had the grace to acknowledge that

---

of interviews. The case of the gold necklace is discussed by Vinit Haksar, *Rights, Communities and Disobedience*, 2nd ed., Delhi, 2001, pp. 190–98.

62. Quoted from an earlier source by Rajmohan Gandhi, *Mohandas*, p. 262.

63. Quoted by Rajmohan Gandhi, *Mohandas*, p. 415, from *Harijan* 9 Apr 1938, in *CW*, vol. 73, p. 457.

64. Gandhi, "The law of swadeshi," 31 May 1931, *CW*, vol. 46, p. 255.

65. Ashoka Gupta, *In the Path of Service*, Kolkata 2008, p. 96.

66. "The fiery ordeal," *Young India* 4 Oct 1928, repr. Iyer, *Writings*, vol. 2, pp. 271–72; "Jain ahimsa," *Young India* 25 Oct 1928, cited in chapter 1 above.

67. Gandhi, *Discourses on the Gita*, Nov 1926, *CW*, vol. 32, p. 370; *Autobiography*, part 1, ch. 2.

68. Gandhi, 22 Apr 1914, *CW*, vol. 12, pp. 410–11, cited in Gopalkrishna Gandhi, *Essential Writings*, p. 170.

he had produced alienation and scars in those he loved.[69] He also recommended his son Ramdas to avoid the strictness he had shown to his own wife, before he had made more progress towards treating her as an equal.[70]

THE LARGER FAMILY OF GANDHI'S ASHRAM AND CLOSEST ASSOCIATES: GREATER LOVING ATTENTION, BUT EQUALLY HARSH REQUIREMENTS

Gandhi extended to the larger family of his ashram communities and to his closest followers the same restrictions as he placed on his family. Many loved him and spoke of his loving attention to them, seemingly greater than that to his family,[71] but they could also speak of his harshness.[72] They had taken vows. We might compare Christian monasteries. In the ancient desert monasteries of Egypt, mothers were turned away and not even allowed to visit their sons. We shall see in chapter 6, on the other hand, that Gandhi urged people to think carefully about their individual duty (*svadharma*) before committing themselves, and he tested new arrivals whom he thought might be merely curious by having them clean latrines.[73]

Celibacy was one of the eleven vows taken even by married couples in the ashrams, and when Gandhi first heard of a breach, he was horrified and reacted by fasting.[74] Quite apart from the need for emotional detachment in order to face the hazards of nonviolent resistance, and celibacy to gain spiritual strength, another of Gandhi's rationales for celibacy was that one could not love and serve all humanity if one were preoccupied with a spouse or children. One who would obey the law of nonviolence cannot marry.[75] In a number of cases he forbade the marriages of his helpers. With Sucheta Kripalani he had many discussions urging her not to marry one of his righthand men J. B. Kripalani and "divert his mind from the struggles." She replied that, with herself, he would gain two workers in place of one. He was not convinced and she finally agreed not to marry because of love and regard for Gandhi. But when he asked her to marry someone else, to avoid diverting J. B. Kripalani, she refused. Eventually, Gandhi found that the burden of not

69. Gandhi, Bombay theater meeting 31 Aug 1924; *Young India* 4 Sep 1924, *CW*, vol. 29, pp. 65, 75, cited by Rajmohan Gandhi, *Mohandas*, pp. 283, 293.

70. Nilam Parikh, *Gandhi Wrote*, p. 168.

71. Thakkar and Mehta, *Understanding Gandhi*, pp. 162–63, 432, 463.

72. Thakkar and Mehta, *Understanding Gandhi*, pp. 371, 432.

73. Recorded in Thakkar and Mehta, *Understanding Gandhi*.

74. *Autobiography*, part 4, ch. 36.

75. *Autobiography* 1929, part 4, ch. 25, *CW*, vol. 39, 252–53: and letter to Narandas Gandhi, 3–5 Aug 1930, *CW*, vol. 44, pp. 68–69.

marrying did divert J. B. Kripalani, and he wrote and agreed to the marriage. To fulfill the promise that he would gain two workers, they lived happily as two friends and had no family.[76] Even after that, he later proposed that she sacrifice her husband in order to continue her work in the dangerous region of Noakhali.[77] It was as a member of the ashram that Gandhi forbade ornaments to his wife: with young girls it was because of the ashram's vow of *brahmacharya*, celibacy even in thought, but he offered the same counsel to a daughter-in-law.[78]

Tolstoy had proposed very much the same argument, its preoccupying character, against marriage in 1890 in the afterword to his novella portraying the horrors of a marriage, *The Kreutzer Sonata*.[79] One might think that Tolstoy could not possibly believe what his character says in the novella. But his own view in the postscript turns out to be even more extreme. Carnal love and marriage are a hindrance to the service of God and to people and hence are for Christians a degradation and a sin. Marriage with its consequence, the birth of children, defines a limited form of service and sphere of activity confined to the resulting children. It is better accompanied by a return to celibacy. His attack is more sweeping than Gandhi's. Falling in love and carnal love are a degrading state of bestiality, and care and labor over children are an expiation. Even marriage for the sake of perpetuating the human race is unjustified, when support is needed for millions of children already in existence but perishing for want of sustenance.

If Gandhi's workers were already married with children, he expected risks to be taken with the children, as we have seen with one of the workers at Noakhali.[80] In the case of Sucheta Kripalani, the first visitor to Noakhali, he extended this requirement to her assistants, ignoring her plea that they were boys and girls, some not grownup.[81]

CHRIST AND DETACHMENT FROM FAMILY AS INEVITABLE

None of what I have said is in any way intended to belittle Gandhi. He would have found at least as strong a detachment from family, based on different grounds, in another advocate of love for all: Christ. One of Gandhi's

76. Thakkar and Mehta, *Understanding Gandhi:* pp. 435–39.

77. Thakkar and Mehta, *Understanding Gandhi*, pp. 477–78.

78. Thakkar and Mehta, *Understanding Gandhi*, p. 478; Nilam Parikh, *Gandhi Wrote*, p. 14.

79. Afterword, translated by Robert Edwards and repr. with revisions in Leo Tolstoy, *The Kreutzer Sonata and Other Stories*, Oxford 1998, pp. 163–77.

80. Ashoka Gupta, *In the Path of Service*, Kolkata 2008, p. 96.

81. Thakkar and Mehta, *Understanding Gandhi*, p. 414.

favorite books was the Gospel of St. Matthew, on which he gave a series of lectures.[82] Christ is represented there as forbidding a disciple to stay and bury his father. Christ declared that any who loved mother, father, son, or daughter more than they loved him was not worthy of him, and that he had come to set family members against each other. When told that his mother and brothers were outside the door waiting to speak to him, he pointed to his disciples and replied, "Here are my mother and my brothers." Those who had left brothers, sisters, father, mother, or children for his name's sake would inherit eternal life.[83]

Gandhi's love for all humans, like Christ's, was not merely good will exercised as the occasion arose. It entered into a life of continuous nonviolent campaigning, and was exercised towards his opponents as well as towards those whom he was supporting. The campaigns would not have provided opportunity for ordinary family life with its "preoccupations," to use his own term. They might involve long periods in remote villages or years of imprisonment. Ordinary family love might have been possible, if the love for all humans had taken a less revolutionary form, but then it would not have had the same impact on the world.

GANDHI'S DEVIATION FROM THE GITA? IMPARTIALITY VERSUS DISFAVOR TOWARDS RELATIVES

But did Gandhi always rest content with the Gita's impartiality towards relatives? There are signs that he went further and positively *disfavored* relatives.[84] Commenting on the Gita's insistence on Arjuna's not sparing his own relatives, Gandhi added the word "*first*": "if one must kill, one should kill one's people first."[85] He wrote, when his son Devdas urged him not to fast, "You are of course a friend and a friend of a very high order at that. But you cannot get over the son in you. [. . .] Your affection is rooted in attachment."[86] He refused to accept a visit in prison from two sons at the end of a fast, saying, "As the Government know, I make no distinction between sons born to me and numerous others who are as dear to me even as they are." He also refused the attendance of relatives at his wife's death

82. Lectures recorded in *Day to Day*, vol. 8.

83. Matthew 8:21–22, 10:35–37, 12:46, 19:29.

84. I am grateful to Faisal Devji, who first alerted me to this.

85. Gandhi, *Discourses on the Gita*, *CW*, vol. 32, p. 103.

86. Cited in Gopalkrishna Gandhi, *Essential Writings* p. 676, from Pyarelal, ed., *Mahatma Gandhi, Last Phase*, vol. 2, Ahmedabad 1956, pp. 703–5.

ceremonies in prison, if that was not allowed also to friends.[87] He will have admired Socrates, if he read Plato's *Phaedo* 60A, for sending away his wife and little son before his execution, so that he could discuss the nature of death with his friends. Rajchandra persuaded Gandhi that Mrs. Gladstone's devotion to Gladstone was "perfectly natural," and that a servant's devotion would have been "a thousand times more praiseworthy."[88] In his early days, in a conversation with Mrs. Polak in South Africa in 1909, Gandhi insisted rather peremptorily that a wife, and in general one's nearest, do not need to be always thought about or specially attended to, because they are part of oneself, like one's arm. This is "identification, as all true love should be." Mrs. Polak put her point by saying, "I think I sometimes prefer to be thought of, then, as someone a little further away. I don't want to be put on one side as an unconscious bit of the body by those I love. [. . .] I think it wrong to omit the acts of thoughtful courtesy and self-control to those who have the first claim upon our consideration, and to reserve our smiling best for the stranger. I see it happen and it vexes me, for I cannot justify it." Gandhi replied, "Then do not worry yourself by thinking about it!"

This does not seem to be endorsed by the Gita, or by the Stoics. It might be different if Gandhi's wife herself had identified herself as Gandhi's arm, or had taken a vow to serve as Gandhi's arm. But it would not be possible for each spouse to view the other as their arm. Seneca's Stoic view about parts is not that one person is part of another, but that each individual is part of the wider community of rational beings like a stone in an arch.[89]

GANDHI'S DEVIATION FROM STOICISM: *SVADHARMA*, *PERSONA*, AND THE INDIVIDUAL'S DUTY TO WIFE AND CHILDREN

Although the Stoics' universal love is in a certain way detached, the Stoics do insist on our carrying out our duty as father, brother, husband. These roles are part of our identity (*persona* or *prosôpon*), and so help to reveal where our duty lies.[90] Epictetus is very scornful of a father who left home, because he could not bear to see his little daughter dangerously ill. As a father he should, like the mother, have stayed with the child (Epictetus' Stoic teacher, Musonius Rufus, called for equality between men and women).[91]

87. *CW*, vol. 77, pp. 70, 236, cited in Gopalkrishna Gandhi, *Essential Writings* pp. 515, 520.
88. *Autobiography*, part 3, ch. 7, pp. 194–95.
89. Seneca, *Letters* 95, 53.
90. Epictetus, *Discourses* 1.11, 2.10.
91. Musonius Rufus, *Fragments*, ed. Hense, 3, 4, 12, 13A.

The Stoics are able to combine a certain distance towards relatives with attachment to all because they believe in seeking the target energetically—saving the sick child or securing the other conventional objectives for it—even though in the end it is the seeking that most matters.

On the other side it must be acknowledged that Gandhi did help nurse his children when he was at home. Moreover, not unlike Epictetus, he scolded as selfishly motivated a man who proposed euthanasia for his incurably sick four-month-old baby on the grounds that he had a large family to feed and could not bear to see its sufferings.[92] But he differed from the Stoics if he saw his duty as calling for the *sacrifice* of relatives and of some of those closest to him, as did the *dharma* of Arjuna. In another context, he discussed the special duty (*svadharma*) of the householder to protect his family.[93] He may not at that stage have regarded himself as still being a householder. But we shall see in chapter 4 that he accepted an analogous duty to protect from threatening animals the larger family of his ashram.

CONCLUSIONS

We can now answer the question we started with. The universal love for all humans in which both Gandhi and the Stoics believe is compatible with emotional detachment because it is a comparatively *detached* love. The Stoics, moreover, have a positive reason for calling it love, and indeed a *truer* kind of love, in that it can never become hate. In this respect the Stoics might provide support for Gandhi. That is a first conclusion, but it is not the only conclusion we can draw, because I think we can also see that Gandhi and the Stoics throw mutual light on each other elsewhere too.

They shed light on each other in several ways. Gandhi had a *scriptural* basis in the Gita for belief in maintaining a certain equidistance from friend and foe, kin and non-kin, and in nonattachment to the fruit of action. Stoicism also maintained a certain distance from each, and could supply a *philosophical* basis for doing so. On the other hand, the Stoics would not be in total agreement. Their message was different, insofar as it required energetic *pursuit* of natural objectives for oneself and others, family included. What had less importance was not the *pursuit*, but the *securing*. Moreover, Stoicism would not approve Gandhi's actually *disfavoring* or *sacrificing*

92. "Some More Posers in *Ahimsa*," *Young India* 22 Nov 1928, repr. Iyer, *Writings*, vol. 2, p. 282. For further reference to family duty, see p. 71 below.

93. "Is This Humanity?," 1926, in *Day to Day*, vol. 8, p. 280.

close friends or kin. At most, in its sterner versions, it regarded only the good as *true* kin.

In his turn Gandhi throws light on the Stoics. They both believed that few things matter in the end. The Stoics focused on character. Gandhi thought character and a small range of other things important. Since I believe that hundreds of things are important, I used to think that the belief in few was simply part of the unacceptable face of Stoicism. A good mother or father thinks it important whether their son wins at football tomorrow. Even if winning can appear trivial from one perspective, the support is not. But reflection on Gandhi has shown me that, if one wants to have a liberator of one's country or a reformer of society, it may be necessary to have one or two people who think that few things matter. It is best if they are not in one's family. But to Gandhi his physical freedom did not matter, nor even his life. This meant that it was the viceroy, not Gandhi, who was afraid when he was sent to prison.

Gandhi also provides a picture of what the Stoic sage might be like at least in certain respects if he ever existed. He further shows how far certain Stoic aspirations might be *possible* in spite of their impractical appearance. Stoic love for all humans, which was detached in the ways described, might seem an *impossibility*, especially as the Stoics admitted that it had not been realized. But Gandhi did achieve a similarly detached love for all. Gandhi was an experimenter and this was not the only respect in which he put to the test ideals of a Stoic type. Some Stoics, we shall see in chapter 9, show an attraction for a past or future without private property, and for a future without law courts or armies. Gandhi's experiments and thought experiments reveal something about how far this might be practical or impractical.

CHAPTER TWO

Emotional detachment: how to square it with politics in the Stoics and Gandhi

I turn now to a further problem. How could the Stoics and Gandhi remain emotionally detached if they were to engage in action, above all in political action? For goals in politics are typically urgent; is that compatible with detachment?

For the Stoics, two different kinds of answer might be canvassed. On one view, brilliantly expressed by Isaiah Berlin, the Stoics, starting with their founder Zeno, gave up political theory and confined themselves to personal ethics. Berlin congratulates Zeno for introducing one of the three great revolutions of Western political theory by substituting personal for political values. The Stoics gave up not only political theory, but also political life. This would make them very unlike Gandhi. I do not agree with this claim of Stoic depoliticization as it stands, but it needs addressing and I shall return to it in chapter 10 below. For now I want instead to describe a much more general explanation that the Stoics offered of how to remain detached while pursuing objectives.

THE STOICS ON GOALS OF ACTION

Their recipe for the unemotional pursuit of objectives was most fully worked out by one of the later Stoics. The idea was brilliant, although it is not one that I could live up to myself. It took the model of archery practice. One needs a *target* (*skopos, propositum*), or there will be no archery practice at all. But the important thing, the *goal* (*telos, ultimum*) is not hitting the target. What if a bad aim hits the target because of an unpredictable gust of wind? Equally it does not matter if a perfect aim misses the target because of an unpredictable gust. What matters, the real goal, is *aiming* right.[1] At the same time, the Stoic who introduced this idea, Antipater, head of the school from 152 to 129 BC, insisted that you should do everything in your power (*kath' hauton*) to hit the target.[2] The same used to be taught to English schoolboys about cricket. You play very hard to win, but what if you lose? Then "the game's the thing." It matters how you played, and how you lost, with grace and recognition of the other side. Playing the game was the real goal, winning merely the target. This value spread to American football too. In the immortal words of Grantland Rice,

> And when the last Great Scorer comes to mark against your name,
> He asks not if you won or lost, but how you played the game.

This attitude makes a tremendous demand of us. We are working to gain our degree, or complete our dissertation, or publish our next book. But that is only a target to make the activity of researching possible. What matters is the goal, the activity of researching. The great advantage of this idea is that it gives no hostages to fortune. Even if death strikes you down the next moment, you have achieved the *goal* of researching. What is lost is only the *target* of completing the current task. The Stoic, then, does not pin hopes on the future, but is content with the present. How many readers are capable of this recipe for serenity in action? Not myself, I have to confess, but I can appreciate its point. It combines doing everything in your power to attain a target with detachment from whether you attain it.

The Stoic's detachment is not an elimination of desires. What is eliminated is *emotional* desire. The desire that remains in a perfect Stoic is unemotional because it sees the objectives for what they are: things *indifferent*, although natural and right to pursue as far as lies in your power. The Stoics even coined a word to designate this detached kind of desire. It *selects* (*eklegesthai*), rather than *choosing* (*haireisthai*), naturally preferred objectives.[3]

GANDHI ON GOALS OF ACTION

In discussing commitment to goals of action, Gandhi sometimes speaks in ways like the Stoics. He quotes the Christian hymn, "One step enough

1. Cicero, *On Ends* 3.22; Plutarch, *On Common Conceptions* 1070F–1071E.
2. Stobaeus, vol. 2, pp. 76.9–15.
3. Stobaeus, vol. 2, pp. 84.18–85.11; Diogenes Laertius, *Lives* 7.105; Cicero, *On Ends* 3.20.

for me," and adds, "To think of some remote future is building castles in the air. [. . .] The present means our duty at this moment. If we put all our strength into doing our duty, as we know it at this moment, we shall have made the highest human effort."[4] He also says, referring to the Gita's detachment from the fruits of action, "To be detached is never to abandon action because the contemplated result may not follow."[5] He applies this to the hoped-for reform of his son Harilal.[6] In the search for self-rule (*swaraj*), he says, the joy lies in the fight, even if it takes generations.[7] Indeed, swaraj is a state of *mind* and consists in the effort to attain it ("it," I think, being *political* self-rule).[8] All this is congenial to Stoicism.

But Gandhi also appealed to non-Stoic ideas. He continued the quotation about acting whether or not the result would follow by saying, "On the contrary, it is proof of the immovable faith in the certainty of the contemplated result following in due course." The Stoics would never have sought assurance from the future, but viewed the future, like Gandhi in the earlier quotation, as offering so many castles in the air. Again, the Stoics did not believe in the soul's immortality, whereas Gandhi is able to say that achieving a truly nonviolent mind may take several incarnations,[9] and again that his son's misbehavior was partly due to his (Gandhi's) own failures in past incarnations.[10]

GANDHI AND DETACHMENT FROM *POLITICAL* GOALS

Gandhi's ways of detaching himself from goals of action seem to work well enough for the goal of achieving a truly nonviolent mind. But what about political goals, which tend to involve a strict timetable, such as removing British rule from India? Sometimes Gandhi spoke as if achieving true nonviolence of mind was a prerequisite for political independence. But in 1920 and 1921 he repeatedly suggested the political goal might be achieved in a

4. Gandhi, letter of 1927 in Mahadev Desai, mss. of Mahadev Desai's diary, repr. Iyer, *Writings*, vol. 2, no. 33, p. 70.

5. Gandhi, "Still at It," *Young India* 15 March 1928, repr. Iyer, *Essential Writings*, p. 273.

6. Gandhi, reply to a question, 5 Aug 1940, in *Harijan* 18 Aug 1940, repr. Gopalkrishna Gandhi, *Essential Writings*, p. 457.

7. *Harijan* 23 Dec 1939, *CW*, vol. 71, pp. 44–45.

8. "My notes," *Navajivan* on or before 10 March 1922, *CW*, vol. 23, pp. 71–72.

9. Gandhi, *Harijan* Mar 1936, cited by Iyer, *Thought*, p. 101; *Young India* vol. 3, *Ganesan*, repr. in D. G. Tendulkar, *Mahatma*, Bombay 1951–54, vol. 5, pp. 392–93.

10. Gandhi, reply to a question, 5 Aug 1940, in *Harijan* 18 Aug 1940, repr. Gopalkrishna Gandhi, *Essential Writings*, p. 457.

year.[11] Moreover, before launching his "Quit India" movement in 1942, he felt he could not wait. In his words:

> I always thought that I would have to wait till the country was ready for a non-violent struggle. But my attitude has undergone a change. I feel that if I continue to wait I might have to wait till doomsday [. . .] and in the meantime I may be enveloped and overwhelmed by the flames of violence that are spreading all around.[12]

Gandhi is thought of as more political than the Stoics. Although the latter believed that they should normally engage in politics, we shall see[13] that after Zeno few of the Greek heads of the school did so, and in the first century of Roman imperial rule, Stoics in politics were often unable to take on projects with a timetable. But Gandhi was surely the great politician, the one who liberated his country. How then could he possibly be detached from the timetabled goals of politics? We noticed in chapter 1 that politics did in fact sometimes make Gandhi despondent or angry.

"MY POLITICS ARE SUBSERVIENT TO MY RELIGION"

To the extent that he avoided this, an explanation may lie in the work of others. They have urged that Gandhi's innovative attitude treated political life not only as *compatible* with spiritual or inner life, as has already been said,[14] but as actually *subordinate* to it,[15] and this line of thought has been developed much further in recent work.[16] Although the Stoics' inner life

11. For 1920, see below, "Swaraj in one year?," *Young India* 22 Sep 1920, *CW*, vol. 18, p. 272. The claim features also in "On the wrong track," cited for a different purpose below from *Young India* 8 Dec 1920, *eCW*, vol. 22, p. 63. For 1921, the *CW* index lists *CW*, vol. 19, pp. 219, 221, 246, 250, 257, 267–68, 293–95, 339, 474, 500, 507, 533, 544, 545, 553.

12. Speech to the Rashtriya Yuvak Sangh, Sevagram, 28 May 1942, *CW*, vol. 82, p. 338.

13. Chapter 10.

14. See introduction, which cites Chatterjee, *Religious Thought*, ch. 9; Parekh, *Political Philosophy*, p. 100 ff; Anthony J. Parel, *Gandhi's Philosophy and the Quest for Harmony*, Cambridge 2006.

15. Parekh, *Political Philosophy*, pp. 101–9.

16. I greatly benefited from being allowed to see the Ph.D. dissertation of Mohamed Mehdi, "The Political Dimension of the Contemplative Life: Engagement and Disengagement in Plato, Seneca and Gandhi," McGill University 2007, and his subsequent paper, "Political action and cosmopolitanism in Gandhi and Seneca," along with papers by Faisal Devji, "Gandhi: Morality in the shadow of politics," and by Uday Mehta, "Gandhi: War, violence and the logic of inevitability." These three papers provided a common theme with the present chapter at conferences that I held in New York and Oxford in October and November 2009, and I am very grateful to the participants for our discussions.

was ethical rather than spiritual in emphasis, Berlin's claim about them has a similar structure, when he says that they subordinated political to ethical life. But Gandhi is explicit about the subordination of both his politics and his patriotism to his religion. He uses the same phrase of each. "My politics are subservient to my religion. [. . .] I should discard them if they hindered it" (1924). "If India makes violence her creed, [. . .] I would not care to live in India. She will cease to evoke any pride in me. My patriotism is subservient to my religion" (1921).[17] I think this confirms the recent claims about his priorities.

In Gandhi we can distinguish different kinds of subordination of the political to the spiritual. (i) First, he had a number of different reasons for insisting on the priority of moral transformation. For one thing, of the two kinds of self-rule (swaraj) that he considered, he thought the psychological kind to be truer self-rule than the political kind.[18] Confronting his followers' disappointment at abandoning civil disobedience, he told them that noncooperation with the British was all they needed in order to gain the swaraj of psychological self-rule. That swaraj could even be exemplified in the attitude of a slave who no longer saluted his master.[19] When noncooperation replaced dependence on the British, Indians would be psychologically ready for self-government.[20] By making Indians strong and reliant, noncooperation could replace Indian hatred of the British with pity for them.[21] However, his followers must not forget the importance of nonviolence. He called off the apparently successful campaign of tax refusal in Bardoli in 1922, because it had failed the test of nonviolence. He later called nonviolence "the greatest spiritual force that mankind has known," and implied that it was "the only thing that counts."[22] He prized it for itself, but also valued it, we shall see in chapter 4, because the suffering of nonviolent protestors could open the rulers' ears,[23] whereas, as chapter 4 will also bring out, he thought that political self-rule gained by violence would merely replace one violent regime

17. Gandhi, *Young India* 19 June 1924, *eCW*, vol. 28, p. 178; "A taxing examiner," *Young India* 6 Apr 1921, *eCW*, vol. 23, p. 5.

18. *Hind Swaraj*, chs. 14 and 20, pp. 73, 118, *CW*, vol. 10, pp. 39, 64; Gandhi, "*Sarvodaya*," conclusion, repr. Iyer, *Writings*, vol. 3, pp. 410–32, at p. 431, version with a few verbal alterations suggested by Verrier Elwyn published in Ahmedabad 1956, available on the Internet under www.peace.ca/UntoThisLast-Gandhi.doc.

19. "My notes," *Navajivan* on or before 10 March 1922, *CW*, vol. 23, pp. 71–72.

20. "Swaraj in one year?," *Young India* 22 Sep 1920, *CW*, vol. 18, pp. 272–73.

21. "On the wrong track," *Young India* 8 Dec 1920, *eCW*, vol. 22, pp. 63–65.

22. *Harijan* March 1936, cited by Iyer, *Thought*, p. 101.

23. Speech at Birmingham meeting, 18 Oct 1931, *Young India* 5 Nov 1931, *eCW*, vol. 54, p. 48.

with another. But he was not satisfied with nonviolence adopted merely as a political tactic, so long as it was politically useful. For him non-violence was a *creed*, not a tactic, the mission of his life, and the only true nonviolence.[24] He further thought that the *means* of achieving political change needed to be pure, because this affected whether the change would be of the right sort, and here he brought in a different consideration. Political activity needed to be "spiritualised," so that it could lead to *moksha*, spiritual liberation.[25] That is already a large number of considerations, but there were others too.

(ii) There would *always* be a need for spiritual values. A nonviolent attitude would be required long after nonviolent resistance to imperial rule was over, and freedom would be needed from passions long after freedom from an imperial power had been gained.

(iii) Then there was the matter of Gandhi's personal preference. He positively *preferred* the nonpolitical and declared that he found politics a "botheration."[26] Elsewhere he said, "The politician in me has never dominated a single decision of mine, and if I seem to take part in politics, it is only because politics encircle us today like the coil of a snake from which one cannot get out, no matter how much one tries. I wish therefore to wrestle with the snake."[27]

(iv) In other texts again, Gandhi declared that his primary aim was *moksha* (spiritual liberation), already cited above as a constraint on political tactics. He thought that his form of political activity could subserve the aim of achieving *moksha*.[28] "For me even the effort of attaining swaraj [home rule] is a part of the effort for *moksha*. Writing this [letter] to you is also a part of the same effort. If I find it a hindrance in the path of *moksha*, my pen would drop down this very moment, such is my yearning for *moksha*." "What I want to achieve [. . .] is [. . .] to attain *moksha*. I live and move and have my being in pursuit of this goal. All that I do by way of speaking and writing,

24. E.g. "Both happy and unhappy," *Harijan* 29 June 1940, repr. Iyer, *Essential Writings*, pp. 248–51; "Is this humanity?," translated for *Young India* from the Gujarati in *Navajivan* Oct–Nov 1926, by Mahadev Desai and recorded also in his *Day to Day with Gandhi*, vol. 8, p. 273. See also Bhikhu Parekh, *Colonialism, Tradition and Reform*, rev. ed. New Delhi 1999, ch. 4.

25. Foreword to volume of Gokhale's speeches, written before 19 Feb 1918, repr. Iyer, *Writings*, vol. 1, p. 138.

26. Speech to the Gandhi Seva Sangh, 21 Feb 1940, repr. Iyer, *Writings*, vol. 1, p. 419.

27. "Saint or politician," *Young India* 12 May 1920, repr. Iyer, *Writings*, vol. 1, p. 42, cited by Anthony J. Parel, *Harmony*, pp. 200 and 177, and by Mohamed Mehdi, "The Political Dimension," p. 242.

28. Letter to Mathuradas Trikumji, 1 Nov 1921, *CW*, vol. 21, and introduction to *Autobiography*, p. 14, both cited by Mehdi, "The Political Dimension," pp. 240–41; *Harijan* 29 Aug 1936.

and all my ventures in the political field are directed to this same end." "Man's ultimate aim is the realisation of God, and all his activities, social, political, religious, have to be guided by the ultimate aim of the vision of God." *Moksha* here seems to play the role of a dominating goal, which the Stoics would accord instead to virtue.

(v) Finally, where political success was impossible in the face of certain extermination at the hands of the Nazis or the atomic bomb, Gandhi still looked for a moral success on the part of those about to die.[29] This illustrates the Bhagavadgita's insistence on detachment from the fruit of action, which is a point of convergence with Stoicism.

This evidence certainly shows Gandhi's subordination in various different ways of political to spiritual goals. But we should not conclude that after all Gandhi was not a politician. Even in a single action, the pursuit of one goal does not rule out the pursuit of another. People could join Gandhi's "Salt March," both to make the British withdraw their tax on salt, and to practice confronting danger, while retaining good will towards their British adversaries. There would be a test of whether they had the second, spiritual motive. If it became clear that the march would be politically ineffective, would they continue with it? If they would, that would be evidence that they had the further, nonpolitical motive. There would also be a test of whether one motive was subordinate. Would they give up the march if it encouraged violence in the participants? That was what Gandhi did in Bardoli, and doubtless would have done here. So there was an asymmetry: loss of the political objective would not call off the march, loss of the spiritual objective would. This once again suggests that the spiritual goal was more important and that the political goal was not indeed missing, but dependent on the spiritual goal.

In a number of cases, the spiritual and political pursuits supported each other. Psychological self-rule was needed as a means to the political kind, but was also said by Gandhi to *consist* (in that context) in the effort to attain political self-rule. Further, nonviolent suffering opened political ears, but its use in political resistance could also *strengthen* the nonviolent attitude of mind. In another case of the spiritual and the political being needed for each other, Gandhi argued that after the troubles in Ahmedabad even a holy man who had taken a vow of silence would be unable to achieve spiritual

29. Faisal Devji, *The Terrorist in Search of Humanity*, London 2008, pp. 215–20. See the end of chapter 4 below.

liberation, *moksha*, if he did not at least through his thoughts influence the political atmosphere.[30]

The Bhagavadgita did not require Gandhi to give up political goals. When it urges nonattachment to the fruit of action, it is not instructing us not to collect the fruit, but only not to be attached to it, not to be hung up about it. As Gandhi says, it does not require us to disown the fruits.[31] Being *ready* to disown them is the spirit that Gandhi showed in calling off his campaign in Bardoli, even if not the spirit he showed in his remarks before the Quit India campaign, nor the attitude he took in his campaign to secure dignity for the Dalits, or, more controversially, when he used the threat of a fatal fast to secure the "Poona Pact" about the Dalits' future.[32]

But often Gandhi advocated spiritual pursuits without reference to any political objectives. This was true of his belief in nonviolence as a creed, not a tactic, of some of his statements about inner swaraj being the truer freedom, again about his recommendations to the victims of Hitler and of the atomic bomb to seek a moral victory. Moreover, his quest for *moksha* is never, I believe, presented as a means to political ends, and could hardly be so presented, since *moksha* involves final release from the world.

CONCLUSION

I conclude that Gandhi's double motivation, spiritual and political, with the political motivation subordinate, might provide him with a solution to the problem under discussion: how to pursue political goals while retaining emotional detachment from them. He might retain a certain detachment if he was ready to abandon the political goal when it obstructed the spiritual one, and if, while he pursued it, he thought it less important. His spiritual values often required him to pursue political goals, but the spiritual values came first, and they were free from the tight timetable that makes political objectives so emotional. Like the Stoics, he could afford to die in the attempt to implement them, and unlike the Stoics he could be reborn to try again.

30. Gandhi in *Day to Day*, vol. 1, Nov. 1917 to Mar. 1918, pp. 181–82, quoted by Anthony Parel, in the introduction to his (ed.) *Gandhi, Freedom and Self-Rule*, Lanham, Md. 200, p. 23. Cf. "Gokhale's ideal of service," in Iyer, *Writings*, vol. 1, p. 137 f., cited by Parekh, *Political Philosophy*, p. 100.

31. Gandhi, *Harijan* March 1936, cited by Iyer, *Thought*, p. 101.

32. Gandhi used the threat of his fast in negotiating to substitute his own political strategy for Dalits for that of the Dalits' leader, Dr. Ambedkar. Gandhi objected to Ambedkar's plan for separate Dalit electorates. On this see Vinit Haksar, *Rights, Communities and Disobedience*, enlarged 2nd ed., Delhi 2001.

QUESTION: POLITICAL GOALS FOR THE FUTURE, OR SPIRITUAL GOALS FOR THE PRESENT?

I need, however, to address a challenge put to me in conversation by Faisal Devji to my chosen example of a political goal with a timetable: political self-rule within a year. Could Gandhi instead have been referring only to *psychological* self-rule within a year? He even once said that if his advice was followed, Indians could be free in a single day. The absurdity of a single day, or even a single year, could suggest that Gandhi was not really talking about swaraj in the political sense of future home rule for India, but, as I agree sometimes happens, about swaraj in the other sense he distinguishes,[33] an inner control of one's own mind that could be achieved in the immediate present. Similarly, his repeatedly expressed intention of living to 125 is too absurd, if taken as an intention for a future objective. It is better taken, on this interpretation, as an assertion of moral possibilities in the present.

It is true that in a passage drawn to my attention by Devji, Gandhi is able to accelerate swaraj by splitting his program into two stages.[34] Indians would be ready to govern themselves if they gave up the use of British schools, law courts, and legislative councils. This could be done quickly, but I do not think that even this could be done in a day. The next stage of putting an end to British rule involved asking government civil servants and the military to resign, and all to withhold tax. If not only soldiers and civil servants resigned, but police and everyone who serviced government buildings, the second stage of ending British rule would also follow quickly. But both stages would involve future political goals, and both would require more than a year.

In nonpolitical spheres too, I think that Gandhi pursued future goals. We have seen above that he considered a truly nonviolent attitude might take several incarnations to achieve. And his aspiration for a future India consisting of villages was a future goal more remote than the ending of British rule.[35]

As regards Gandhi's intention of living to 125, his confidence about the effect of true *brahmacharya*, celibacy, on the aging process was such[36] that

33. *Hind Swaraj*, pp. 73, 118, *CW*, vol. 10, pp. 39, 62.

34. "Swaraj in one year?" *Young India* 22 Sep 1920, *CW*, vol. 18, pp. 272–73.

35. E.g. talk with Manu Gandhi, 15 Apr 1947, and letter to Nehru, 5 Oct 1945, repr. Iyer, *Writings*, vol. 3, pp. 582–83, vol. 1, pp. 285–88; also interview 12 July 1946, *CW*, vol. 85, pp. 32–34, repr. Anthony J. Parel, ed., *Hind Swaraj and Other Writings*, Cambridge 1997, pp. 188–89.

36. Gandhi, "Walls of protection," *Harijan* 15 June 1947, *CW*, vol. 87, p. 102; Gandhi, *Key to Health*, Ahmedabad 1948, p. 48 ff.

I think he could have taken literally the possibility of even an imperfect *brahmachari*, as he regarded himself, setting himself the future goal of living to 125.

MARCUS AURELIUS AND GANDHI: POLITICS A STEPMOTHER WHO MUST BE SERVED

I think that Gandhi's attitude to politics may have been like that of the Stoic Roman Emperor Marcus Aurelius in the second century CE. Marcus said to himself, "If you had a stepmother and a mother, you would serve the first, but you would still continually be returning to your mother. These are what the Palace and Philosophy are for you. So return often and take your rest in her through whom palace affairs appear bearable, and you appear bearable in palace affairs."[37]

37. Marcus Aurelius, *Meditations* 6.12.

CHAPTER THREE

Gandhi's individual freedom and Isaiah Berlin on Zeno's—sour grapes?

ISAIAH BERLIN ON FREEDOM IN STOICISM

Isaiah Berlin's seminal inaugural lecture of 1958, "Two concepts of liberty," picked out two kinds of freedom, positive and negative. He himself favored negative freedom, and assigned to the Stoics one type of positive freedom that he deplored. Later, in 1962, he described Stoic freedom further and connected it with a revolution in thought that freed the individual from the demands of political life by directing him to inner consciousness instead. I shall disagree both about the value of the Stoic freedom that Berlin deplored, and about his redescription of it as liberation from political activity in favor of inner consciousness.

The freedom that Berlin favored, negative freedom, was freedom from interference by other humans, especially by the State, but he acknowledged that this aspiration was not found until long after Zeno's time.[1] The other kind of freedom, the positive kind, was described as deriving from the wish to be one's own master, and to have authority in one's own hands.[2] This could take two forms,[3] a drive towards self-abnegation, which Berlin ascribed to the Stoics, and in particular to the Stoic Epictetus,[4] and a drive for self-realization. Being one's own master, the positive freedom, is very close

1. Inaugural lecture Oxford, 1958, first printed in *Four Essays on Liberty*, Oxford 1969, repr. with revision in his most comprehensive set of papers on liberty, Isaiah Berlin, *Liberty*, ed. Henry Hardy, Oxford 2002. The revision at *Liberty*, pp. 216–17, is designed, according to p. 50, to remove the impression of an unqualified defense or blank endorsement of negative liberty. For the lateness of the idea of negative freedom, see in *Liberty*, the introduction to *Five Essays on Liberty*, pp. 33–34, the revised version of "Two concepts of liberty," p. 176, and "The birth of Greek individualism," pp. 318–19. Berlin uses the terms "freedom" and "liberty" interchangeably.

2. Berlin, "Two concepts of liberty," in *Liberty*, pp. 178–79, 212.

3. Berlin, "Two concepts," in *Liberty* p. 181.

4. Berlin, introduction and "Two concepts," in *Liberty* pp. 31, 182, 186.

to the Stoic definition, to be discussed below, of freedom as *autopragia*—being one's own agent.[5] But although Berlin saw the idea of self-mastery as "initially perhaps quite harmless at first," or in a later correction as "a valid universal goal,"[6] he thought that in practice it had led to unfreedom.[7] The Stoics did enable you to remain your own master, but they did so by eliminating all desires that someone else could frustrate, not by restricting the interference of a tyrant. This he deplored as a doctrine of "sour grapes," referring to Aesop's fable in which the fox declares the desirable but unattainable grapes to be sour anyway.[8] In his later correction, he conceded that it was a type of freedom, but sought to exclude it from consideration on the different ground that it was not a social or political freedom.[9] Berlin's other form of positive freedom as self-realization sounds extremely different, but it has in common that it allows for tyranny. One way in which it can do so is by allowing the tyrant to define the idea of a *true self.* In its self-realization version, positive freedom allows the tyrant to define the true self as something approved by himself.[10] The Stoic positive idea of freedom also invoked a true self narrowed down to a rational self that contained no frustratable desires.[11] In neither version could the positive idea of freedom be counted on to restrict interference by a tyrant, as required by negative freedom. Conversely, negative freedom's restriction on interference did not necessarily seek mastery for oneself.

So far Berlin had connected the Stoics, rightly I believe, with a positive kind of freedom, one that gave mastery by narrowing the idea of the true self so as to exclude frustratable desires. My disagreement will be with his deploring that kind of freedom, initially leaving it obscure whether it was freedom at all, and eventually characterizing it as a nonpolitical freedom.

In the later Storrs lecture of 1962,[12] Berlin gave a much more favorable account of the Stoics, even though their freedom was still of the positive

5. I thank Henry Hardy, who pointed this out to me.

6. Introduction and "Two concepts," in *Liberty*, pp. 39, 179.

7. Introduction and "Two concepts," in *Liberty*, pp. 36–37, 39, 179–81.

8. "Two concepts," in *Liberty*, p. 186.

9. Introduction, in *Liberty*, pp. 31–32.

10. Introduction, in *Liberty*, pp. 36–37, 41

11. Introduction and "Two concepts," in *Liberty*, pp. 36, 182.

12. Three Storrs lectures were given at Yale in 1962 as "Three turning-points in political thought." The first was called "The Greeks," and published by Henry Hardy in *Common Knowledge* 7, 1998, 187–214, as "A turning-point in political thought." Hardy reprinted it in *Liberty* as "The birth of Greek individualism: a turning-point in the history of political thought," at pp. 287–321 (the page numbers used below). I am grateful to Henry Hardy for first showing me the lecture.

kind. He credited the founder of Stoicism, Zeno, with identifying a new kind of individual freedom, which he connected with the revolution he ascribed to Zeno of freeing the wise person from the demands of political activity—the subject of chapter 10 below. This freedom, according to Berlin, depended exclusively on inner consciousness, and ignored the external world. In particular it ignored the call of political life in the way to be described in chapter 10. To quote Berlin, "A man is not a man unless his acts are dictated by himself and not forced upon him by a despot from without or by circumstances which he cannot control. The only portion of himself that is within his control is his inner consciousness. If he trains that consciousness to ignore and reject what it cannot control, he acquires independence from the external world. Only the independent are free, and only the free can satisfy their desires, that is, attain to peace and happiness. Such independence can be attained only by understanding the nature of reality. But whereas for Aristotle this reality contains public life—the State—as intrinsic parts of it, for the Hellenistic philosophers[13] it does not; hence the decay of political philosophy until Roman needs and Roman practice cause a specious revival in it."[14]

My disagreement here is with the contrast between inner consciousness and externals, especially political externals, as forming the basis of Zeno's idea of freedom. But Berlin's seminal statement led me to notice that Zeno was advocating a certain kind of freedom, and although it was one that had been partially exemplified earlier, it had not before been given a theoretical structure. I do not think, however, that this freedom required inattention to public life, or the ignoring or rejecting of externals. It called for a more qualified form of detachment, and that not only from externals, but also from such inner indifferents as pleasure and pain. It required seeing all indifferents for what they were: indifferents to be preferred or dis-preferred.

ZENO

What did Zeno say about freedom? The one explicit surviving statement about Zeno himself (as opposed to the Stoics in general) tells us no more than that "he calls all who are not good "enemies, foes, *slaves*, and aliens.' " Again in the *Republic*, he presents only the good as "citizens, friends, kin,

13. Those of the three centuries after the death of Alexander the Great and Aristotle in 323 and 322 BC.

14. Berlin, "The birth of Greek individualism," p. 318

and *free.*"[15] Berlin's interpretation was based not on this statement, but on some less explicit evidence. I will need to return once again to Zeno's idea of indifference and explain more about its content and development.

To bring out Zeno's contribution on freedom, it will be useful to contrast it with that of the Cynics with whom he studied first. The first and most famous of the Cynics, the teacher of Zeno's teacher, was Diogenes of Sinope. Diogenes did not think that he needed to wait for any change in society before he would be free. He claimed to be free even when captured and sold as a slave. At least the story is recorded of him that when he was put up for sale as a slave and asked what he was good at, he replied, "governing men."[16] Diogenes was said to like nothing more than freedom (*eleutheria*) and free speech (*parrhesia*).[17] Other anecdotes about him are not so explicitly about freedom and slavery, but they show why his reputation was connected with freedom. He saw no need for having a house and lived in a big wine jar. Alexander the Great, conqueror of the known world, was impressed, and coming to see him in Corinth, said, "Ask of me what you like." "Get out of my light," was Diogenes' reply.[18] All he needed was the sunlight that was supplied by nature, not by the conqueror of the world.

Cynicism gave freedom to a few exceptional eccentrics. Zeno, I believe, did the philosophical work to convert it into a way of life for respectable citizens. On reaching Athens, Zeno had studied under Diogenes' Cynic disciple, Crates,[19] and when he set up his own Stoic school, he chose a word that could well describe the Cynic position. They treated conventional objectives as "indifferent" (*adiaphoron*).[20] The word was not used in that sense by the Cynics themselves,[21] but it could capture what they were doing and it was used by Zeno as a key term in his own elaborate theory. At least on one interpretation of that theory, nearly all objectives were indifferent, according to Zeno. In humans what mattered without qualification was good character. Other objectives had a certain value (*axia*) if they were natural objectives.[22] Humans were given by divine Providence a natural tendency from birth to seek self-preservation, so that life, health, and food had a

15. Diogenes Laertius, *Lives* 7.32–33.

16. Diogenes Laertius, *Lives* 6.29–30, 6.74.

17. Diogenes Laertius, *Lives* 6.69, 6.71.

18. Diogenes Laertius, *Lives* 6.23, 6.38.

19. Diogenes Laertius, *Lives* 7.2–4.

20. Stobaeus, vol. 2, pp. 57.8–58.4, 84.18–85.11.

21. Marie-Odile Goulet-Cazé, *Les Kynica du stoïcisme*, Hermes Einzelschriften 89, Stuttgart 2003, pp. 112–19.

22. Diogenes Laertius, *Lives* 7.105; Stobaeus vol. 2, 84.18–2.85.11; Cicero, *On Ends* 3.20.

certain value.[23] But these natural objectives should be transcended in favor of another natural objective, good character, and, in the light of that, their chief value would turn out to be derivative from the fact that it was the mark of good character to pursue the other natural objectives for oneself and others. The objectives could not be called "good," because they were not important enough for that.[24] In humans, only character was important enough to be called "good" or "bad." This was the background to what we have seen, that the other natural objectives, though "indifferent," were "naturally preferred," or "naturally dis-preferred,"[25] Zeno's own term.[26] It was normally right to pursue the naturally preferred ones, but that pursuit should not be dignified with the word "choice." To distinguish it from the choice of what was really good, we saw, it should be called by the more neutral name "selection" (*eklogê*).[27] To select something was to see it for what it was: indifferent, but naturally preferred. Thus there would be no emotional overestimation of its worth, but neither would there be a quiescent lack of motivation to engage in action. Under pressure, the later Stoic, Antipater, as we also saw, made it clear how it could be an actual duty to pursue natural objectives for oneself and others, and even to do everything in one's power (*pan to kath' hauton*) to secure them. The eventual indifference of such objectives would emerge only retrospectively if, through no fault of one's own, one failed to attain them. The important value would still have been attained, since it lay in the correct pursuit.

Thus the Cynic position was modified. People had admired the eccentric Diogenes, but it would not be respectable to live like that oneself. Zeno was now identifying in Cynicism, and was preserving, the idea of indifference, but allowing a certain value after all to natural objectives. Stoics could appear outwardly to be living normal lives, pursuing the same objectives as respectable citizens. Stoics, unlike Cynics, ought normally to marry—this is ascribed to Zeno—have children, and engage in public life (*politeuesthai*).[28] But they would have a fortitude that other citizens lacked in the face of the loss of ordinary natural objectives.

23. Cicero, *On Ends* 3.20.

24. In the Stoic view they did not even contribute to happiness or unhappiness. Diogenes Laertius, *Lives* 7.104, Stobaeus, vol. 2. pp. 84.18–2.85.11.

25. Cicero, *On Ends* 3.17–22, 51; Diogenes Laertius, *Lives* 7.104–6; Stobaeus, vol. 2, pp. 84.18–85.11.

26. Stobaeus, vol. 2, p. 84.22.

27. Stobaeus, vol. 2, pp. 84.18–2.85.11; Diogenes Laertius, *Lives* 7.105; Cicero, *On Ends* 3.20.

28. Stobaeus, vol. 2, pp. 94.8–11, 109.15–18, 111.5–9; Diogenes Laertius, *Lives* 7.121; Cicero, *On Ends* 3.68.

This was not the only case in which Zeno transmuted the Cynic way of life into a respectable one. According to one source, Zeno "was the first to say that living in agreement with nature was the goal [*telos*: the goal of life], which is living in accordance with virtue."[29] If he really said this, then he cleverly picked up the Cynic preference for the natural as opposed to the conventional, but made it respectable by adding that the result would conform with *virtue*. Another source says that Zeno did not mention nature but represented the end only as living in agreement, in other words, living with consistent rationality. It was his immediate successor who added the reference to nature.[30] Even in that case, virtue would have been given a more central emphasis than is found in the Cynics, and the Stoics went on to define the virtues.[31] Although Zeno made virtue practically unattainable, he compensated by introducing the name *kathêkonta* for a range of duties within the compass of an ordinary person.[32] Accusations that he endorsed Cynic violations of conventional morality may be calumnies.[33] At any rate, he required that a young man (*neanias*) should look modestly presentable, and avoid looking seductive.[34]

It was by regarding most natural objectives as indifferent that the Stoic was expected to remain serene in the face of failure to secure those objectives. In other words, it was by a change of attitude to things, not by gritting the teeth. Anyone who had to grit teeth had not learnt the Stoic attitude.

We can now see why in his one surviving remark about freedom, quoted above, Zeno might have held that only good people are free. Only people with the right values, who see what is genuinely good and what is indifferent, can be free like Diogenes even when they are enslaved.

ZENO'S "INDIFFERENTS" AS SUPPLEMENTING SOCRATES

It needs a little explanation to see why people with the right values should be called good. Might they not instead have an agonized conscience through recognition that they forever fail to live up to their values? But Zeno, like the Cynics but in a different way, was in the tradition of Socrates. Socrates

29. Diogenes Laertius, *Lives* 7. 87.

30. Stobaeus, vol. 2, pp. 75.11–76.6.

31. Diogenes Laertius, *Lives* 7.126; Stobaeus, vol. 2, pp. 60.9–62.6.

32. Diogenes Laertius, *Lives* 7.108.

33. See Katja Vogt, *Law, Reason and the Cosmic City*, Oxford 2008, ch. 1, developing Malcolm Schofield, *The Stoic Idea of the City*, Cambridge 1991.

34. Clement of Alexandria, *Paedagogus*, book 3, ch.11.74, secs 3–4. One translator thought the reference was to young women.

is said to have argued that no one will even want (*ethelein*) a course of action that he does not think (*oiesthai*) the better course.[35] This might be called an intellectualist position, because thinking or opinion is expected to control wanting. Zeno is in effect making this a little bit more plausible than it appears to be in Socrates by bringing in the notion of indifference. If you could really regard most natural objectives as indifferent, then you would no longer *want* an indifferent objective, when you thought a rival objective to be good. The Stoics go even further in supplementing Socrates, when they actually define ordinary wanting—appetite (*epithumia*)—as a kind of judgment. It is a mistaken judgment about something indifferent that it is an imminent good and that it is appropriate to reach for it.[36] This closes the gap between judgment and appetite by identifying them.

In other cases too the Stoics could be seen as supplementing Socrates. Socrates is said to have held that it is more wretched to perpetrate injustice than to suffer it[37] and that the good man cannot be harmed by injustice.[38] The Stoics not only agree with this. By introducing the idea of preferred and dis-preferred indifferents, they provide a basis for it. For their idea is that there is nothing you could do against a person with the right values that he would see as a harm to himself rather than indifferent, unless you could make him go against his values and commit injustice. Here the idea of indifference can be seen for a second time as supplementing Socrates' claims. By a further process called "reversal" the Stoic would even *welcome* injustices that befell him.[39]

THREE STOIC KINDS OF FREEDOM

After Zeno claimed that only people with the right values could have his sort of freedom, the Stoics at some date went on to distinguish three kinds of freedom (*eleutheria*).[40] Only the wise were said to possess the first kind: the ability to be one's own agent (*exousia autopragias*), roughly Berlin's positive freedom. A second kind was the absence of subordination (*hupo-*

35. Plato, *Protagoras* 358 B–E; cf. *Gorgias* 468B–D; *Meno* 77E–78B.

36. Cicero, *Tusculan Disputations* 4.14; Diogenes Laertius, *Lives* 7.110–14; Pseudo-Andronicus, *On Emotions* 1–5. These are analyzed in Richard Sorabji, *Emotion and Peace of Mind*, Oxford 2000, ch. 2.

37. Plato, *Gorgias* 469B–C, 473A–474B, 508B–509C, 527B.

38. Plato, *Apology* 30C–D.

39. Jacques Brunschwig, "Sur deux notions de l'éthique stoïcienne: de la 'réserve' au 'renversement,'" in G. Rhomeyer-Dherbey and J.-B. Gourinet, *Les Stoïciens*, Paris 2005, 149–77.

40. Diogenes Laertius, *Lives* 7.121.

taxis). The difference between these two could perhaps be illustrated by what the Stoic Epictetus says about some Roman senators who defied the Roman emperor.[41] One, Helvidius Priscus, accepted a certain subordination when he said to the emperor, "It is up to you and it is your part to remove me from the Senate or to put me to death." But he nonetheless insisted, as a wise man would, on being his own agent (*autopragia*) by defying the emperor's wishes. The third kind of freedom was not being owned (*ktêsis*). Diogenes, the Cynic, was owned when he was sold into slavery, but in one way was not subordinate. Helvidius Priscus the senator was subordinate to the emperor, but not owned. Each, moreover, was his own agent, if we may for present purposes treat them as if they were wise men.

EPICTETUS ON FREE VS. FREE BY NATURE

The Stoic Epictetus nearly lived 400 years after Zeno, in the first century CE, but nonetheless seems to hark back to Zeno and to complete some of Zeno's fragmentary remarks, albeit in rather different conceptual terms. Sometimes he argues that you and your will (a very imperfect rendering of *prohairesis*) are unimpeded, uncompelled, unobstructed, and (2.15.1) by nature free because even if you are subjected to duress and the threat of death, it is not the threat that compels. Only your desire or your will to live can overcome your desire or will to do the right thing.[42] At other times he speaks as if only the most exceptional effort could make you and your will free. He hopes that at death he will be still engaged in making his will free.[43] To achieve this you have to avoid desiring or longing for anything that is not up to you. Otherwise you will not be free, but will be tossed about with what you long for or seek to avoid, and will be subordinate (*hupotaxis*) to those who can procure it or prevent it.[44] I once thought that two types of freedom were being introduced, but I now think that the free by nature is what *would* be free *if* you make enough effort.

Epictetus tells us the exercises by which he makes his students set aside from consideration anything that is not under the control of their wills.[45] You have even to narrow your conception of yourself down so that it no longer includes your body, but only a rightly directed will. Thus Epictetus imagines an exchange with a threatening tyrant: "I will put you in chains."

41. Epictetus, *Discourses* 1.2.19–24.

42. Epictetus, *Discourses* 1.17.23–26.

43. Epictetus, *Discourses* 3.5.7.

44. Epictetus, *Discourses* 1.4.19, 4.4.1–2.

45. Epictetus, *Discourses* 3.3.14–19.

"What did you say, man? Put *me* in chains? My *leg* you will put in chains, but my *will* not even God can conquer."[46] The person who can say this is free and so is his will. Everyone, then, is free by nature, but as Zeno said, only the person who has become truly good is actually free. It is this exceptional kind of freedom that Epictetus mostly discusses.

The exceptional freedom makes you free not only from tyrants, but from more intimate threats to freedom, which Epictetus calls tyrants as well. He names as tyrants to be set aside: your body, its parts, your faculties, your possessions, your reputation, offices, honors, children, brothers, friends. All these should be seen as not belonging to you (*allotria*).[47] *Discourse* 4.1, from which this injunction comes, is called *On Freedom* (*eleutheria*). It opens with Zeno's doctrine that no bad man is free. No one wants to live distressed, in fear, envy, pity, desiring things and failing to get them, avoiding things and falling into them.[48] We fear death, exile, loss of goods, prison, disfranchisement, and we love wealth and offices; and that is what gives the emperor control over us[49]—as Tolstoy would later say of the British king-emperor of India.[50] It is not under our control whether our body remains whole, well, or even alive. Nor is possession of our farm under our control, or of our slaves, our clothes, our house, our horses. Nor is the life of our children, wife, brother, or friends. The only thing under our control is giving or withholding the assent (*sunkatathesis*) of our reason to the right things. If we confine our desire to what is under the control of our will, we shall avoid fear.[51]

Epictetus finishes his discourse by giving two examples of people who were free: Diogenes the Cynic and before him Socrates. Socrates was different from the eccentric Diogenes, because he had a wife and children, and performed military and legislative service for Athens. But he had the right attitude to these commitments. He refused to carry out an illegal demand of the Athenian assembly or parliament, but when unjustly accused and sentenced on another charge, he equally refused to escape from prison and execution for the sake of his children. He had the right sense of shame (*aidêmon*)—a term somewhat analogous to our "conscience."[52] In his references to children and family, Epictetus does not here mention the aspect of

46. Epictetus, *Discourses* 1.17. 23–26.
47. Epictetus, *Discourses* 4.1.87.
48. Epictetus, *Discourses* 4.1.5.
49. Epictetus, *Discourses* 4.1.60.
50. I thank Mohamed Mehdi for the comparison.
51. Epictetus, *Discourses* 4.1.66–85; cf. 1.1.10–12, 4..4.29; *Handbook* 1.
52. Epictetus, *Discourses* 4.1.152–69.

Stoicism that Antipater had stressed, that it is one's duty to do everything in one's power to secure natural objectives for one's family, even while regarding those objectives as indifferent, although he does refer to that sort of idea elsewhere.[53]

The choice of Socrates and Diogenes as examples seems justified. Socrates, like Diogenes, surely was his own agent, which is the wise person's kind of freedom. At the same time, in refusing to escape from prison, he acknowledged a certain subordination to the laws of Athens, but he did so because he valued right conduct most highly. It is not clear that Diogenes acknowledged subordination at all.

Epictetus is advocating an insurmountable kind of freedom that makes it actually *impossible* for the tyrant to master you.[54] One who has decided not to try does not have freedom under a benevolent despot. Quentin Skinner has described insurmountable freedom in a different context. But he was interested in freedom to take action against the *tyrant* and he found this kind of freedom only in Cicero's *Philippics*[55] and then in Machiavelli. Epictetus' version is different, because it requires you to change *yourself*, not the tyrant, so that he will have no power over you.

The freedom of which Epictetus is talking has nothing to do with determinism, the question of whether our *acts* are determined or necessitated in advance by long chains of causes or other factors like Zeus or Fate. The Stoics proclaim that they are so necessitated,[56] but I doubt if Epictetus' discourse on freedom, 4.1, even mentions determinism. That is discussed in treatises with a different title, *On Fate*, and chiefly in terms of whether determinism clashes with our acts being *up-to-us*, so that the words for freedom are not even the preferred terms of discussion. Epictetus' question, by contrast, is whether the *person* and his will (*prohairesis*) is free, and the freedom desiderated is not a freedom from necessitating causes. The idea is partly that no one could *frustrate* a will that is rightly directed to what is under its control, and further that if one has *identified* oneself with a will so directed, one's agency is *self*-agency—*autopragia*, to use the Stoic term. Such a person is not *dependent* in the way that others are, even if his will shares the universal dependence on Zeus or Fate.

No one is allowed to escape the implications of Epictetus' view on freedom. For academics, students, and intellectuals he has a special example

53. Epictetus, *Discourses* 2.5.1–21.

54. Epictetus, *Discourses* 4.1.56

55. Cicero, *Philippics* 8.4.12, cited by Quentin Skinner, *Visions of Politics*, Cambridge 2002, vol. 2, ch. 12, "Classical liberty, Renaissance translation and the English civil war," at pp. 314–15.

56. I have discussed this in *Necessity, Cause and Blame*, London 1980, Chicago 2006.

in another discourse, which is about how even the desire for peace of mind rather than political office can make one subservient (*hupotaxis*):[57]

> Remember that it is not only the appetite for office and wealth that makes people servile and subordinate (*hupotetagmenoi*), but also the appetite for peace, leisure, travel, and scholarship. For in general, whatever the external thing is, the value set on it makes one subordinate to another. What difference, then, does it make whether one's appetite is for being a senator or not being a senator; what difference whether it is for holding office or not holding office? What difference does it make whether one says, "I am in a bad way; I have no active role, but am tied to my books like a corpse," or whether one says, "I am in a bad way; I have no leisure to read"?

In Chapter 6, we shall encounter another admonition to writers and researchers, when Galen, who respected the use of Stoic techniques among others, explains how he avoided distress at losing his manuscripts, just before he had planned to create backup copies.

ISAIAH BERLIN AGAIN AND CATO

Against Isaiah Berlin's view I want to argue that Stoic and Gandhian freedom of the individual was a genuine freedom of a sort that is sometimes needed in adverse circumstances. I think that Epictetus' examples of Diogenes and Socrates support this claim, and so does the example of Cato the Younger, who will be discussed further in chapter 10. He saw his suicide, when Caesar became invincible, as a guarantee of his freedom.[58] It is true that Berlin eventually conceded that the Stoics achieved a sort of freedom, while dismissing it from his purview as not political freedom. But Cato's capacity to oppose the subverters of the Roman constitution without sharing in the almost universal fear felt by his colleagues gave him for a long time a freedom in *political* maneuver.

57. Epictetus, *Discourses*.4.4.1–2. Compare Marcus Aurelius, *Meditations* 2.2, where books are classed among the strings that pull humans like automata: Sylvia Berryman, "The puppet and the sage: images of the self in Marcus Aurelius," *Oxford Studies in Ancient Philosophy*, 38, 2010, pp. 187–209.

58. Plutarch, *Life of Cato the Younger* 67.1, 70.2.

ADMIRAL STOCKDALE AND EPICTETUS

Turning to a modern example, I shall tell the story of Admiral Jim Stockdale only briefly, since I have told it elsewhere.[59] He became a candidate for the vice-presidency of the USA after his heroism as a prisoner for eight years in Vietnam from 1965 to 1973, where he survived four years of solitary confinement and nineteen occasions of physical torture. He claimed to have done so by following the principles of Epictetus.[60] His plane was shot down, and his parachute was fired at, so that the impact of his fall broke his leg. This, he realized, gave him something in common with Epictetus, whose leg had been broken when he was a slave. Under chaining and torture the broken leg made very relevant Epictetus' remark, "You can chain my leg, but not *me*." What above all he conveyed from Epictetus to his fellow-captives was the importance of distinguishing between what was in their power and what was not. Under torture each had blurted out more than his name and number, which was all that military regulations allowed them to reveal. The extra information was not what the captors found useful, but rather the shame that they felt for giving it. They were too ashamed to face each other, and the captors were then able to exploit the shame to obtain the thing they really wanted: denunciations on television of the US invasion of Vietnam. Stockdale, though not happy about the pretext for the invasion, was determined not to give in. As the senior American captive, he told his men that it was not in their power to avoid giving away extra information under torture. He had done so himself. But they had overlooked something that was in their power, getting themselves tortured again, by small acts of disobedience to their captors. Silence was not in their power, but, as Epictetus would put it, assent to the new plan was. Stockdale persuaded a group of the men to follow the plan and he did so himself. None of the men in this group ever appeared on Vietnamese television. Although the men were imprisoned and tortured, their captors never acquired the only power over them that they were seeking. Correspondingly, the men retained a certain freedom, consciously based on the principles of Epictetus. I will now turn to still clearer cases, those of Tolstoy and Gandhi.

59. Richard Sorabji, *Emotion and Peace of Mind*, Oxford and Chicago 2000, pp. 225–27, records also a conversation with Stockdale's wife on their visit to King's College and the Institute of Classical Studies, London.

60. J. B. Stockdale, "Testing Epictetus' doctrines in a laboratory of human behaviour," *Bulletin of the Institute of Classical Studies*, 40, 1995, 1–13.

TOLSTOY AND FREEDOM

Tolstoy enormously influenced Gandhi, chiefly through his book published in 1893, *The Kingdom of God Is Within You.* The record of books marked with underlinings in Tolstoy's library includes a book about Epictetus and other Greek thinkers,[61] and one of his remarks about freedom in chapter 9 of *The Kingdom* seems very like what Epictetus was quoted as saying above. In Aylmer Maude's English translation, he writes, "It is impossible for a man to be placed against his will in a situation repugnant to his conscience."[62] Tolstoy is arguing here that Christians are free to reject violence and to adopt the "law of love" preached by Christ in the Sermon on the Mount.[63] He says that this freedom is the Christian's inalienable possession. In chapter 12, added later, he qualifies this: the freedom is rather to recognize the truth that the role you play in a violent society is not needed for the public good. Once you recognize that, your situation will inevitably change of itself.[64]

By 1908 Tolstoy had written a manuscript, *Letter to a Hindoo,* and Gandhi, who very much agreed with the copy he saw, got Tolstoy's permission in 1909 to print it. Tolstoy said that a few thousand British could not have enslaved millions of Indians. Indians had enslaved themselves by rejecting the law of love and collaborating in the violent institutions of their rulers. As soon as they stopped they would be free:

> Is it not the same thing with the millions of people who submit to thousands, or even hundreds, of others—of their own or other nations? If the people of India are enslaved by violence it is only because they themselves live and have lived by violence, and do not recognise the eternal law of love inherent in humanity.
>
> *"Pitiful and foolish is the man who seeks what he already has, and does not know that he has it. Yes, pitiful and foolish is he who does not know the bliss of love which surrounds him and which I have given him." Krishna.*
>
> As soon as men live entirely in accord with the law of love natural to their hearts and now revealed to them, which excludes all resistance by violence—as soon as this happens, not only will hundreds be unable to

61. I thank my Oxford colleague Julie Curtis for showing me the website, http://tolstoy-nasledie.ru/index.php?doc=48.

62. Tolstoy, *Kingdom,* ch. 9 (tr. Maude, p. 439; tr. Garnett, p. 321).

63. Matthew 5:38–40; cf. Luke 6:29.

64. Tolstoy, *Kingdom,* ch. 12 (tr. Maude, pp. 424, 442; tr. Garnett, pp. 312, 323–24).

enslave millions, but not even millions will be able to enslave a single individual. Do not resist the evil-doer and take no part in doing so, either in the violent deeds of the administration, in the law courts, the collection of taxes, or above all in soldiering, and no one in the world will be able to enslave you."

Although Tolstoy was talking about political freedom, it was to be acquired by something internal, the assimilation of the law of love, which provided an inner freedom as well. Gandhi's preface to the letter in his South African newspaper, *Indian Opinion*, repeated Tolstoy's view as being that "We are our own slaves, not of the British."[65]

GANDHI AND INDIVIDUAL FREEDOM

Gandhi believed something that sounds like Epictetus and Tolstoy, that "no power on earth can make a person do a thing against his will."[66] Again, an individual becomes irresistible and his action becomes all-pervasive in its effect when he voluntarily reduces himself to zero.[67] This last reduction sounds parallel to the reduction of one's wants in Epictetus, and Gandhi connects the reduction to zero with freedom elsewhere too.[68] Gandhi even shares Epictetus' view that I should not regard the body as being myself, or even mine, but should be prepared to die,[69] although he, unlike Epictetus, does not connect that surrender with freedom.

Gandhi was very much influenced by a scriptural text, the Bhagavadgita, cited in chapter 1. In Mahadev Desai's translation of Gandhi's Gujarati translation, the Gita advocates a certain kind of detached indifference as between opposite outcomes. While the Stoics spoke of *outcomes* as indifferent, the Gita is speaking of our *attitudes to* opposite outcomes. For example:

12.18 Who is same to foe and friend, who regards alike respect and disrespect, cold and heat, pleasure and pain, who is free from attachment;

65. Repr. Iyer, *Writings*, vol. 1, no. 54, pp. 108–11, repr. Iyer, *Essential Writings*, no. 28, pp. 73–75.

66. "The topic of the hour," *Young India* 8 Feb 1926, *eCW*, vol. 34, p. 303.

67. Talk with an American journalist, *Harijan* 6 Oct 1946, *eCW*, vol. 92, p. 232.

68. "The eternal duel," *Young India* 20 Dec 1928, *eCW*, vol. 43, p. 417.

69. Speech at ashram on Ramanavami Day, *Navajivan* 1 Apr 1928, *CW*, vol. 36, p. 165; speech at Guildhouse Church, 23 Sep 1931, *CW*, vol. 48, pp. 50–58, at 54; also interview with Nirmal Kumar Bose, *Hindustan Times* 17 Oct 1935, repr. Iyer, *Writings*, vol. 3, p. 598.

> 14.24 He who holds pleasure and pain alike, who is sedate, who regards as same earth, stone and gold, who is wise and weighs in equal scale things pleasant and unpleasant, who is even-minded in praise and blame;
> 2.57 Who owns attachment nowhere, who feels neither joy nor resentment whether good or bad comes his way—that man's understanding is secure.

Gandhi did not acquire this attitude of equanimity simply by reading. A whole way of life was needed. I shall come back more than once to another text he wrote at the same time as his introduction to Tolstoy's letter in 1909, *Hind Swaraj (Indian Home Rule)*. There he picks out the importance for would-be passive resisters to "observe perfect chastity, adopt poverty, follow truth and cultivate fearlessness."[70] With equanimity thus solidly based, Gandhi gained from it a sort of individual freedom in two different contexts. First, in his struggle against the British Raj, when he faced imprisonment, or death in prison through fasting, it was the British who were afraid, not Gandhi. This gave him a kind of freedom in prison that the British lacked after putting him there. He thus provides an even clearer example of individual freedom than Socrates, Diogenes, or Stockdale. But as with Epictetus, his freedom was exemplified not only in resistance to an empire. It was exemplified also in his freedom from fear in the new situation of communal massacres after India had gained its independence.

This individual freedom was not the same as political freedom from the British. He called political independence by the name swaraj or "home rule." It was more like what the Stoics called absence of subordination (*hupotaxis*), whereas being one's own agent (*autopragia*) he possessed already. Individual and political freedom, then, were different for Gandhi.

Nonetheless, Gandhi did think that political freedom from the British could not be gained, and would not constitute much advantage,[71] until an individual inner freedom had been acquired first. He even called the inner freedom the real swaraj in his *Hind Swaraj* (*Indian Home Rule*) of 1909: "It is Swaraj when we learn to rule ourselves. It is therefore in the palm of our hands. [. . .] After we have once realised it, we will endeavour to the

70. *Hind Swaraj*, pp. 96–98.

71. "Not much advantage" is the message from the paraphrase of Ruskin about to be cited: Gandhi, "*Sarvodaya*," conclusion. "Could not be gained" is suggested by the two stages of political liberation, to be recapitulated almost immediately after that, in which the first stage gives Indians self-reliance.

end of our life time to persuade others to do likewise. But such Swaraj has to be experienced by each one for himself." "Real home-rule is self-rule or self-control," or in a more literal rendering of the Gujarati, "One's rule over one's own mind is real swaraj."[72]

In the previous year, 1908, in his paraphrase of Ruskin's *Unto This Last*, Gandhi had already written about this kind of swaraj:[73] "Real *swarajya* consists in restraint. He alone is capable of this who leads a moral life, does not cheat anyone, does not forsake truth and does his duty to his parents, his wife, his children, his servant and his neighbour. Such a man will enjoy *swarajya* wherever he may happen to live. A nation that has many such men always enjoys *swarajya*. It is wrong normally [*sic*, not as we might have expected "morally"] for one nation to rule over another. British rule in India is an evil but we need not believe that any very great advantage would accrue to the Indians if the British were to leave India. The reason why they rule over us is to be found in ourselves; that reason is our disunity, our immorality and our ignorance. If these three things were to disappear, not only would the British leave India without the rustling of a leaf, but it would be real *swarajya* that we would enjoy."

In notes of 1922 he repeated:[74]

> Swaraj is a state of mind to be experienced by us. We have to win it by our own strength. If this is true, there is no reason at all for disappointment. Swaraj consists in our efforts to win it.

The stages of inner freedom and political freedom may correspond to the two stages mentioned in chapter 2. First, Indians would be ready to govern themselves, if they gave up the use of British schools, law courts, and legislative councils. Ending British rule would require withdrawal of cooperation from a more extensive range of British services.[75]

Gandhi's discussion of true swaraj over one's own mind shows him not only practicing, but also recognizing, an inner freedom different from any approved by Berlin.

72. *Hind Swaraj*, chs. 14 and 20, pp. 73, 118, *CW*, vol. 10, pp. 39, 64.

73. Gandhi, "*Sarvodaya*," conclusion, repr. Iyer, *Writings*, vol. 3, pp. 410–32, at p. 431; version with alterations suggested by Verrier Elwin published in Ahmedabad 1956, available on the Internet at www.peace.ca/UntoThisLast-Gandhi.doc.

74. Gandhi, "My notes," *Navajivan*, 12 March 1922, *CW*, vol. 23, pp. 71–72.

75. Gandhi, "Swaraj in one year," *Young India* 22 Sep 1920, *CW*, vol. 18, p. 272.

Gandhi also believed in a different kind of freedom that has no parallel in Stoicism, the spiritual liberation called *moksha*. I have argued in the introduction that Gandhi saw *moksha* in the conventional way as a liberation from rebirth. He saw it also as involving a full vision of God. But others have rightly emphasized something startlingly unusual about his view. He thought that *moksha* was to be acquired not by a retreat from the world, in the traditional Indian manner, but by engagement with the oppressed, and that the hoped-for vision of God could be anticipated by a glimpse of God in the face of those suffering. There is another startling innovation when Gandhi says in a comment of 1920 that the truest swaraj, psychological self-rule, is after all *synonymous* with *moksha*.[76] Psychological self-rule was close to the Stoic ideal, whereas spiritual liberation was remote from their interests. But perhaps it was because Gandhi had made *moksha* attainable through immersion in the world that he felt able to equate it with worldly self-command.

GANDHI'S KNOWLEDGE OF PLATO'S *APOLOGY*

Gandhi did not know the Stoics, apart from the one book he read about them in jail between 1922 and 1924. Mahadev Desai did know them, as we shall see in chapter 6. But what Gandhi did know was Plato's text about Socrates, the *Apology*, which includes a passage that reads as a sort of prototype of the Stoic idea of indifferents. The Stoics will have reflected in devising their theory on this text among others. In defending himself from his unjust accusers, Meletus and Anytus, Socrates is represented as saying:

> Know that if you kill me, I being a man such as I say I am, you will not harm me more than you harm yourselves. For neither Meletus nor Anytus could harm me at all. It would not even be possible, because it is not permitted for a better man to be harmed by a worse. He might still perhaps kill me, or exile me, or ban me from office. But while he perhaps and, I suppose, others might think these things great harms, I think that way not of them, but much rather of doing what he is now doing: trying to kill a man unjustly.[77]

Here Plato represents Socrates as treating the performance of unjust action as a harm to the perpetrator, but suffering unjust execution, exile,

76. "On the wrong track," *Young India* 8 Dec 1920, *eCW*, vol. 22, pp. 63–65.
77. Plato, *Apology* 30 C–D.

and denial of office as being, in later Stoic terms, merely indifferent. This will have chimed with the attitudes that Gandhi had already imbibed from the Gita, and made Plato's *Apology* all the more congenial to him. The resulting individual freedom might be called equally Zenonian freedom or Gandhian freedom.

CHAPTER FOUR

Nonviolence as universal love: origins and Gandhi's supplements to Tolstoy—dilemmas,successes, and failures

NONVIOLENT ATTITUDES AND NONVIOLENT RESISTANCE DISTINGUISHED

I turn now to Gandhi's unexpected conception of nonviolence as universal love. Gandhi's nonviolence was originally coupled with *resistance* to rule first in South Africa and then in India, but his interest in nonviolence spread to all contexts. He valued it equally whether coupled with resistance against violent rule or not. Even in the context of a liberated India, he thought of it as something still to be practiced in daily life. What he learned from Tolstoy, we have seen, was to think of nonviolence as an inner psychological state of good will to all, or universal love. Moreover, he considered it a psychological state that could only be achieved by the kind of emotional detachment he found in the Gita, as described in chapter 1.

GREEK PHILOSOPHY: EPICTETUS ON THE CYNIC WHO LOVES HIS PERSECUTORS

I shall come shortly to the influence on Gandhi of Tolstoy and the Christian tradition. But was there no influence on him from the tradition of Greek philosophy, and from the Stoics in particular? It is known from underlinings in the books in Tolstoy's library that he, Tolstoy, had read translations of Cynics and Stoics.[1] But Greek philosophical appeals to nonviolence were more limited than those of Christ, even though a Stoic text provides the closest parallel I know.

1. I thank Julie Curtis for directing me to the website http://tolstoy-nasledie.ru/index.php?doc=48.

One Greek tradition stems from Socrates, who spoke about injustices, including violent ones. He argued that it was unjust (*ou dikaion*) to return evil for evil,[2] and a greater harm to one to commit an injustice (*adikein*) than to suffer one.[3] Both claims influenced the Stoics. Epictetus forbids getting even with those who do you an injustice.[4] Seneca repeats that it is more wretched to harm than to be harmed.[5] But Socrates' context was justice and self-interest, whereas the context in Christ's Sermon on the Mount and in Gandhi was universal *love* for other humans. Christ gave an example of violence when he said, "You have heard that it was said, 'An eye for an eye and a tooth for a tooth.' But I say to you, Do not resist one who is evil. But if anyone strikes you on the right cheek, turn to him the other also; and if anyone would sue you and take your coat, let him have your cloak as well."[6] Christ's generalization of the recommendation to turn the other cheek transformed it, because the earlier Judaic reference to turning the other cheek had been merely to the danger of restive young men provoking their oppressors, while the Jews waited in patient hope for their release from Babylonian captivity.[7]

It was the Stoics, not Socrates, who connected justice with universal *love* through their theory of *oikeiôsis*. The theory was that it would accord with nature to extend a sense of affectionate *kinship* to all other human beings. Seneca makes a tacit reference to Socrates' view when he appeals to the self-interest of being just, but he precedes this immediately with a reference to universal *love*.[8] He claims that nature has made all humans akin (*cognati*), and has given us mutual love (*amor*) and sociability (*sociabilis*). He is alluding to the Stoic theory that bases universal justice on the foundation of universal love. The Stoics claim that it is natural to extend *justice* to all humans because it is natural to extend a sense of affectionate kinship by the process of *oikeiôsis* to all humans.

Seneca's fellow-Stoic Epictetus a little later makes the statement that is closest of all to Christ's Sermon on the Mount and to Gandhi. In his treatise praising the ideal Cynic,[9] Epictetus says that if the Cynic is beaten like a

2. Plato, *Crito* 49C, 54C.

3. Plato, *Gorgias* 469B–527B; *Apology* 30C–D.

4. Epictetus, *Discourses* 4.167.

5. Seneca, *Letters* 95, 52.

6. Matthew 5:38–40.

7. Lamentations of Jeremiah 3:30.

8. This will further discussed in chapter 10.

9. Epictetus, *Discourses* 3.22. 54–56. Other aspects of 3.22 are discussed by Malcolm Schofield, "Epictetus on Cynicism," in Theodore Scaltsas and Andrew Mason, eds., *The Philosophy of Epictetus*, Oxford 2007, pp. 71–86.

donkey, he must *love* (*philein*) those who are beating him as if he were the *father* or *brother* of them all. The true Cynic will not appeal to the officers of the law courts, but only to God, who is giving him this trial.

Gandhi would have liked this and he would have been interested if he had known the comment of an early Cynic, Onesicritus on an Indian kingdom, now Sind in Pakistan. Onesicritus accompanied Alexander the Great in his invasion of India and was very impressed that in the land of King Musicanus contracts were not disputed in the law courts, but only cases of murder or defamation.[10]

Whether or not Tolstoy knew of Epictetus' Cynic, it was the Christian background that he stressed in his account of nonviolence, and it was Tolstoy who influenced Gandhi.

EARLY CHRISTIAN REACTIONS TO CHRIST ON OFFERING THE OTHER CHEEK

Another example often cited of Christ's advocacy of nonviolence was his telling a disciple (Peter) not to defend him with a sword, because all who take the sword will perish by the sword.[11] But in this case Christ had authorized self-defense, because he had arranged for the swords to be bought for that purpose.[12]

The early Church followed Christ on turning the other cheek. Pacifism is such an emotional subject that there has been much dispute over the bans by early Christian thinkers on soldiery as a profession for Christians.[13] But it was only in the fourth century that it became hard to advocate Christian pacifism, once Christianity gained the support of the emperor, Constantine. Before that there are plenty of texts that appear to say that people would not be accepted as Christians if they joined the army. Even later there are texts that exclude Christians from their sacrament of communion if they had already joined the army and shed blood. But after Constantine, Augustine

10. Strabo, *Geographica* 15.1.34 and 54; M. H. Fisch, "Alexander and the Stoics," part 4, *American Journal of Philology*, 58, 1937, pp. 129–44, esp. 133.

11. E.g. Matthew 26:52.

12. Matthew 10:9; Luke 22:35–36.

13. Apparent bans include: third century CE, Tertullian, *On the Crown* 11; *On Idolatry*, ch. 19; his pupil Cyprian, *Letter* 60, *On the Good of Patience* 14; Hippolytus, *Apostolic Tradition* 16; Origen, *Against Celsus* 7.25–26, 8.73. Fourth century: Arnobius, *Against the Pagans* 1.6; his pupil Lactantius, *Divine Institutes* 5.17, 6.20. Fifth century: Basil of Caesarea, *Canonical Epistles*, *Letter* 188 (= Canonical Letter 1), Canon 13; Pseudo-Hippolytus, *Canon* 13 and 14.

in the Western Latin-speaking Church, with the support of Cicero's writings, introduced the idea of *just* war as legitimate.[14] This was a conscious *alternative* to pacifism, and it gave a legitimate place to certain types of war. Augustine reinterpreted Christ's injunction to offer the other cheek as a warning not against fighting, but against having the wrong inward disposition towards enemies. He would have rejected the familiar kind of demonization of them. Augustine's insistence on the right inward disposition was taken up by Thomas Aquinas under the heading of "right intention."[15]

TOLSTOY'S ACKNOWLEDGED INFLUENCE ON GANDHI

Gandhi called Tolstoy the second greatest influence among men who had influenced his life.[16] Among Tolstoy's works, he continued, the one with the greatest effect was *The Kingdom of God Is Within You* (1893), a book whose title Tolstoy had taken from scripture (Luke 17:20–21). Gandhi confessed that he had been "a votary of violence" until he read that book. "I know of no author in the West," he wrote, "who has written as much and as effectively for the cause of non-violence as Tolstoy has done." Gandhi continued by rejecting the conception of nonviolence he had heard in India in favor of Tolstoy's conception. "Our non-violence is an unworthy thing. We see its utmost limit in refraining somehow from destroying bugs, mosquitos and fleas, or from killing birds and animals. We do not care if these creatures suffer, nor even if we partly contribute to their suffering. On the contrary, we think it a heinous sin if anyone releases or helps in releasing a creature that suffers. I have already written and explained that this is not non-violence, and I take this occasion, when I am speaking about Tolstoy, to repeat that that is not the meaning of non-violence. Non-violence means an ocean of compassion, it means shedding from us every trace of ill-will for others." Achieving this attitude, he continued, requires the same humility

14. For one of many accounts, see Richard Sorabji, "Just war from ancient origins to the Conquistadors debate and its modern relevance," ch. 1 of Richard Sorabji and David Rodin, eds., *The Ethics of War: Shared Problems in Different Traditions*, Aldershot 2006. Augustine, *City of God* 19.21, preserves Cicero's defense of Rome's conquests on the basis of the idea that some people are natural slaves. Cicero also appeals to Roman fetial law to give an enemy time to offer reparations. *On Duties* 1.26; *Republic* Book 3, ch. 23. sections 34–35.

15. See Richard Sorabji, ch. 1, pp. 15–16, and Anthony Coates, ch. 11, *The Ethics of War: Shared Problems in Different Traditions*. For Augustine, I cited *Against Faustus* 22.74–79; *Letter* 138,2, and 13–15; *On the Sermon on the Mount* 1.19.59.

16. The first was Rajchandra: see chapter 1. Gandhi, speech of 10 Sep 1928 for the anniversary of Tolstoy's birth, *Navajivan* 16 Sep 1928, repr. Iyer, *Writings*, vol. 1, no. 59, see pp. 115–19.

or emptiness as Indian sages require for the achievement of *moksha* (spiritual liberation), and then he used a central concept of Christianity to say that such emptiness cannot be attained without God's *grace*.

Tolstoy's influence on Gandhi was enormous. When in 1908 Tolstoy applied his views to the case of British rule in India, in the manuscript of *Letter to a Hindoo*, Gandhi wrote to Tolstoy and obtained his permission to have it printed, which he did in twenty thousand copies.[17] In South Africa in 1910, Gandhi set up his 1,100-acre site for satyagrahis and their families, the nonviolent resisters against the South African regime, and he called it Tolstoy Farm.

TOLSTOY'S FAR-REACHING INFERENCES FROM OFFERING THE OTHER CHEEK

In the *Kingdom of God Is Within You*, Tolstoy postulated a thesis that was to be echoed by Gandhi. There were three stages, which Tolstoy considered inevitable, in the history of mankind. At first each man was concerned only with himself. In the second stage, concern spread to family, to tribe, and even to one's country. There it halted until eighteen hundred years before Tolstoy, Christ put forward the law of love, a new concern that did not stop at the artificial frontier of country. This was a doctrine of universal brotherhood, community of property (Tolstoy tried to give away his own), and not resisting evil by violence. National distinctions led to violence and should be eliminated (Gandhi did not go as far as that). The transition from each stage to the next is slow and seems strange and impossible, until the old attitude becomes too uncomfortable to maintain. That time is already coming because there is an increasingly intolerable conflict between the old attitude of the second stage and our consciences, which already contain the law of the brotherhood of men. It is evidenced by the thousands of suicides every year among military men in Europe (still a serious problem), who are required to go out and kill other people who have done them no harm.[18] The creation of temples (which the founder of Stoicism sought to abolish for his own different reasons) was merely a hypnotic device of the second stage to keep people loyal to country.[19] Clearly the influence on Tolstoy's book was

17. Rajmohan Gandhi, *Mohandas*, p. 151; see also 157.

18. Tolstoy, *Kingdom*, ch. 5 (tr. Maude, pp. 130–37, 157–59; tr. Garnett, pp. 97–102, 115).

19. Tolstoy, *Kingdom*, ch. 12 (tr. Maude, p. 231; tr. Garnett, p. 171). For the Stoics on temples, see chapter 10.

first and foremost that of the Christian tradition, despite his acquaintance with Cynics and Stoics.

Tolstoy went on to oppose Russia's violent revolutionaries. Revolution only leads to a more despotic government. Any anticipated advantage of the new government's restraining violence is superseded when they have to restrain their rivals and their oppressed subjects.[20] It is in this context that Tolstoy speaks of the topic discussed in chapter 3, the need to recognize our freedom to refuse to cooperate in violence.

Tolstoy added a final twelfth chapter in the light of two horrific incidents at Tula and Oryël, after he had interviewed personally the authorities and soldiers who were traveling to carry out one of these atrocities at Tula. At Oryël the peasants were starving after having tried to resist a magistrate's order confirming the confiscation by a wealthy landlord of the natural facilities that provided their livelihood. They had now submitted, but the local governor sent soldiers to execute a savage beating upon twelve peasants selected by the landowner. The beatings at Oryël were carried out in front of the families, and the governor refused to stop where the doctor recommended, when the first victim fell unconscious at fifty blows, but went on to seventy blows for each of the twelve. At Tula, Tolstoy found that the soldiers looked ashamed when a woman in the train questioned their errand to the place of punishment half an hour away. In their consciences they knew. Tolstoy later witnessed at Tula the compulsory annual enlistment of peasant lads to serve in this very army, and the apparent inability of anyone to refuse or to resist the loss of five years of family and earnings.[21]

Tolstoy tells us in the first chapter of *The Kingdom of God* of his familiarity with pacifist groups. Among them were Protestant Christians—the Mennonites dating from sixteenth-century Holland and the Quakers dating from seventeenth-century England—and among dissident Russian Christians, the Molokans and the Dukhobors, for the last of whom Tolstoy gained safe conduct from Russia to Canada.

Tolstoy's conclusion was that one should refuse to work in government, policing, or the army, and should refuse to pay taxes.[22] A short book translated into English in 1900 as *Slavery of our Times* was still more far-reaching. One should not accept any payment derived from taxes, nor

20. Tolstoy, *Kingdom*, chs. 7 and 8 (tr. Maude, pp. 201–6, 234; tr. Garnett, pp. 148–52, 173).

21. Tolstoy, *Kingdom*, ch. 12 (tr. Maude, pp. 339–43, 347–53, 366–69; tr. Garnett, pp. 249–56, 259–63, 272–76).

22. Tolstoy, *Kingdom*, chs. 11 and 12 (tr. Maude, pp. 289, 314, 327, 371; tr. Garnett, pp. 215, 232, 242, 272).

government defense of possessions or near ones, and instead of law courts one should appeal only at most to arbitration tribunals.[23]

In his *Letter to a Hindoo* of 1908, quoted in the last chapter, Tolstoy wrote that millions of Indians could not have been enslaved by a few hundred or thousand British. They were-self-enslaved because they ignored the law of love, which would have prevented them cooperating with the violence of implementing British administration, law, tax-collection, and military action. As soon as they stopped they would be free.[24]

GANDHI'S ACCEPTANCE OF TOLSTOY

Many of Gandhi's statements right through to the 1930s follow Tolstoy very closely. The three stages of mankind are represented in a piece from 1922, coupled in the same paragraph with a warning that revolution will only increase subsequent violence. "Some day we must extend the national law to the universe, even as we have extended the family law to form nations—a larger family. . . . Power seized by violence will only result in their greater grinding."[25] Speaking in 1931 of the *law of love* as inevitable, Gandhi wrote, "Whether mankind will consciously follow the law of love I do not know. But that need not perturb us. The law will work, just as the law of gravitation will work whether we accept it or no."[26] In 1936, Gandhi described love as "the law of life" and the law of love as "the Supreme law of our Being."[27] Noncooperation was seen by Gandhi as like seeking first the kingdom of God, after which everything else would be added.[28]

Gandhi, like Tolstoy, rejected law courts as based on violence. In 1909 in *Hind Swaraj*, he wrote an attack on his own profession as lawyer. Not only did lawyers keep the British in power in India, but quite generally lawyers promote quarreling instead of having people settle quarrels among them-

23. Tolstoy, *Slavery of our Times*, 1890, translated Aylmer Maude, New York 1900, Oxford World Classics edition, pp. 9–63.

24. Tolstoy, *Letter to a Hindoo*, 14 Dec 1908, ed. Christian Bartolf, Berlin 1997, p. 26.

25. "Notes," *Young India* 2 March 1922, repr. *Young India 1919–1922*, Madras 1924, p. 285.

26. Gandhi, *Young India* 1 Oct 1931, recorded by Mahadev Desai from a prayer meeting aboard S. S. Rajputana en route to the second Round Table Conference in London, repr. Iyer, *The Esential Writings of Mahatma Gandhi*, no. 151, p. 243. Repeated by Gandhi in speech to Gandhi Seva Sangh, 22 Feb 1940, repr. Iyer, *Writings*, vol. 1, no. 150, at p. 437.

27. Gandhi, "The law of our being," *Harijan* 26 Sep 1936, from a letter of 2 May 1935, recorded in Mahadev Desai, mss. of *Day to Day with Gandhi*, repr. Iyer, *Writings*, vol. 2, pp. 324–27.

28. *Young India* June 1920, cited by Iyer, *Thought*, p. 285.

selves.[29] This leaves some people destitute and hands power to the British rulers. The rulers, however, depend for their power on the use of Indian judges and pleaders. In 1920 and 1921, Gandhi recommended as an alternative model the village panchayat, or council of five elders, for arbitrating quarrels. Such councils must be careful to resort to no punitive measures. They should use only the force of public opinion, including excommunication.[30] Gandhi may here have underestimated the violent effects, including suicide, of public opinion and excommunication, which are portrayed in films about village life by Anantamurthy, *Samskara* and *Ghata Shradda.* Nonetheless, out of the two major nationalist leaders dominant in the law courts of northern India, Gandhi persuaded one, to give up his law practice, Matilal Nehru, father of the future prime minister, though not the other, Tej Bahadur Sapru.

Starting in 1918, Gandhi urged Indians to boycott not only the law-courts, but also everything that supported a regime that ruled by violence, whether it was in itself violent or not. They should boycott the law-courts first along with government-controlled schools and seats on legislative councils and later the army, police, administration, and even menial government services. They should also refuse government honors.[31] A good number, not all, gave up seats on legislative councils or gave back their honors to the British government. Persuading warrior peoples to leave the army was harder, but I have myself met someone whose father, Mr. Bhatt, was persuaded by Gandhi to give up his army career and consequently his pension.

DIVERGENCE FROM TOLSTOY ON PACIFISM AND NATIONALISM

On some matters Gandhi differed from Tolstoy. We shall see more clearly when we come to his countenancing some cases of violent killing that Gandhi was not, like Tolstoy, a pacifist. He even went so far as to insist that the British should hand over to Indians control of the army and defense as

29. He could have found the same advice in St. Paul's First Letter to the Corinthians, 6:1–8.

30. *Hind Swaraj*, ch. 11, pp. 58–62; extract from Gandhi's *Young India* printed in *Young India 1919–1922*, Madras 1924, under "Boycott of courts," p. 363, with a footnote quoting a second extract from *Young India* 16 March 1921.

31. See *CW*, index under "boycott." Selected extracts are printed also in the collection *Young India 1919–1922*, Madras 1924, p. 149, from *Young India* 10 March 1920, under "The question of questions" (about Khilafat), and pp. 228–29, from *Young India* 23 Feb 1921, under "Noncooperation—its theory and practice." For the division into two phases of boycott, see "Swaraj in one year?" *Young India* 22 Sep 1920, *CW*, vol. 18, pp. 272–73.

being the essence of a nation's existence and required for responsible government.[32] As for nationalism, Tolstoy had rejected it uncompromisingly, because it called for violence against other nations. Gandhi's rejection of ordinary nationalism was more subtle. As he wrote in 1935, "My nationalism includes the love of all the nations of the earth irrespective of creed."[33]

THE BEHAVIORAL CONCEPT OF VIOLENCE RECURS, BUT IS OVERRIDDEN BY THE ATTITUDINAL

Although Gandhi accepted Tolstoy's conception of nonviolence as an attitude of good will and compassion, and rejected the behavioral conception he claimed to have learnt in India, he did make use of the behavioral conception sometimes. The latter required one to refrain from killing animals even accidentally. Jains would wear masks or sweep the street ahead of them to avoid accidental killing, even though, according to Gandhi, Indian nonviolence did not care about animal suffering. Occasionally, and not surprisingly, Gandhi slipped into talking about violence in this other way. He did so when he spoke of violence being unavoidable, when, for example, we breathe in microbes. He said that "even the forest-dweller cannot be entirely free from violence, in spite of his limitless compassion. With every breath he commits a certain amount of violence. The body itself is a house of slaughter." Again, "man cannot for a moment live without committing outward *himsa* [violence]. The very fact of his living—eating, drinking and moving about—necessarily involves some *himsa*, destruction of life, be it ever so minute."[34] This is violence in the behavioral, not the attitudinal, sense. But there is no room for confusion here. The attitudinal sense was explicitly introduced in contrast to the rejected behavioral sense, and it was nonviolence in the *attitudinal* sense that Gandhi officially endorsed.

NONVIOLENCE AS *ATTITUDE*: ITS RELATION TO *MOTIVE* AND TO *WISH*

Speaking of his official new concept of nonviolence, *ahimsa*, as *attitude*, Gandhi said in 1928: "whilst it is true that mental attitude is the crucial test of *ahimsa*, it is not the sole test." He meant that there are constraints

32. Extract from Proceedings of Federal Structure Committee Meeting, 17 Nov 1931, *CW*, vol. 48, pp. 304, 307.

33. A letter in manuscript of Mahadev Desai's diary, repr. Iyer, *Essential Writings*, p. 245.

34. "Is this humanity?," in *Day to Day*, vol. 8, Oct–Nov 1926, p. 270; *Autobiography*, part 4, ch. 29.

on motive as well. Repeating his fullest statement of criteria for nonviolent *killing* from 1926, he said that killing will be violence, unless it is done *for the sake of* the victim, and there will still be violence if someone with a different motive *would* kill if he could.[35]

GANDHI'S SUPPLEMENTATION OF TOLSTOY ON NONVIOLENT METHODS

Gandhi developed a battery of methods for nonviolent resistance that went beyond anything in Tolstoy. For one thing, he saw the need to address directly the *suffering* that the nonviolent resister must expect to meet. The preparation in emotional detachment that was described in chapter 1 was not an unconnected feature of Gandhi's approach, since only with the right detachment can the nonviolent resister persist when trouble begins. Moreover, we shall see[36] that he applied his idea of *svadharma*, individual duty, to say that people should be *selected* for this, because only some, not others, were suited for it. Further, he saw actual value in the punishment undergone. It could appeal to *conscience* and make an important contribution to persuading opponents. In 1931 he wrote it could *open their ears*:[37]

> Since then the conviction has been growing upon me, that things of fundamental importance to the people are not secured by reason alone but have to be purchased with their suffering. [. . .] Suffering is infinitely more powerful than the law of the jungle for converting the opponent and opening his ears, which are otherwise shut, to the voice of reason. [. . .] The appeal of reason is more to the head but the penetration of the heart comes from suffering. It opens up the inner understanding in man.

Another feature of Gandhi's armory that has been pointed out was his good will, because if people feel good will, they listen better to a reasoned case.[38] A third feature was that these encouragements to listen were accompanied by the threat of mass protest. It has been pointed out, fourthly, that Gandhi was good at choosing particular issues on which popular sentiment already existed—though he did not do so in advising self-sacrifice to the victims of Hitler.

35. "Himsa and ahimsa," *Young India* 18 Oct 1928, repr. Iyer, *Writings*, vol. 2, pp. 276–78.

36. Chapter 7 below.

37. Speech at Birmingham meeting, 18 Oct 1931, *Young India* 5 Nov 1931, *eCW*, vol. 54, p. 48, quoted by Chatterjee, *Religious Thought*, p. 78.

38. Parekh, *Political Philosophy*, pp. 143–44.

Of these methods, the first two obviously, but perhaps even the others, involved an insistence on truth, *satyagraha*. The suffering and the good will help opponents to reflect on what they believe in. It has been argued that even breaking the law in civil disobedience might be construed as an invitation to the authorities to reflect on the truth.[39]

As regards civil disobedience (for example not paying taxes that support violent institutions), Gandhi distinguished it from noncooperation, as in the boycott of British facilities described above. Tolstoy had offered examples of each in *The Kingdom of God Is Within You* in 1893, the year of Gandhi's arrival in South Africa, though he had not hived them off under a distinct name. The term "civil disobedience" came from Thoreau. But Gandhi claimed to have thought of both methods for himself. He said that Thoreau's work only gave him scientific confirmation of what he was already doing in South Africa.[40] About noncooperation he claimed, "The idea of non-cooperation was conceived first by me."[41]

But Gandhi later played down the utility of civil disobedience and said that it could never on its own achieve political independence. It can be used only for particular issues intelligible to the opponent and within the opponent's power to concede. For political independence one needs something that again goes beyond Tolstoy, a "constructive programme" involving millions of Indians.[42] The program would include Indians spinning their own clothes, running their own schools, and learning to look after themselves independently of their rulers, eventually in twenty-one different ways.[43] Gandhi claimed that it would bring "complete independence" (*poorna swaraj*), of which he could give only a set of complementary definitions, but it would include the ousting of foreign domination.[44]

39. Vinit Haksar, *Rights, Communities and Disobedience*, enlarged 2nd ed., Delhi 2001, ch. 5, pp. 109–37.

40. Letter to Kodanda Rao, 10 Sep 1935, *eCW*, vol. 67, p. 400; letter to American friends, 3 Aug 1942, *eCW*, vol. 83, p. 163.

41. Gandhi, "My dharma," 20 Dec 1929, *CW*, vol. 29, p. 334.

42. "Gandhi, "Constructive programme," Dec 1941, originally addressed to the Indian National Congress, *CW*, vol. 75, pp. 146–66, partially repr. in Anthony J. Parel, ed., *Hind Swaraj,and Other Writings*, Cambridge 1997, pp. 170–81, at 179–80; cited also by Judith Brown, "Gandhi and human rights: in search of true humanity," in Anthony J. Parel, ed., *Gandhi, Freedom and Self-Rule*, Lanham, Md. 2000, p. 97.

43. Sucheta Kripalani in Thakkar and Mehta, *Understanding Gandhi*, p. 457, adds village industry, Hindu-Muslim unity, uplift of women, uplift of Dalits, uplift of villages, and teaching Hindi.

44. Statement to the press, Wardaganj, 17 Sep 1934; foreword to "Constructive programme: its meaning and place," Poona, 13 Nov 1945, revised from 12 Dec 1941, *eCW*, vol. 65, p. 9, vol. 88, p. 325.

NONVIOLENT *KILLING* CALLS FOR A SECOND RESTRICTION: BESIDES TOLSTOY'S GOOD WILL, KILL ONLY FOR THE SAKE OF THE KILLED

Gandhi had to face the question whether *killing* could ever be nonviolent. This arose in such contexts as violent killing in self-defence, killing dangerous animals, killing to protect the life or chastity of others, and killing in fulfillment of a vow to the gods. In order for actual *killing*, as opposed to mere resistance, to be nonviolent, he came to feel that an extra restriction was necessary.

I have been quoting partly from Gandhi's fullest treatment of nonviolence towards dangerous animals. In October to November 1926, he wrote a series of seven articles in his Gujarati journal *Navajivan*, translated into English for *Young India* in November 1926, in favor of a decision to kill sixty stray dogs to prevent the spread of rabies among dogs and humans. The title of the series was "Is this humanity?" In 1946 he was to refer a correspondent back to this as his main treatment of the subject.[45] The discussion eventually formulated on two successive pages what is probably his fullest statement of criteria for nonviolent *killing*. We are familiar with his Tolstoyan criterion for nonviolence: an ocean of compassion and shedding every trace of ill will. Though inspiring as far as it goes, this criterion of the absence of ill will and presence of good will is dangerously limited. It is found twice in the present discussion. On p. 282, he says, "That is violence which springs out of anger and desire to do evil to the creature killed," and adds "wanton destruction for its own sake." The reference to anger is repeated on p. 296, but already there is something extra: that nonviolence excludes a selfish motive, while p. 297 offers the more demanding criterion that nonviolence requires acting *for the sake of* the target of forcible action. The second criterion is presented by way of summing up the present discussion. I think he intended it not to replace the first criterion, but to supplement it. The criteria overlap in the rejection of selfish motives as violent. Both criteria are in the spirit of Tolstoyan love and he would not silently drop in the space of two pages the first criterion that had been with him since he read Tolstoy's book early in his career, and that he would reaffirm two years later in 1928 in his commemoration of Tolstoy quoted above.

45. "Is this humanity?," seven articles, Oct–Nov 1926, translated from *Navajivan* Oct–Nov 1926, for *Young India* by Mahadev Desai and recorded with replies to objections in *Day to Day*, vol. 8; "Ahimsa and the sanctity of life," *Harijan* 9 June 1946, repr. Iyer, *Writings* 2, p. 257.

The more demanding criterion also appears elsewhere. It is repeated, for example, in an article already cited from 1928, and it had appeared in 1925, and would appear again, explicitly associated with love in 1931.[46] Here is his wording on pp. 296–97:

> p. 296: The fact is that *ahimsa* does not simply mean nonkilling. *Himsa* means causing pain to or killing any life out of anger, or from a selfish purpose, or with the intention of injuring it. Refraining from doing so is *ahimsa*. [. . .] He who refrains from killing a murderer who is about to kill his ward (when he cannot prevent him otherwise) earns no merit, but commits a sin, he practises no *ahimsa* but *himsa* out of a fatuous sense of *ahimsa*.
>
> p. 297: "Thus we arrive at the following result from the foregoing:
>
> (1) It is impossible to sustain one's body without the destruction of other bodies to some extent.
>
> (2) All have to destroy some life
>
> (a) for sustaining their own bodies,
>
> (b) for protecting those under their care; or
>
> (c) sometimes for the sake of those whose life is taken.
>
> (3) (a) and (b) in (2) mean *himsa* to a greater or less extent. (c) means no *himsa* and is, therefore, *ahimsa*. *Himsa* in (a) and (b) is unavoidable.
>
> (4) A progressive *ahimsaist* will, therefore, commit the *himsa* contained in (a) and (b) as little as possible, only when it is unavoidable, and after full and mature deliberation, and having exhausted all remedies to avoid it.
>
> The destruction of dogs that I have suggested comes under (4) and can, therefore, be resorted to only when it is unavoidable, when there is no other remedy and after mature deliberation. But I have not the slightest doubt that refraining from that destruction when it is unavoidable is worse than destruction.[47]

INCONSISTENT ON HARISHCHANDRA?

The criterion of good will on its own will prove defective from the point of view of many readers. It would allow as nonviolent the attempted killing

46. "Himsa and ahimsa," *Young India* 18 Oct 1928, repr. Iyer, *Writings*, vol. 2, 276–78; "On the verge of it," *Young India* 21 May 1925, repr. Iyer, *Writings*, vol. 2, p. 308; discussion with Romain Rolland, on or after 10 Dec 1931, from the mss. of Mahadev Desai's diary, in Iyer, *Writings*, vol. 2, p. 286.

47. Gandhi recognizes that there could be self-deceit about what was unavoidable, "Problem of nonviolence," *Navajivan* 6 June 1926, repr. Iyer, *Writings*, vol. 2, p. 347.

of his wife by the legendary Harishchandra solely in fulfillment of a vow. Gandhi had admired this figure from childhood as a model of truth,[48] and in 1926, the same year as he wrote the papers on dangerous animals, he called his austerity "a beacon-light to guide us."[49] Again in 1926, Gandhi described Harishchandra's act as nonviolent, for he had a heart filled with compassion—the poet was wrong to say he hardened his heart: he hardened only his hand. Moreover, "he saw he had to cut off the dear head of her whom he adored."[50] Exonerating Harishchandra as nonviolent will have been important to Gandhi. He would not want the signal truthfulness of Harishchandra ever to conflict with his other ideal of nonviolence. But there is something dangerous here in making nonviolence depend on good will, or the absence of ill will. The danger can be illustrated by the later very different context of legality in interrogation methods against suspected terrorists in Northern Ireland. An English judge rightly criticized the criterion of reluctance to harm a suspect as irrelevant. It would have permitted interrogators to cut off a suspect's fingers one by one, provided they did so with extreme regret. This is not quite the same as Gandhi's criterion of nonviolence that ill will should be absent. But his criterion runs the same risk of allowing disproportionate damage.

The stronger constraints on p. 297 provide a revision that would solve the problem: killing is violent, unless it is actually for the sake of the being one kills. The new constraint would have treated as violent Harishchandra's attempt to behead his wife. So Gandhi would have had to rely on the other defenses of his hero, of which he supplies several in his *Discourses on the Gita* alone. Better was his recognition in the same *Discourses* that Harishchandra did not aspire to nonviolence in the first place.[51]

Even the stronger constraints allow, on Gandhi's personal view, that there could be nonviolent killing of women to protect them from rape. He cites this as happening with the Rajput burning of wives to protect their chastity at Chittor in the face of a Muslim invasion.[52] No doubt he would regard as nonviolent also his own declared willingness to kill a daughter, if

48. *Autobiography*, part 1, ch. 2.

49. Lectures on Matthew 1–6, 1926, in *Day to Day*, vol. 8, p. 267.

50. *Discourses on the Gita*, Feb–Nov 1926, *CW*, vol. 32, pp. 179, 370.

51. *CW*, vol. 32, pp. 324, 339: Harishchandra only carried out the Lord's order. More significantly, he was not committed to nonviolence—he had killed people in the past, and could even now have resorted to nonviolent *satyagraha*, if what repelled him had been the beheading itself, rather than beheading his wife—a self-interested consideration.

52. *CW*, pp. 282, 296, 297.

he had one, in the context of rape.[53] But distasteful as these verdicts will be to most readers, they do not result from the idea that killing is violent if not for the sake of the being one kills. They result from Gandhi's conception of what would be most in a woman's interest. The stronger constraint does improve Gandhi's criteria of what should count as violent and nonviolent.

The killing of dangerous animals, on the stronger criterion, will be nonviolent only in cases where the animal is killed for its own sake. If it is killed for the sake of sustaining one's body or for protecting other humans or animals in one's care, then there is violence to a greater or lesser extent, but it is in many cases unavoidable. Sometimes, he says on pp. 270 and 295, it is a duty.

KILLING COUNTENANCED FOR FOUR REASONS, THOUGH NOT FOR THE SAKE OF THE KILLED

(i) AVOIDING THE WORSE COURSE IN A MORAL DOUBLE-BIND

The duty to be violent means that there may be a moral double-bind: you will be doing violence or allowing violence whichever course you take, whether you protect your ward by violence or not, although one course may be clearly *worse*, as with rabid dogs, or a *graver sin*, than the other. Gandhi explicitly recognizes this on an earlier page, 270: "a city-dweller who is responsible for the protection of lives under his care [. . .] is faced with a conflict of duties. If he kills the dog he commits a sin. If he does not kill it, he commits a graver sin. So he prefers to commit the lesser one and save himself from the graver." Similarly with protecting humans, Gandhi said in a discussion with pacifists in 1940 that the use of tear gas was not justified, or rather that it was not justified *"in terms of the non-violent ideal,"* but that God would not excuse him if his nonviolent creed deterred him from using it to protect a girl from violation, or to prevent an infuriated crowd from indulging in madness.[54] In other words, Gandhi *countenances* this use of violence, even though he thinks it wrong.

A double-bind may have no resolution. It will then be a problem for all of us, not merely for the person who recognizes it, who is to be congratu-

53. "The fiery ordeal," *Young India* 4 Oct 1928, repr. Iyer, *Writings*, vol. 2, pp. 271–72; "Jain ahimsa," *Young India* 25 Oct 1928, cited in chapter 1 above.

54. Discussion with pacifists, *Harijan* 9 March 1940, *CW*, vol. 71, p. 225.

lated for seeing the problem. But Gandhi has also offered positive moral advice: avoid the worse course in a moral double-bind.

(ii) A COUNSEL OF PERFECTION FOR THE IMPERFECT

Gandhi goes on immediately from his example of tear gas to make the choice between evils easier. Although he calls it an eternal principle with no exceptions that "the use of force is wrong in whatever degree and under whatever circumstances," he says that he means this in a relative sense. It turns out that he intends it as a counsel of perfection. He admits that he has not sufficient nonviolence in him, but he prefers the principle to allow no exceptions, so as to spur him to perfect himself in the technique of nonviolence.

> Therefore, when I say that that the use of force is wrong in whatever degree and under whatever circumstances, I mean it in a relative sense. It is much better for me to say I have not sufficient non-violence in me, than to admit exceptions to an eternal principle. Moreover my refusal to admit exceptions spurs me to perfect myself in the technique of non-violence.[55]

Gandhi's preference for an unreachable ideal represents a different approach to a problem that had also been put to the Stoics. They were asked, as we shall see in chapter 6, what use was an ethics that described a perfect sagehood that no one was able to realize. Their response was to switch from describing the perfect sage to advising on imperfect progress that might be made by imperfect people.[56] Gandhi saw the situation in a more positive way in terms of a challenge that an imperfect person might sometimes live up to.

Gandhi combines his counsel of perfection with a repeated stress on our imperfection. In the seven articles of 1926, he appeals to our current imperfection repeatedly, first to explain why we have to kill rabid dogs. He says that it is only because of our present ignorance of ourselves that we cannot live with dangerous animals. A yogi who, unlike us, is almost perfected should *not* kill a man who has run amuck. The best that can be done by a follower of nonviolence who is "progressive" is to aim at using the permitted

55. Continuation of same passage.

56. Cicero, *On Duties* 1.46.

violence as little as possible. I take it that the progressive is making progress but not perfected.[57] Gandhi appeals to human imperfection also to explain why his ashrams had to kill animals that spoiled their harvest,[58] and why it would be necessary, at least for a while, to retain an army and police in India after independence from Britain. It was an imperfection in Congress, we saw, not to have found a more peaceful way. He wrote: "I would support the formation of a militia under *swaraj* if only because I realise that people cannot be made non-violent by compulsion. But it is one thing to adopt non-violence for a specific purpose in a time of crisis, and quite another to advocate its adoption by all for all time as a philosophy of life. Not that I consider such adoption to be impossible. But I lack the strength for such a mission. I may not therefore resist the formation of a national militia. Only I cannot join it myself. I feel quite clearly within me that a militia is unnecessary but I have not the word that would carry conviction to others."[59] Again: "I have conceded that even in a non-violent State a police force may be necessary. This, I admit, is a sign of my imperfect *ahimsa* (non-violence). I have not the courage to declare that we carry on without a police force as I have in respect of an army. Of course I can and do envisage a state where the police will not be necessary; but whether we shall succeed in realising it, the future alone will show. The police of my conception will, however, be of a wholly different pattern from the present-day force. Its ranks will be composed of believers in non-violence. They will be servants, not masters of the people. The people will instinctively render them every help, and through mutual cooperation they will increasingly deal with the ever-decreasing disturbances. The police force will have some kind of arms, but they will be rarely used, if at all. In fact the policemen will be reformers. Their police work will be confined primarily to robbers and dacoits (armed brigands). Quarrels between labour and capital and strikes will be few and far between in a non-violent state, because the influence of the non-violent majority will be so great as to command the respect of the principal elements in society. Similarly there will be no room for communal disturbances."[60] Once again, there is no inconsistency in saying that something is wrong, but that we are as yet too imperfect to live accordingly.

57. "Is this humanity?" pp. 269, 293, 295, 297.

58. A letter, *eCW*, vol. 98, pp. 349–50.

59. Gandhi, in *Young India* 10 Jan 1929, repr. Iyer, *Writings*, vol. 2, no. 265, p. 391.

60. Gandhi on nonviolent police force, 10 Aug 1940, *Harijan* 1 Sep 1940, repr. Iyer, *Essential Writings*, no. 166, pp. 264–65.

(iii) WITHOUT REFUSAL OF GOVERNMENT BENEFITS, ONE CANNOT REFUSE TO SUPPORT THE GOVERNMENT'S WAR EFFORT

Gandhi gives another reason why he had originally been obliged to support British war efforts. He held that he was obliged to support Britain in the Boer War and the First World War because he had not yet given up the benefits of cooperation with the British.[61]

(iv) DIFFERENT *SVADHARMA*

A major reason why Gandhi sometimes countenances violence is connected with *svadharma* and differences of individual duty. In the seven articles of 1926, he repeatedly appeals to this idea. The city dweller and the householder both have to protect people. They are not like the recluse, who might be able to heal a rabid dog, or the yogi almost perfected, who might be able to subdue the fury of a man who has run amuck, and so would have a different duty. Muslims, he thought, accepted as their *dharma* not nonviolence, but beating a man who beat them. Neither they, nor the municipal councils on which they sat, could therefore be expected to follow nonviolence as a creed. He thought the same true of Afghans.[62] In this he did not foresee that in 1929 a Pathan from the Afghan frontier, Ghaffar Khan, would become one of his closest allies, founding the Khudai Khidmatgars as devotees of nonviolence. Different from the Khidmatgars were the Hindu tradesmen, also on the frontier with Afghanistan. He was able to tell them that they were entitled to defend themselves from attacks by Afghan tribes, and he would prefer self-defense to cowardice, and he often repeated this sort of view.[63] It might be thought that Gandhi was inconsistent at least when he spoke to the unarmed Khidmatgars in 1938 and forbade them to use violence against Afghan raiders. Instead, he insisted, if the raiders come despite your efforts at dissuasion, "tell them that they can take away all your belongings, but they shall touch the property of your Hindu neighbours only over your dead body." In fact Gandhi was being consistent, because the Khidmatgars,

61. *Young India* 13 Sep 1928, *CW*, vol. 37, pp. 270–71.

62. "Is this humanity?," pp. 270, 272–73, 276, 280, 295, 321.

63. Speech at Bannu, *Harijan* 5 Nov 1938, *eCW*, vol. 74, p. 157. See also "The doctrine of the sword," *Young India* 11 Aug 1920; "Chaos v. misrule," *Young India* 1 March 1928; letter, 18 Apr 1932; discussion with pacifists, *Harijan* 9 March 1940; "What to do?" Harijan 15 Sep 1946, these five repr. Iyer, *Writings*, vol. 2, pp. 298, 384, 286–87, 431, 451.

unlike the others, had taken a vow of nonviolence.[64] In general he required such strict nonviolence only from those who *believed* in it.[65]

People will have a different *svadharma* if they have accepted a ministerial position in politics, or own a factory. It may then become their duty to order shooting and have a few men shot, to quell an intercommunal riot, or to call for the police to prevent violent picketing. Of course this would not have been inevitable. If they had practiced noncooperation with the British, they would not have accepted a ministry. Further, it was a failure on the part of the Congress Party that it had not discovered a peaceful method of dealing with violent crimes. But in the meantime, Congress ministers had a duty to authorize the relevant type of violence.[66] The stress on different duties for different people so far from being an inconsistency, I shall argue in chapters 6 and 7, is a positive merit of Gandhi's approach.

The violence that Gandhi allows to some people need not usually be the violence of ill will—his weaker criterion. What he normally allows is violence that fails to meet his stronger criterion of acting for the sake of the target of one's action. On the other hand, it may be hard to see how he could require good will on the part of those who regard retaliation as a virtue.

NEED GANDHI BE SEEN AS INCONSISTENT?

Gandhi was concerned to meet charges of inconsistency. In his article of 1938, "My so-called inconsistencies," after invoking Emerson's *bon mot*, "Foolish consistency is the hobgoblin of little minds," he nonetheless defends himself vigorously. I have been asking if Gandhi need be seen as inconsistent. There was no problem in his distinguishing a behavior-based form of nonviolence from an attitude-based form, and opting clearly for the latter, even if he continued referring occasionally to the unintentional *behavior* as violence. The only problem arose in his defending Harishchandra's attempted killing for the sake of a vow, by omitting his supplementary criterion of nonviolence. For this omission would allow too many cases of killing to be nonviolent. But there was no comparable inconsistency in his advice on following the lesser evil, in his recognition that nonviolence as defined by the supplementary criterion could be followed only by the per-

64. Talks to Khudai Khidmatgars at Paniala, 1 Nov 1938, and at Tank, *Harijan* 19 Nov 1938, *CW*, vol. 68, pp. 81–82, and 83.

65. E.g., letter to a friend, 1 Aug 1925, repr. Iyer, *Writings*, vol 2, p. 266.

66. Speech at Gandhi Seva Sangh meeting, 27 March 1938; "My so-called inconsistencies," *Harijan* 27 Aug 1938, *CW*, vol. 66, pp. 438–39, and vol. 67, 285.

fected, in his insistence on consistency in noncooperation, and in his sensitivity to differences of *svadharma*. These represent a healthy recognition of how to adapt moral advice to particular circumstances. This realism about possibilities may admittedly look like a retreat from his echoing of Tolstoy when he wrote that the law of love would work with the inevitability of the law of gravitation. That brings us to the question how many people can be expected to achieve nonviolence.

HOW MANY CAN ACHIEVE GANDHIAN NONVIOLENCE, 30,000 OR 1?

In 1931 at the second Round Table Conference in London, Cornelia Sorabji interviewed Gandhi[67] and asked him how many believers in nonviolence he had following him. He replied 30,000. That was a remarkable figure, if correct, even though Gandhi would have been talking about the temporary adoption of nonviolence as a political tactic, not as a creed filling the whole of life.[68] The numbers of those would be much smaller. Numbers would also be limited by the difference that he recognized in the *svadharma*, or distinctive duty, of different people. He also wrote: "I don't believe that a large number will become non-violent all at once. I am a believer in the law of '*karma*' (—a man's actions in his past births colour his thinking, action, etc. and bear fruit in this). How then is it possible for the meritorious deeds of each and every one to ripen at one and the same time?"[69] By 1940 he found that even his own party, the Congress Party, was willing to join Britain in the war against Hitler, if the right terms were offered on Independence—which, in the event, they were not. But when Gandhi asked Congress to restate its commitment to nonviolence as a creed, the Congress working party stated in a resolution "that they are unable to go the full length with Gandhiji. But they recognise that he should be free to pursue his great ideal in his own way." Finding himself alone in taking nonviolence as a creed, he left his Congress Party, but he acknowledged, in an article that he called "Both happy and unhappy," that everyone had taken the course that was right for

67. Cornelia Sorabji, interview with Gandhi, *Atlantic Monthly* Apr 1932, pp. 453–58. Her failure to appreciate Gandhi is explained in my biography of her, *Opening Doors*, London and New Delhi 2010, pp. 343–47.

68. E.g., "Both happy and unhappy," *Harijan* 29 June, 1940, repr. Iyer, *Essential Writings*, pp. 248–51; "Is this humanity?," translated for *Young India* from the Gujarati in *Navajivan* Oct–Nov 1926, by Mahadev Desai and recorded also in *Day to Day*, vol. 8, p. 273. See also Bhikhu Parekh, *Colonialism, Tradition and Reform*, rev. ed., New Delhi 1999, ch. 4.

69. *Day to Day*, vol. 8, p. 273.

them.[70] In other words, they had followed their *svadharma*. But nonviolence as a creed, he felt at that moment, was followed not by 30,000, but by 1.

NONVIOLENCE AND NONVIOLENT RESISTANCE: THEIR SUCCESSES AND FAILURES

DISADVANTAGES FOR THE FAMILY

I shall conclude with a word about the successes and failures of Gandhi's nonviolence. I claimed in chapter 1 that the detached love or good will to all men that we have now seen equated with the nonviolent attitude had disastrous effects for close family, but often benign effects on international relations. But we need to take separately nonviolent *attitudes* and nonviolent *resistance*. Gandhi valued both for their effects, and nonviolent attitudes also for their own sake. I shall start with nonviolent resistance.

(I) NONVIOLENT RESISTANCE

Gandhi's first interest was in *moral* effects, but the question asked by historians is also relevant, what *political* effect Gandhi's campaigns had, and the answer may be different for his first campaign in South Africa and his later campaign in India. It is also relevant to consider how far Gandhi provided a moral or political model for *others* elsewhere. Gandhi's nonviolent *resistance* was later to inspire the effective Montgomery bus boycott led by Martin Luther King in the USA as an early step in the liberation of black people. King first thought that nonviolence applied only to relations between individuals, not to politics. But he was converted from violence to nonviolent resistance after learning from a lecture about Gandhi.[71] King said that Christian love furnished the motivation and Gandhi the method. Of course, Tolstoy's account, which influenced Gandhi, was already based on the idea of Christian love, as expressed by Christ in a passage that was also one of Gandhi's favorites. King knew of Gandhi's enthusiasm, but he had the extra advantage that the message of Christian love resonated in the churches of the black population.

The most comprehensive writer on nonviolent movements, Gene Sharp, whose work has been used by several movements as a handbook, has described campaigns of nonviolent resistance of the eighteenth to nineteenth

70. "Both happy and unhappy," *Harijan* 29 June 1940, repr. Iyer, *Essential Writings*, pp. 248–51

71. Martin Luther King, *Stride Toward Freedom*, New York 1958.

centuries, and in a follow-up book twenty-three movements of the twentieth century. These included Gandhi's movement and others up to 2005. More than half of these cases, including Gandhi's, he describes in successful terms.[72] Success, Sharp argues, can depend on the disciplined avoidance of violence. Even then, nonviolent resistance works only sometimes. But where military odds are overwhelming, it may be the only strategy available, and even when unsuccessful, it may produce fewer casualties than violent resistance. There are also protracted conflicts still unresolved in which nonviolent resistance has been tried. In two countries with governments as different as those of Burma and of Israel and Palestine, it has been tried with contrasting degrees of consistency, and the outcome remains undecided.

A more recent study has modified the position by arguing that the political success or failure of nonviolent resistance is typically dependent on other factors, including the availability or unavailability of violence within a country or outside it.[73] The relevance of violence elsewhere is nicely illustrated by Judith Brown's contribution to the study on Gandhi's political campaign against British rule in India.[74] Gandhi surely gained many concessions from the British, but for a long time they fell short of independence from British rule. Against popular conceptions, Brown argues that the British Raj was safe by 1938 from Gandhi's nonviolent campaign, and could have remained so, but for a violent turn of fortune elsewhere, the Second World War, coupled with further economic factors. She allows that Gandhi had "a brilliant strategy to undermine the practical and moral foundations of British power." But despite this, she concludes that "civil resistance had not made British rule impossible, or been a critical factor in the British decision to leave India."

72. Gene Sharp, *The Politics of Nonviolent Action*, Boston 1973, later published as three volumes by the same publisher (*Power and Struggle, The Methods of Nonviolent Action, The Dynamics of Nonviolent Action*) and *Waging Nonviolent Struggle*, Boston 2005. Besides the movements of Gandhi and Martin Luther King, the later book describes in successful terms: the Norwegian teachers' movement against the Nazis (1942); the ousting of General Jorge Ubico from Guatemala (1944); the campaign of California grape workers (1965–70); the liberation from the Soviet Union of Czechoslovakia (1989) and of Latvia (1991); the liberation of Poland through the Solidarity movement (1980–89); the replacement of President Marcos in the Philippines (1986); the defense with civilian support by Yeltsin and others against the military overthrow of Gorbachev's regime in the Soviet Union (1991); the removal of a Thai military coup (1991–92); and the removal of President Milosevic from Serbia (1996–2000).

73. Adam Roberts and Timothy Garton Ash, eds., *Civil Resistance and Power Politics*, Oxford 2009, introduction by Adam Roberts, pp. 1–24.

74. Brown in *Civil Resistance and Power Politics*, ch. 3, "Gandhi and civil resistance in India 1917–47: key issues," pp. 43–57.

This is an important finding for a standard conception of civil resistance. But I have been looking at Gandhi's conception of civil resistance, and ascribing to him a *rich* conception, which *included* the aim of undermining the moral foundations of British power. I endorsed the view in chapter 2 above that moral effects were actually Gandhi's dominant interest, quite apart from their essential role for obtaining political results. In the present chapter I have seen his nonviolent resistance as intended to restore the morale of Indians at home, overcome the British sense of moral superiority, and capture the moral sympathy of the international community through a multiple approach. The approach included not only the conventional politics of noncooperation and civil disobedience, but also constructive work and unfailing good will towards the opponent. I would have expected that, when Britain was weakened by the Second World War, Gandhi's reversal of the parties' moral confidence was a significant contributory cause of withdrawal. Perhaps it can be shown that British withdrawal from India was overdetermined, because economic considerations would have made it inevitable anyhow. But even in that case, I take it that Gandhi's moral and psychological effect would have been one factor that combined with others to produce one of the overdetermining causes of British withdrawal.

I am interested also in whether there was a certain *moral* effect of Gandhi's nonviolent resistance. Did it make relations between Britain and India more harmonious than one would ever have expected in a gradually retreating colonial power? Certainly two Viceroys, Lord Reading and Lord Irwin (later Lord Halifax), and a secretary of state for India, Lord Montague, were very impressed by Gandhi.[75] The final parting appeared amicable between the two countries, and, even more strikingly, there seemed to be very little animosity amongst Indians after Independence towards their former rulers.

(II) NONVIOLENCE OUTSIDE THE CONTEXT OF RESISTANCE

If we turn to the effects of Gandhi's nonviolence as applied not to *resistance* against a ruling power, but to other issues, we find different results. When Gandhi tried to halt religious killing in the 1947 partition of India, he succeeded with great courage, in the few areas that he was able to visit, in securing temporary peace. But he could not ward off the wider communal

75. There was a rumor that Lord Irwin said his greatest regret was that he had not joined Gandhi in a fast, recorded in Cornelia Sorabji's papers: Richard Sorabji, *Opening Doors*, ch. 20.

killings.[76] Nor did he persuade independent India to follow his particular conception of a nonviolent future.

There were two further cases on which Gandhi expressed a view, where *resistance* was not in question for the different reason that it was hopeless, and he looked only for a moral victory. These cases have been superbly analyzed by Devji.[77] How could nonviolent resistance succeed for Jews against Hitler's program of extermination, or for the Japanese against the 1946 dropping on two cities of the atomic bomb? Of course, *violent* resistance by the Jews or Japanese was not going to succeed either. But nonviolent resistance had depended in India on dialogue, and there was no possibility of dialogue with Hitler or with an atomic bomber. What Devji points out is that in the case of Hitler and the Jews, Gandhi urged that they should choose with calm determination to be gunned down in nonviolent defiance, rather than removed from sight as passive victims. This would give other Jews inner strength and self-respect. It would earn the subsequent admiration of the world, and would prove their title to be the truer Germans. What kind of success would this be? They would have been exterminated, but as moral agents, not passive victims. This would be a clear example of what was discussed in chapter 2, Gandhi's advocacy of a moral goal, when the immediate political goal was unattainable.

On the atomic bomb, Gandhi was interviewed in the very last hours before his assassination by Margaret Bourke-White. Gandhi's recommendation was that for those awaiting attack by atomic bomber it was better not to seek shelter, but to come out into the open, with a prayer that the pilot should come to no harm. At best that would give the assailant a prospect of redemption, at worst it would be to die a moral agent, not a passive victim.[78] That left very little of Tolstoy's expectation of changing society. But it conformed to the Gita's injunction not to be attached to the fruits of action. The success would again be *moral* success.

Gandhi's proposals about these cases, however, do not seem practical. No one foresaw the first of the two atomic bombs dropped and no one knew where the second one would fall. But in some cases there might have been a *different* point at which nonviolence could have played a role, again not in the form of *resistance*, through considering the role of *survivors*, rather

76. He saw the application of nonviolence, *satyagraha*, to the Hindu-Muslim quarrel of the time as "on the whole a failure": speech at a gathering of students, Calcutta, *Harijan* 31 Aug 1947.

77. Devji, *The Terrorist in Search of Humanity*, pp. 215–20.

78. Devji, *The Terrorist in Search of Humanity*, pp. 215–20, citing Gandhi, "The Jews," *Harijan* 26 Nov 1938; Margaret Bourke-White, *Interview with Gandhi*, Travel Book Club, London 1951, p. 185.

than of immediate victims. What has sometimes happened since Gandhi's death is movements of reconciliation, or in South Africa of reconciliation and truth (confession), on the part of *survivors*. The effectiveness of these movements in terms of reconciliation has been a matter of study and controversy. But if it has produced reconciliation among some victims or relatives of victims, or Gandhi's goal of redemption among some on the side of the users of violence, these individuals will have been able to overcome what happened without in any way adding to the spiral of violence. Survivors will also have achieved Gandhi's project of not remaining victims, but of becoming moral agents, even though the original victims of the atomic bomb did not have the warning to enable them to do so. In Hiroshima itself, the city that received the first atomic bomb, the focus has been not on reconciliation, so much as on peace without recrimination. It should not in any way be expected of survivors that they would find such attitudes possible, or even acceptable, but some appear to have done so.

This history suggests that Gandhian nonviolence, the attitude of universal good will (like his nonviolent *resistance*) may not always achieve the desired effects for large groups of people in all contexts, and cannot play the role that occurred to Gandhi in the last hours before his death. But it may recur in forms he did not foresee with some of the moral effects that he wanted. Moreover, if we turn from *effects* to the value of the attitude for its *own* sake, Gandhi's universal good will provides an inspiring ideal. And if we turn from the unpredictable context of large groups of people to the *individual*, the ideal is not only inspiring in itself, but may also be more reliably rewarding in its effects.

There remains the anomaly that Gandhi treated Tolstoy's two boundaries, family and nation, differently. Of his nationalism he wrote: "Love has no boundaries. My nationalism includes the love of all nations of the earth irrespective of creed."[79] Gandhi found a similar rationale for religious boundaries. He was a Hindu, but he considered that the great insights could be learned, albeit imperfectly, from many faiths. Love of one's own religion was thus compatible with the love of other religions. If only he could have shown similarly how to make ordinary family love compatible with the love of all humans. In chapter 1 above it emerged that he saw family love as incompatible, and it appeared inevitably incompatible, with the kind of nonviolent campaigning to which he devoted his life.[80]

79. A letter from mss. of Mahadev Desai's diaries, repr. Iyer, *Essential Writings*, p. 245.

80. *Autobiography*, part 4, ch. 25, *CW*, vol. 39, 252–53, and letter to Narandas Gandhi, 3–5 Aug 1930, *CW*, vol. 44, pp. 68–69.

CHAPTER FIVE

From universal love to human rights?

THE STOICS

The Stoics took the idea of universal affection for other people in a different direction from Gandhi's. Whereas Gandhi connected it with *non-violence*, the Stoics connected it with universal *justice* to all humans. The directions are different because justice is not normally free from violence. Indeed, Seneca's reformative and deterrent theory of just punishment endorses various kinds of violent execution.[1]

The Stoics argued, we have seen,[2] that it would be in accordance with nature to extend to all humans the sense of affectionate *kinship* that we feel for our nearest. From this they drew the unprecedented and important conclusion that it would also be natural, and therefore right, to extend *justice* to all humans.[3] It was probably realistic of them to base justice on a sense of kinship, because although justice is meant to be extended impartially to people, whether you feel akin to them or not, in practice that is not likely to happen.

It was a wonderful step forward to argue that justice should be extended universally to all humans, even to slaves and to foreigners who spoke no Greek. Would the step be all that much improved if they had conceived their idea in terms of human rights? I shall give a reason shortly for thinking that it would not. But first I need to say that some have thought that the Stoics actually were proposing the idea of human rights, and to explain why I disagree.

1. Seneca, *On Anger* 1.6.4, 1.16.3–5.

2. Chapter 1 above.

3. Cicero, *On Ends* 3. 62–68, esp. 67; Porphyry, *On Abstinence from Killing Animals* 3.19; *Anonymous Commentary on Plato's Theaetetus* 5.18–6.31.

I have argued elsewhere[4] that the Stoics' theory was not one of human rights, although it had at least as beneficial a tendency as such a theory. My central reason was connected with the Stoic theory of indifferents discussed in chapters 1 to 3. The Stoics regard the satisfaction of most human needs as natural objectives, but as in the end *indifferent*, in the qualified sense described in those chapters. As explained in chapter 2, Antipater, the Stoic of the second century BC, says that it is your duty to do everything in your power (*pan to kath' hauton*) to pursue the satisfaction of such natural objectives.[5] But what if you fail to secure them through no fault of your own? It is then that their ultimate indifference emerges, because the important goal (*telos*, Latin *propositum*) will have been achieved, namely your exercise of good character by doing everything in your power to secure them (*panta ta para hauton*). Good character is the only thing that is un-derivatively good. The actual securing of the natural objectives was only a target (*skopos*, Latin *ultimum*) in the sense explained.[6] In archery one needs a target for there to be any activity at all. But the real goal is aiming well. One gets no credit if an unpredictable gust of wind blows one's arrow onto the target and no discredit if it blows one's arrow away. I argued that this is not the position of a believer in human rights. Such a person thinks that it really matters if your intended beneficiaries fail to have their basic human needs satisfied. It does not address this concern that you acted with good character. Suppose through no fault of your own the intended beneficiaries die of starvation. The believer in human rights, unlike the Stoic believer in justice to all, will not think that the thing that ultimately matters has been achieved.

I think the human rights attitude of attaching greater importance to the meeting of human needs may be more attractive than the Stoic prioritization of one's own virtue of character. I would prefer to see it as merely a fall-back position, when one can only meet the needs of others at great disadvantage to oneself, to ask oneself what sort of person one wants to be. Aspirations to character can then offset the disincentives. However, the beneficial effect for human needs of the Stoic prioritization of good character may be no less than that of the other attitude.

The fullest opposition to my denial that the Stoics were advocating human rights (as to my view in chapter 7 below on rules of conduct) has come from Phillip Mitsis.[7] For one thing, I evidently gave the impression that the

4. Richard Sorabji, *Animal Minds and Human Morals*, London 1993, ch. 1.

5. Stobaeus, vol. 2, pp. 76.9–15.

6. Chapter 2 above: Plutarch, *On Common Conceptions* 1071C; Cicero, *On Ends* 3.22.

7. Phillip Mitsis, "The Stoic origin of natural rights," in Katerina Ierodiakonou, ed., *Topics in Stoic Philosophy*, ch. 6, pp. 153–77.

Stoic of good character is not concerned for any beneficiary, nor concerned for that beneficiary as a human. But I wanted to say that the good Stoic is indeed so concerned. The crucial distinction is rather that he takes the needs of the intended beneficiary as a target, not a goal.

Mitsis expresses my view as an ascription to the Stoics of an ethics of duty rather than an ethics of rights, and Myles Burnyeat has described the Stoics in similar terms, saying that they made any rights to be due to duties; duties were not due to rights.[8] Although I think this sounds true, it was not how I first thought of the matter, because I was thinking about the Stoics' ultimate goal (*telos*), achieved only by the sage, which involves going beyond one's duty and actually performing duties in a *virtuous* way. This is an ethics of virtue, and it is *virtue* that seeks to satisfy human needs, but eventually takes precedence over them.

I gave some further reasons why the Stoic theory of justice to all was not intended as a theory of human rights. For one thing, the motive for inventing a first theory of human rights was reduced by the Stoic belief in divine Providence, which covered many human needs by extending selectively even to individual humans.[9] Further, the individual was subordinated to the community and once compared to the stones in an arch.[10]

Nonetheless, I asked if there was not a class of individuals who have very important needs, those individuals who are progressing towards virtue, which is agreed not to be a matter of indifference. Seneca says that such people need some indulgence from fortune. His own personal wealth could help them. They need food and they need the liberal arts. They need precepts from a suitable mentor.[11] It is true that these needs do have a special importance, but they do not amount to a recognition of human rights. For one thing, they are the needs not of all humans as humans, but of a very small class of people. Seneca calls them the most worthy (*dignissimi*).[12] They need to have learned philosophy and to have a chance of acquiring wisdom.[13] Seneca envisages them as having slaves and a small amount of property.[14] He even thinks that they will never be able to exercise the full

8. Myles Burnyeat, "Did the ancient Greeks have the concept of human rights?" *Polis* 13, 1994, 1–11 (originally a 1992 radio broadcast).

9. Cicero, *On the Nature of the Gods* 2.164–67.

10. Sorabji, *Animal Minds*, pp. 143–44. See Cicero, *On Ends* 3.64; *On Duties* 3.22; Seneca, *Letters* 95, 53; Hierocles in Stobaeus, vol. 3, p. 723.1–13.

11. Sorabji, *Animal Minds*, pp. 148–49: Seneca, *On the Happy Life* 16.3, 23.5; *Letters* 88.31, 94–95.

12. Seneca, *On the Happy Life* 23.5.

13. Seneca, *Letters* 94.52, 95.1, 95.11–12, 95.34, 95.37–40, 95.44–46, 95.58–64.

14. Seneca, *Letters* 94.54, 95.72.

set of virtues without wealth.[15] Second, there would not be enough qualified teachers to go around to provide everyone with training for the rare quality of virtue, and there cannot be a right to what is impossible. Third, this is not due to a reluctance on the part of the teachers available. For nature has providentially inclined us to teach the rational basis (*rationes*) of wisdom.[16] So we do not have the modern phenomenon of needing to appeal to human rights in order to motivate inattentive helpers.

Mitsis has raised the question whether I do not have a human right to show indifference to my circumstances, and to take the right attitude to my torturers. But this is not a human right, I believe, for an opposite reason, not because it is impossible, but because according to the Stoics it is perfectly possible. No one is stopping you except yourself.

What I did wish to acknowledge was that there is in Stoicism a stress on concern for other humans *because they are human*, and this is one vital ingredient in the idea of human rights. Examples will be given in chapter 7 from Cicero's and Seneca's formulations of the moral law.[17] But here too the same caveats apply against construing the Stoic attitude in terms of human rights, rather than of justice for all. The list of situations for rescuing people is a set of targets; the goal remains the rescuer's virtue. Moreover, Cicero says that we are impelled (*impellimur*) by nature to benefit people.[18] So we are already doing all we can. In Seneca the assistance required is described as small (*quantulum*): sharing a crust of bread with the starving, showing the way to someone lost, or helping the shipwrecked is not a need that is left unmet.

The Stoic definition of justice is sometimes translated in a way that might suggest a connection with rights and even with human rights, so long as it is said to be connected with distributing things to people according to what is *due*.[19] The word is *axion*, or in Latin *dignum*. A better translation for some cases might be "according to *desert*," and for others "according to what is *appropriate*." Neither of these carries the same suggestion of rights. Undeserving workers still have a *right* to pay, and highly deserving ones do not necessarily have a right to *more* pay. In fact I think that in the Stoic

15. Seneca, *On the Happy Life* 22.1.

16. Cicero, *On Ends* 3.65–66.

17. Sorabji, *Animal Minds*, pp. 144–46; Cicero, *On Duties* 3.6.27–28, 3.19.63; *On Laws* 1.12.33; Seneca, *Letters* 95.51–53.

18. Cicero, *On Ends* 3.67.

19. Sorabji, *Animal Minds*, pp. 142–43, cites Stobaeus, vol. 2, pp. 59.4, 84.4; Philo, *Allegorical Interpretations of the Laws* 1.87; Plutarch, *On Stoic Self-Contradictions* 1034D; Galen, *Opinions of Plato and Hippocrates* 7.2; Andronicus, *On Emotions*, ed. Glibert-Thirry, p. 241, or Schuhardt, p. 19; Cicero, *On Republic* 3.18–19; *On Duties* 1.42; *de Inventione* 2.160.

definition of justice, "appropriate" is the right translation. The Stoic Diogenes of Babylon offers as his paraphrase *to epiballon*,[20] which means either duties, or what is *appropriate*. Justice is not concerned particularly with distributing duties, so the remaining meaning is the *appropriate*. And this wide term is what is needed. The Stoic theory of punishment concentrates on reform and deterrence. A just punishment, then, will not necessarily aim at what is *due*, but may give more or less according to what is *appropriate* for reforming or deterring.

The term *ius* in Latin sometimes means a right, but not always. When Cicero says that there are bonds of *ius* among humans (*inter homines iuris vincula*), but no *ius* connecting us with animals (*nihil iuris cum*), the point is one about *justice*. It is a Latin rendering of the idea bequeathed by Aristotle to the Stoics that there is no such thing as justice towards (*dikaion pros*) animals.[21] The use of *ius* that has most been thought to refer to *human* rights comes in the phrase *ius gentium*, which is sometimes rendered "law of nations." But in Cicero's use of the phrase *ius gentium*, coupled with plain *ius*, in *On Duties*, book 3, the reference is not to rights, but to the *obligation* not to break the bonds of human society.[22] Meanwhile, it has been shown by others that in Roman law the *ius gentium*, established for international trading relations, could be overridden by civil law, unlike a modern appeal to human rights.[23]

I doubt if the concept of human rights is to be found in other ancient Greek philosophical schools either. It has been well argued by Fred Miller[24] that Aristotle bases some *political* rights on what is natural, and Mitsis rightly points out that Cicero, in a move that Cicero regards not as Stoic but as original, seeks in his *On Laws* to base all civic law on natural law. But the holding of civic posts in a city is not readily considered a *human* right, because it is applicable only to a rather particular type of human community.

Despite my not finding a *concept* of human rights, I think that two *examples* might be given from other ancient thinkers, one of them paradoxical

20. Stobaeus, vol. 2, p. 84.13–17.

21. Cicero, *On Ends* 3.67.

22. Cicero, *On Duties* 3.23, 3.69.

23. Sorabji, *Animal Minds*, pp. 151–53, referring to M. Colish, *The Stoic Tradition from Antiquity to the Early Middle Ages*, Leiden 1985, pp. 356–64; Paul Vander Waerdt, "The Stoic Theory of Natural Law," Ph.D. diss. Princeton 1989, esp. pp. 18–28, 270–83, and "Philosophical influence on Roman jurisprudence? The case of Stoicism and natural law," *Aufstieg und Niedergang der römischen Welt*, part 2, vol. 36, no. 7, Berlin 1994, pp. 4851–4895.

24. Fred Miller, *Nature, Justice and Rights in Aristotle's Politics*, Oxford 1995, ch. 4, pp. 87–139.

since it denies animal rights. The right of humans to hunt animals is recognized as a *ius naturale* by Gratian, in the twefth century, drawing on Isidore, and this might be inferred even earlier from Aristotle's rationale for hunting. Aristotle says that the art of hunting wild animals is by nature just because nature creates animals for the sake of humans.[25] A more acceptable example of a human right is that of a human right to self-defense, which might be derived from Cicero. But this comes from a speech that Cicero did not dare to deliver but wrote up afterwards, in defense of Milo, who killed Cicero's dangerous enemy Clodius. It is therefore a piece of special pleading, rather than something that he was prepared to argue as a philosopher. He says that self-defense is a justification (*ratio*) for the educated, a necessity for barbarians, a custom for foreign nations, and that even to wild beasts nature has prescribed it.[26] Private property is not treated as a human right by the Stoics, if the account in chapter 9 below is right, because the sharing of all property was seen by some Stoics as a past or future possibility.

JOHN CHRYSOSTOM, A STOICIZING CHRISTIAN

John Chrysostom, a major figure in the Greek Orthodox Church, was born around 350 CE in Antioch, and gave there seven sermons on wealth and poverty around 387–88. His theme is remarkably Stoic. Wealth is not really a good, and poverty is not really evil.[27] The virtuous man is never a real slave, the sinful man always is.[28] The rich man is a steward (*hupodektês*) of possessions which are owed for distribution to the poor—his fellow servants—and he is ordered (*epitassesthai*) to make the distribution. The possessions are not his own (*hautou*), but another's (*allotria*), and belong to his fellow servants.[29] The model is that of a king or other master, who entrusts (*empisteuein*) royal or other possessions to a steward to be distributed as and when the master orders. I do not think that this means the poor have a right to the possessions. Rights are not mentioned, but if there were any, they would be those of the master—God. It is he who orders his steward to distribute to the poor, and it would be his right, if anyone's, to withdraw the

25. Sorabji, *Animal Minds*, p. 154; Aristotle, *Politics* 1.8, 1256b 20–26; Gratian, *Decretum*, dist.1, c.7.

26. Cicero, *Pro Milone* 11.30.

27. John Chrysostom, seventh of the sermons *On Lazarus and Wealth*, *PG*, vol. 48, cols 963–1054.

28. Fifth sermon.

29. Second sermon, *PG*, vol. 48, col. 988. For trustee cf. Ambrose, *Duties of Clergy* 2.25-9.

order. Elsewhere[30] John is explicit about this and provides a Stoic-sounding gloss. He speaks directly to the rich and says that he is addressing them "not so much out of concern for the poor as for your souls. For the poor will get comfort, if not from us, at least from elsewhere, and even if no comfort came, but they died of hunger, the price they paid would be nothing great. For how was Lazarus harmed by poverty and being wasted by hunger? But no one will save you from hell if you do not get help from the poor."

This suggests the Stoic idea that it is not poverty that is the real evil, rightly though it is dis-preferred, but the harm done to the souls of the rich, if they do not help the poor, who cannot then save them from hell. Such neglect of the poor would be an injustice, but to treat their deprivations as merely dis-preferred is not to treat them as the subject of a human right.

THE UN DECLARATION

The Universal Declaration of Human Rights was proclaimed by the General Assembly of the United Nations on December 10, 1948, long after the hopes of its predecessor, the League of Nations, had been dashed. Since then, it has become the primary and obvious way to seek justice for all humans, even though it has also been put to cynical uses. But there was no reason why it should have seemed to the Stoics the right way to advocate justice for all humans. What about Gandhi, who died while the United Nations Declaration was being finalized?

GANDHI AND HUMAN RIGHTS

Gandhi regarded various particular rights as important, but like the Stoics, he stayed away from the idea of *human* rights. He did so consciously, and for reasons of his own. On the other side, it has been pointed out that Gandhi helped draft a declaration in 1930 that spoke of the inalienable right of the Indian people and in 1931 another resolution on fundamental rights of the people, that is, of the Indian people, including, incidentally, the right to bear arms in accordance with regulations and reservations. The second resolution he moved in Congress. But he did not raise the question whether these were *human* rights, and I agree with the view that he was often opposed to drawing up lists of rights, human or otherwise.[31] The closest he came to

30. *Homilies on John* 27:3, *PG*, vol. 59, col. 162.

31. Anthony J. Parel makes a case for Gandhi as a supporter of human rights, *Harmony*, pp. 37–38, 53–55, citing among other texts the resolutions above from 10 Jan 1930, *CW*, vol. 42, p. 384, and from 31 March 1931, *CW*, vol. 45, pp. 370–71. I agree with the reply by Judith Brown

implying the existence of human rights may have been in a passage where he did not use the language of rights, but spoke of the *entitlement of all men due to their having been created by God*. At any rate it has been pointed out to me that he said to his great-niece Manu Gandhi: "Lord Krishna preaches the same doctrine in the Gita. One need have in one's possession only what one requires. It means that all men are created by God and therefore entitled to an equal share of food, clothing and housing. [. . .] One should earn just enough to support oneself and one's family."[32]

This looks like an exception, for as early as *Hind Swaraj* in 1909, Gandhi objected that the English gained voting rights in 1832 through the violence of riots, and that therefore they never gained real rights, which are the result of making oneself fit by performing duties.[33] In 1935 he made the nonviolent rationale of his opposition still clearer. The objection, as he stated it then, was that the formulation of rights does, and the performance of duties does not, lead to violence: "Rights follow from a due performance of duties. It is the fashion nowadays to ignore duties and assert or rather usurp rights. [. . .] Definition and performance of duties rule out violence altogether. Violence becomes imperative when an attempt is made to assert right without reference to duties."[34] Gandhi must have been thinking that insistence on one's *own* duties does not lead to violence; insisting on the duties of *others* can do so, although Gandhi aimed to avoid that. Sending a return cable to H. G. Wells about articles Wells published in *The Hindustan Times*, he wrote on 16 April 1940:[35]

> Received your cable. Have carefully read your five articles. You will permit me to say you are on the wrong track. I feel sure that I can draw up a better charter of rights than you have drawn up. But of what good will it be? Who will become its guardian? If you mean propaganda or popular education you have begun at the wrong end. I suggest the right way. Begin with a charter of the Duties of Man (both D and M capitals) and I promise the rights will follow as spring follows winter.

---

in "Gandhi and human rights: in search of true humanity," in Anthony J. Parel, ed., *Gandhi, Freedom and Self-rule*, Lanham, Md. 2000, ch. 4, pp. 87–101, and I draw on the evidence of both of them.

32. I thank Kyle Ferguson for pointing out the implication.

33. *Hind Swaraj*, pp. 80–82.

34. Interview with Nirmal Kumar Bose, 9–10 Nov 1934, repr. in *The Hindustan Times*, 17 Oct 1935, and in Iyer, *Writings*, vol. 3, p. 601.

35. Cable to H. G. Wells, *Hindustan Times* 16 Apr 1940, repr. Gopalkrishna Gandhi, *Essential Writings*, p. 452.

Rights dependent on duties may seem to be precisely what it was argued above[36] human rights could not be; instead human rights flow from human *needs.* The rights create duties on *other* people, but these too flow ultimately from the needs. Gandhi's idea that rights are gained from the performance of duties creates a relationship in the *opposite* direction—from duties to rights. There is in fact no conflict, but what he means is, as usual, unexpected. You might have thought he would mean that, if everyone carries out his or her duties, the human needs of *others* will be met. But, as has been pointed out to me,[37] he seems to speaking about one's *own* needs being met. It is only by performing duties that you can earn and gain rights worth having. For example, through fulfilling the duty of making yourself fit to vote you gain the true right to do so. To gain the right of obedience from your children, or respect from your wife, you need first to do your duty by them. To gain the right of friendship from Muslims, the Hindu must first perform the duties of friendship towards them. Princes will gain the right to rule and tax peasants only by first serving them. In a less happy example, by carrying out the duty to drink milk, the child gains the right to live.[38]

In 1947, the discussion reached a crescendo, because the United Nations was finalizing its Declaration and the Constituent Assembly of India was deliberating on the fundamental rights of citizens. In relation to the Indian deliberation, Gandhi said, "As a matter of fact the proper question is not what the rights of a citizen are, but rather what constitutes the duties of a citizen. Fundamental rights can only be those rights the exercise of which is not only in the interest of the citizen but that of the whole world. Today everyone wants to know what his rights are, but if a man learns to discharge his duties right from childhood and studies the sacred books of his faith he automatically exercises his rights too. I learnt my duties on my mother's lap. [. . .] If I had shirked the obligation to drink milk I would have forfeited my right to live."[39] He goes on to complain that people high and low are interested only in their rights, but that they will earn their rights only by doing their duty. To Julian Huxley in the same year Gandhi wrote, "I learned from my illiterate, but wise, mother that all rights to be deserved and preserved came from a duty well done. The very right to live accrues to us only when we do the duty of citizenship to the world. From this one fundamental statement perhaps it is easy enough to define the duties of

36. In Myles Burnyeat's formulation.

37. I thank Kyle Ferguson for the point.

38. I take here Gandhi's statements of 1909, 28 June 1947 and 6 July 1947, cited above and below.

39. Speech at prayer meeting, 28 June 1947, *CW*, vol. 88, pp. 230–31.

man and woman and correlate every right to some corresponding duty to be first performed. Every other right can be shown to be usurpation hardly worth fighting for."[40] He had used very similar wording in an article "Rights or duties?" published in *Harijan* a few months earlier.[41]

Gandhi's explicit reason, we have seen, for subordinating rights to duties is his nonStoic concern that the search for rights depends on violence. He does agree with the Stoics in treating human duties, not human rights, as the important thing. But he is not emphatic, as they are, that human indignities, such as those suffered by the Dalits, are merely dis-preferred. Nonetheless, even without the Stoic emphasis on the dis-preferred being indifferent, his position finishes up like theirs as one of duties rather than of rights.

Had Gandhi drawn up the Charter of the Duties of Man that he advocated to Wells, he would presumably have had to specify universal duties that applied to everyone. But I want to consider in the next two chapters the interest of both Gandhi and the later Stoics in individual duties that apply only to some people, or even only to one, and their hesitations about universal moral rules.

40. Letter to Julian Huxley, before 17 Oct 1947, *The Hindustan Times* 19 Oct 1947, *CW*, vol. 89, pp. 346–47.

41. *Harijan* and *Harijanbandhu* 8 June 1947, repr. Iyer, *Writings*, vol. 3, pp. 496–98.

CHAPTER SIX

Persona and *svadharma*: is duty universalizable or unique to the individual?

The Stoics and Gandhi both believed in the idea of one's *individual* role in life as determining one's *individual* duty. And both expressed doubts, although for somewhat different reasons, about rules of conduct that applied universally to everyone. This was in spite of the Stoic belief in a divine moral law, and in spite of Gandhi's purported readiness to specify a Charter of the Duties of Man. I shall start and finish with the Stoics.

STOIC PERSONA

The later Stoics held that one's *individual* role in life (Greek *prosôpon*, Latin *persona* are terms drawn from the actor's mask) helps to determine what decisions it would be appropriate for one to take. These are only sometimes *moral* decisions, and then the term for that which is appropriate (*kathêkon, officium*) is often translated as "duty." But philosophy is a way of life and Stoicism is a philosophy for all aspects of life. The doctrine applies to all practical decisions, moral or otherwise. Aristotle had held that what is needed for making good decisions, apart from having the right values, is a kind of perceptivity (*nous*) about what those values call for in particular circumstances and it might seem hard to go beyond that sound remark. But the Stoic theory of personae goes further with a systematic account of considerations relevant in all particular circumstances.

DECISIONS BASED ON PERSONA IN LATER STOICS: PANAETIUS IN CICERO

The theory appears in Cicero *On Duties* in the first century BCE,[1] and he says that in that work he is especially following the Greek Stoic Panaetius from the later part of the preceding century, who had himself written a book *On Duties*.[2] If Cicero himself had devised such a brilliant theory, he would indeed have been a major philosopher. But despite his important influence on political thought, the theory shows more philosophical skill than we find in Cicero elsewhere, and I share the common view that the theory comes from Panaetius. If it had been invented by Cicero, who wrote in Latin, it would have been unlikely to become a central theme of the Greek-speaking Stoic Epictetus in the next century. Since I have interpreted the theory elsewhere,[3] I shall be comparatively brief, except where I have new points to add. But I want to compare Gandhi's use of the idea of *svadharma*, a person's *individual* duty.

According to Cicero, every human has a first persona as a rational being. There are only certain decisions that a being who uses his reason rightly can take. The right use of reason would rule out both stupid and, on the optimistic Stoic view, vicious decisions. So far, our persona as rational beings imposes some restrictions, but the requirement to act as a rational being has been shown in recent criticisms of another great thinker, Kant, to give us too little guidance. It has been objected in relation to Kant that the right action may be quite different for a rational male, a rational female, a rational Indian, or a rational American. Telling us to act as a rational *being* tells us very little, if different types of rational being should act in opposite ways. The Stoics dealt with this problem two thousand years before Kant. They did so by drawing attention to a plurality of more individual personae that mark each of us off from some other humans, or even from all. Subject to the constraints of the first persona, which rules out stupid or vicious decisions, we should also make decisions in the light of our individual personae.[4]

Cicero gives an example concerning a decision that is as much practical as moral: choosing a career. Your father may want you to choose his career. Suppose he was a successful lawyer. Ought you to become a lawyer? Well, you can hardly consider in isolation what a rational being would decide.

1. Cicero, *On Duties* 1., esp. 107–25.

2. Cicero, *On Duties* 2.60,and 3.7.

3. Richard Sorabji, *Self*, Oxford and Chicago 2006, ch. 8, "Individual persona vs. universalisability," pp. 157–71.

4. Cicero, *On Duties* 1.107.

You must rather consider what the rational son of such a father would decide, and, more than that, you must consider whether you would have the right talent to be a lawyer. What would the rational son without legal talent decide?[5] This takes account of more individual personae, and the right decision may be that you would only make a mess of it if you tried to become a lawyer.

Whether to obey your parents in all cases was a subject addressed by a Stoic of the century after Cicero, Musonius Rufus, the teacher of the more famous Stoic Epictetus. The test case for a philosopher like Musonius was what to decide if your father forbade you to study philosophy. His answer was that if you cannot persuade your father by philosophical reason nor by philosophical conduct towards him, you should in the end obey the will of God that you be good, rather than the will of man. For being good and being a philosopher are one and the same.[6]

Returning to Cicero and the personae, we find a very important point: that the same decision is not right for everyone. It depends not only on talent, but on character too. Among the heroes of the Greek war against Troy, Odysseus (called Ulysses in Cicero's Latin) had a very different character from Ajax. Odysseus put up with all sorts of indignities in order to achieve his objective of getting home from Troy, which he succeeded in doing after ten years of frustration. Ajax, by contrast, killed himself rather than endure the shame of a fit of madness in which he killed cattle in the belief that they were Trojans. Neither decision is to be criticized (*vituperandi*): each is right for that character.[7] But everyone may need to consider: *am I an Ajax or an Odysseus?*

Another important consequence flows from the variability in right decisions. Everyone should study his own merits and defects and should not be diverted away from his own nature to pursuits that are better or have more gravity (*graviora*), but to which he cannot attain.[8] We shall find the same warning in Gandhi.

UNIQUE PERSONA AGAINST UNIVERSALIZED MORAL RULES

The next consequence is even more remarkable. Some people may have a unique persona. When Julius Caesar won the Roman Civil War, his tyranny

5. Cicero, *On Duties* 1.120–21.

6. Musonius Rufus, fragment 16, ed. Hense, translated by Cora E. Lutz, *Yale Classical Studies* 10, 1947, pp. 1–147.

7. Cicero, On *Duties* 1.109, 1.113.

8. Cicero, *On Duties* 1.110, 1.114.

threatened the very survival of the Roman Republic. Among those whom Caesar defeated when he marched on Utica there was one and only one person for whom it was right to commit suicide, rather than make an accommodation. That one person was the Stoic Cato, but it would not have been right for anyone else to commit suicide, even (according to some manuscripts) "*in the same circumstances* (*in eadem causa*)."[9] This again sounds like the direct opposite of what Kant was to say two thousand years later. Kant, stressing impartiality, insists that what is right for one must be right for all *in the same circumstances*. This very influential view of Kant's is usually put by saying that assertions about what is right must be *universalizable*. The Stoic stress on *particularity* does not formally contradict Kant's later insistence on universalizability. The Stoics could agree that *if* there were anyone exactly like Cato (and a Kantian could make that one of the relevant "circumstances"), then it would be right for that person in those circumstances to commit suicide. But the interesting point to the Stoics was that there *was* no one else like Cato. He had always stood for an uncompromising austerity, and so he could not compromise and still be true to himself, to his persona.[10]

What was this austerity of Cato's? It is hard for Cicero to put it into words. All he says is that Cato had a certain gravity (*gravitas*), a word we have seen him use already. But Cicero also had a certain gravity, and was also a leading statesman opposed to Caesar. Why was it not right for Cicero to commit suicide over Caesar's victory? The explanation cannot be given by a single description like "gravity," nor even by a series of descriptions. What does the explanatory work here is the proper name "Cato," because that conjures up a whole string of biographical anecdotes—some will be narrated in chapter 10 below—in a way that the word "gravity" could not. It is the whole history of the particular individual that determines what is the right decision, not some small set of characteristics shared by others. This is hard to fit with Kant's interest in rules. Kant wants to find an exceptionless categorical imperative and he also wants us to formulate for ourselves more specific but exceptionless maxims of conduct. Proper names must not enter into these rules, because they would not give the kind of generality he seeks. But if proper names must be avoided and a whole set of anecdotes must be

9. Cicero, *On Duties* 1.112.

10. That this is the interesting point has been brought out with modern examples by Peter Winch, "The universalisability of moral judgement," *Monist* 49, 1965, 196–214.

invoked to show when suicide is the right decision, this will not yield anything of the right length to serve as a *rule* about when suicide is right.

Kant did refer to the example of Cato's suicide in lectures recorded by a student. But the student's notes put the Stoic point that Cato could not have gone on living as Cato only second *after* a very un-Stoic appeal to the bad *consequence* of compromising with Caesar—the consequence of putting an end to the freedom struggle.[11] Kant's knowledge of Cicero's text looks secondhand, and the degree of his interest in Cicero's *On Duties* has been disputed.[12]

The Stoic appeal to one's individual personae does not allow a free-for-all, what Charles Taylor has called "the malaise of modernity."[13] It is not a search for personal fulfillment regardless of others. Each of the personae lays down *constraints* on what one can decide. You are not free to decide on the career of a burglar. The first persona lays down the constraint of our common rational humanity, and the others lay down constraints based partly on the duties to other people that we have acquired from birth, from fortune, or from personal choice.[14]

Although there are scattered references before Panaetius to what he calls persona, or rather *prosôpon* in Greek, none of them added up to a theory like his of how to make decisions in the light of personae. Personae were already mentioned by the Cynic Bion around 300 BCE. Like a good actor who plays well whatever *prosôpon* the poet assigns, the good person must play whatever part *chance* assigns (he does not say "God"), whether it be the principal part or that of a vagabond. Do not wish to play the principal part if you have been given the second.[15] A related warning has been recognized in the atomist philosophers Democritus and Epicurus of the fifth and late fourth centuries BCE. You should not undertake activities beyond your capacity and nature.[16] The Stoics may also have thought about a famous

11. Kant, *Lectures on Ethics*, translated by Louis Infield, London 1930, p. 149; also translated by Peter Heath in Kant, *Lectures on Ethics*, Cambridge 1997.

12. It was played up by Klaus Reich in "Kant and Greek ethics," part 2, *Mind* 48, 1939, pp. 446–63, and has been played down by Allen Wood in "The supreme principle of morality," in P. Guyer, ed., *The Cambridge Companion to Kant and Modern Philosophy*, Cambridge 2006.

13. Charles Taylor, *The Malaise of Modernity*, Concord, Ont. 1991.

14. Cicero, *On Duties* 1.107, 1.115–19.

15. Teles fragment 2, Hense, pp. 5.1–6.1.

16. Democritus, fragment 3, Diels-Kranz; Epicurus fragment given by Diogenes of Oenoanda, cited in Diels-Kranz, vol. 2, p. 132, n. to line 1, both cited by Christopher Gill, "Peace of mind and being yourself: Panaetius to Plutarch," in *Aufstieg und Niedergang der römischen Welt* 2.36.7, Berlin 1994, pp. 4599–4640.

example of deciding in accordance with individual past choices. Plato represents Socrates as arguing that he should not escape to another city from his death sentence in Athens because of his personal choices never to abandon Athens in the past.[17] None of this, however, gave us a general theory like that of Panaetius.

DECISIONS BASED ON PERSONA IN EPICTETUS

In the first century BCE Epictetus continues the discussion very near the beginning of his *Discourses*.[18] Epictetus tends to use the word "nature" instead of the Greek equivalent (*prosôpon*) for "persona," whereas Cicero, drawing on Panaetius, had distinguished the two, saying that one's nature has even more importance than one's chance characteristics in decisions about one's career. However, Cicero treated both as personae.[19] Epictetus asks: should a slave refuse to hold the chamber pot for his master? There is no one right answer. He must not refuse if he cannot withstand the subsequent starvation and beating. Epictetus describes two Stoic senators who, at personal risk, refused to do the emperor's bidding. One, Helvidius Priscus, even made the emperor back down. Helvidius is described as almost unique: had the emperor offered another man a way out of the confrontation *in such circumstances*,—the phrase recurs—he would have leaped at it with gratitude. Epictetus imagines himself conversing with a tyrant who tells him to shave off his beard, the philosopher's badge. It is better, says Epictetus, for the philosopher to lose his head than his beard. The badge of philosophy was taken seriously in those days, even though it was acquired through a misunderstanding. The first three philosophers the Romans heard in 155 BCE were Athenians, and Athenians wore beards. The Romans inferred that a beard was the mark of philosophers.[20]

Epictetus speaks of the unique persona elsewhere. Only Agamemnon could have led the Greek army against Troy; only Achilles could have fought a duel with the leading Trojan warrior. If Thersites (who recommended abandoning the war) had asked for the command, either he would not have got it, or he would have disgraced himself. In this passage among

17. Plato, *Crito* 52 A–B; relevance drawn to my attention by Alex Cohen.

18. Epictetus, *Discourses* 1.2, esp. 8–29.

19. Cicero, *On Duties* 1.120.

20. The story is well told by John Sellars, *The Art of Living: The Stoics on the Nature and Function of Philosophy*, Aldershot 2003, pp. 16–17.

others, Epictetus adds to Cicero's record that personae can be thought of as assigned by God.[21]

Different personae are incompatible. If you choose to be a philosopher—which in antiquity involved a way of life—you cannot live like a tax gatherer, an orator, or a procurator of the emperor.[22]

DECISIONS BASED ON PERSONA IN ATHENODORUS, SENECA, AND PLUTARCH

The last point had already been made by Epictetus' older contemporary, the Platonist Plutarch in his *On Tranquillity of Mind*. Plutarch recalls the maxim displayed at Delphi, "Know thyself," and tells us to use that self for what *nature* has made us fitted, rather than emulating incompatible alien exploits. Another older contemporary, the Stoic Seneca, had said in his *On Tranquillity of Mind* that whether you engage in public life has to depend on your *nature*.[23] They may both have been drawing on the lost *On Tranquillity of Mind* (*peri euthumias*) of the Stoic Panaetius. Seneca's appeal to one's nature for deciding whether to engage in public life will be illustrated in chapter 10 below, and we will see him also referring to his own older Stoic contemporary, Athenodorus, adviser to the Emperor Augustus, for discussion of the same subject.[24]

The decisions we make about our careers, as Seneca brings out, have implications for further decisions. I shall come shortly to his advice about what form of physical exercise one should take, if one has made the decision to be a philosopher.

I think it is one of the most important messages that the Stoics have to offer to young people, and to older ones, that in making decisions in life we must consider who we are and who we want to be. This has been a major theme in post-Freudian psychology, thanks to the ideas of Erik Erikson, first introduced in his "Eight stages of man."[25] He saw life as concerned with the successful or unsuccessful establishment of personal identity. A successor, James Marcia, recognized as one of four types a situation called "foreclosure," in which identities are passively adopted on the basis of

21. Epictetus, *Discourses* 3.22.4–8; compare 1.29.41–47, 4.7.13; *Handbook* 17.
22. Epictetus, *Discourses* 3.15.10–13.
23. Plutarch, *On Tranquillity of Mind* 472C–F; Seneca, *On Tranquillity of Mind* 6–7.2.
24. Seneca, *On Tranquillity* 3.1–8 (Athenodorus), 6.1–4 and 7.2; *On Leisure* 1.4, 3.3–4.
25. Erik Erikson, "Eight stages of man," in his *Childhood and Society*, New York 1950.

other people's views.[26] The Stoic advice on persona would have been of the greatest value for the *active* establishment of identity, if it had been widely available.

LATER STOIC INTEREST IN THE IMPERFECT PERSON

The interest of certain later Stoics in personae is explained by Cicero's narrative, presumably drawn again from the Stoic Panaetius. Earlier Stoics had tended to focus on what the ideal Stoic sage would do. But the Stoics had to admit to their critics that the ideal Stoic sage had never existed. This is the probable background to the admission recorded in Cicero that we do not live with people who are perfect and absolutely (*plane*) wise, but with people who are doing well if there is some semblance (*simulacrum*) of virtue in them. No one should be neglected if some indication (*significatio*) of virtue appears in them.[27] This interest in people who are less than ideal is likely to have encouraged the later Stoic interest in the individual strengths, weaknesses, and foibles of different personae.

Admittedly, ever since their foundation by Zeno, the Stoics had taken an interest in the possibility of moral *progress*[28]—a term used also by other schools, and due to reappear, thanks to the Pythagoreans, in a famous Christian work, John Bunyan's *The Pilgrim's Progress*.[29] But compatibly with recognizing progress, they held the doctrine that all those who were short of perfection were equally vicious, and that all sins were equal. You are drowning equally if you are an arm's length below or five hundred fathoms.[30] "Vicious" and "drowning" exclude the idea that the progressor might be neither virtuous nor vicious, or a bit of both. The doctrine is so depressing that it might put one off Stoic ethics altogether if it had not allowed for qualifications. Only one of the five texts cited for this doctrine in the footnote below (one of them qualified by an "if') mentions getting closer to virtue. But even then, virtue was acquired only at the end of the progress, and the Stoics held

26. J. E. Marcia, "Identity in adolescence," in J. Adelson, ed., *Handbook of Adolescent Psychology*, New York 1980.

27. Cicero, *On Duties* 1.46.

28. Zeno, in Plutarch, *How to Observe One's Progress in Virtue* 82F.

29. I learned of the influence of the Pythagorean *Tablet of Cebes* from Michael Trapp, when he first delivered his paper, "On the Tablet of Cebes," in Richard Sorabji, ed., *Aristotle and After*, supplement 68 to the *Bulletin of the Institute of Classical Studies*, 1997, pp. 159–78.

30. Diogenes Laertius, *Lives* 7.120 and 7.127; Pliny, *Lettters* 8.2 (with an "if"); Plutarch, *On How to Observe One's Progress on Virtue* 75C; Plutarch, *On Common Conceptions* 1063A–B (getting closer); Alexander, *On Fate* 199, 18–19.

that there were no degrees so virtue,[31] so one did not acquire a little virtue on the way. It is presented as a novelty when Heraclides of Tarsus, a fellow-pupil of Antipater of Tarsus, the teacher of Panaetius, *denied* that all sins are equal. So did a later Stoic, Athenodorus,[32] but neither of these was a very influential Stoic. In the next century, the first century CE, Seneca went much further in recognizing a qualitative change that comes about as progress brings you "within sight of wisdom" and "in striking distance." Already you are in harbor and cease to wander about or be blown backwards in your decisions, even though you are not on dry land, where presumably not even a storm would shake your decisions. For the person in sight of land, Seneca goes further. He is *not* in the worst position; he is *not* sick, but he is not well. All virtues have weak beginnings and time gives them strength.[33] An equally big concession is made by Cicero in the passage we started with, *On Duties* 1.46, and hence by Panaetius if Cicero is faithfully reflecting him. Not only does he say that in imperfect people there can appear semblances (*simulacra*) and an indication (*significatio*) of virtue, but there are after all even *degrees* of virtue, because it is said that the person *most* adorned with propriety, temperance, and justice should be most cultivated.

The later Stoic interest in the imperfect person gives their ethics a certain immediacy. That is to some extent true in other later schools as well, for example of the Platonist Plutarch in the same century as Seneca and Epictetus. But he may have been influenced by the Stoic Panaetius. I have treated elsewhere the later Stoics' development of cognitive therapy, most fully described by Seneca, a therapy designed to free one from unwanted emotions by rational techniques that anyone can learn.[34] They also addressed the imperfect individual's concerns in other ways and in doing so, the later Stoics seem to be tapping one on the shoulder. Some years ago my doctor advised me to take exercise systematically in a way that I had not. I went through a series of thoughts about what sort of exercise would be suitable for a philosopher. I then found that Seneca had been through

31. Porphyry, *On Aristotle's Categories* 137,29–138,4; Simplicius, *On Aristotle's Categories* 284,32–285,1.

32. Diogenes Laertius, *Lives* 7.121. The two best known Stoics of that name are also from Tarsus, but in the next century, the first century BCE. On Athenodorus son of Sandon and Athenodorus Cordylion, see Richard Goulet's authoritative *Dictionnaire des philosophes antiques*, and further discussion in Michael Griffin, "The reception of Aristotle's categories, 80 BCE–CE 220," D.Phil. dissertation, Oxford 2009, pp. 278–83, and his book *Aristotle's* Categories *in the Early Roman Empire*, Oxford, forthcoming.

33. Seneca, *Letters* 72,9–11; *On Tranquillity of Mind* 1. 2–3 and 17; compare 35.4.

34. Richard Sorabji, *Emotion and Peace of Mind*, Oxford University Press 2000, discussing Seneca, *On Anger* 2.2–4.

this entire sequence of thoughts two thousand years earlier, and had added one that would not have occurred to me. A philosopher, he wrote, should not build up muscles. It is the mind that needs feeding, not the body. Nor should the exercise distract you for long from reading. Running, lifting weights, and jumping can be done quickly. Walking has an even greater advantage for the philosopher: you need not interrupt reading, dictating, speaking, or listening at all while you walk. But more than once Seneca recommends something that shares with walking the advantage of not interrupting philosophy, but that can be even more vigorous: being carried in a litter exercises all your muscles, as the litter throws you about.[35] Since I had just been reading similar descriptions of being carried in a palanquin through the jungles of India, I was ready to appreciate that I had stopped short in deciding on walking.

Seneca's letters will also advise on how to treat anxieties about health, and whether and in what way to take early retirement.[36] Panaetius, we have just seen, advises sons on following their father's career, and Musonius Rufus counsels young people on whether and when to obey their parents. Epictetus, the pupil of Musonius, has a particular warning, we saw, that applies to scholars and academics. You must not be enslaved to books.[37] But perhaps the most excruciating advice to academics comes from someone who was not a Stoic, but who accepted Stoic cognitive therapy for calming emotions as part of the right treatment, provided that he, as a doctor, had corrected physical diet first. A lost work—*On Avoiding Distress*—by the doctor Galen of the second century CE has been discovered and was published in 2008.[38] The example that Galen gives is that he had not yet made backup copies of his work, but he had set aside the coming summer to go to the country to do so. Meanwhile, he stored his only manuscripts in the safest place in Rome, the imperial depository, built of stone and protected by armed guards. There was a disastrous fire that burnt the whole lot, and Galen tells the aching modern scholar how his cognitive techniques saved him from distress.

35. Seneca, *Letters* 15.2–6, 55.1–2.

36. Seneca, *Letters* 19; 68.1, and 3–4; 78.

37. Chapter 3, above; Epictetus, *Discourses* 4.4.1–2; compare Seneca, *Letters* 62.1.

38. Galen, *On Avoiding Distress*, Greek edited with French translation by Véronique Boudon-Millot, ed. Boudon-Millot et al., *La science médicale antique: nouveaux regards; études réunies en l'honneur de Jaques Jouanna*, Beauchesne, Paris 2008, English translation by Vivian Nutton forthcoming. Galen's insistence on diet is in his *Quod animi mores* 67,2–16 in Galen, *Scripta Minora*, vol. 2, Teubner edition. Stoic-style cognitive therapy for anger is the recommendation of Galen's *On the Passions and Errors of the Soul.*

GANDHI ON *SVADHARMA* IN THE GITA

The idea of one's *personal* dharma or duty, *svadharma*, is discussed in the Gita. When Mahadev Desai translated Gandhi's Gujarati version of the Gita into English, he added his own learned comments and he noticed the similarities to Stoicism.[39]

In Desai's rendering of Gandhi, the Gita says that it is better to die performing one's own humble duty; performing another's duty (*paradharma*) is fraught with danger (3.35). It is sinless and better to perform one's own duty, even if uninviting and more difficult than another's (18.47). Second, one should not abandon the duty to which one is born because of its imperfection, since all action is at first enveloped in imperfection (18.48).

Desai notices in the first statement the similarity to Epictetus's *Handbook* 17, where God is said to assign us parts as if to actors, and our business is to play the assigned part well. In connection with the second statement about imperfection, Desai compares the Stoic Roman emperor of the second century CE, Marcus Aurelius, when Gandhi says, in Desai's rendering, "Be not ashamed of any action which is in accordance with nature and never be misled by fear of censure or reproach." The connection with persona will be maintained if Desai is assuming that Marcus is talking of each person's *individual* nature.

Gandhi himself discussed the concept of *svadharma* in these Gita passages in his discourses on the Gita at his Ahmedabad ashram in 1926.[40] One may have to perform one's *svadharma* even if it means one's death. An obvious example is taken in order to throw light on cases we might overlook. The prime minister and the commander-in-chief should each perform his own *dharma*. It is for the prime minister to give orders, for the commander-in-chief to give effect to them. It would be dangerous for the country if either took on the other's *dharma*. We may be reminded of Epictetus on Agamemnon and Achilles. Neither *dharma* should be considered *superior* to the other, just as Cicero's Stoic is not to be diverted to a role that seems to have more *gravity* than his own. In the Ramayana the outcaste Guha and the tribal woman Shabari, however lowly, attained the supreme state by each performing their own *dharma*. The work of the lowliest may turn out to have helped the loftiest. Just as with the Stoic persona, following one's own *dharma* is not a matter of a free-for-all. It is, says Gandhi (reminding us of Seneca's stones in an arch), to subordinate oneself to society. One

39. Translated by Mahadev Desai 1933–34, published posthumously 1946.
40. Gandhi, "Discourses on the Gita," *CW*, vol. 32, pp. 367–70.

must follow one's *conscience* and in place of "I" must put God, just as it is God, in Epictetus' conception, who assigns personae. One must perform one's personal *dharma*, one's *svadharma*, even if it smells of violence. Harishchandra, in the story, had to be ready to slay his own wife and son in order to be true to a vow taken to a god. Gandhi is not here diverging from the Stoic aim of excluding immoral decisions—in the Stoic case by appealing to a first persona of common human rationality. Gandhi considers Harishchandra's action highly moral.

There is even a word in the Gita occupying the place of persona. Members of the four main castes or varnas are said to have their own distinctive nature (*sva-bhava* or *swa-bhava*). But Gandhi does not appear to have made so much use of this term.[41]

GANDHI'S APPLICATIONS OF THE IDEA OF *SVADHARMA*

Gandhi applied the idea of *svadharma* to the contemporary situation. For a start, he probably applied to himself the lesson that is given to Arjuna by the god Krishna. It is Arjuna's duty as a warrior to fight and to kill his relatives, even, on Gandhi's interpretation, to kill them *first*.[42] Gandhi himself had a special role that, we have seen,[43] often involved disfavoring (though not killing) relatives.

SVADHARMA OF SOME PEOPLE RARE, BUT NOT UNIQUE

Gandhi's use of the idea of individual duty is startling in a different way from the Stoic use. He did not look for duties that were unique to one single person, from which the Stoics derived so much philosophical interest. At most he spoke of a duty as being *rare*, as when a terminally sick person voluntarily left the ashram to spare the members nursing him. Other people, he said, should not necessarily follow that, but only do what they can.[44]

To find an example of a unique *svadharma*, we could look rather to the Mahabharata's example of Karna. If in that epic Karna had accepted the throne he was offered, he would have averted the whole long destructive war, which left most members of the rival families dead. Why did he refuse?

41. Gandhi does not draw attention to it in discussing that part of the Gita. It is introduced into a brief conversation of 1938 by Rajagopalachari in "talk with C. Rajagopalachari" 7 Jan 1938 in *Harijan* 15 Jan 1938, *eCW*, vol. 72, p. 424.

42. Gandhi, "Discourses on the 'Gita,'" *CW*, vol. 32, pp. 103–4.

43. Chapter 1.

44. Gandhi, letter to Vasumati Pandit, 27 Oct 1932, *CW*, vol. 51, pp. 305–6.

It was in order to acknowledge the couple who had brought him up, rather than his biological parents.[45] This was in a certain way acting on a unique *svadharma* of indebtedness to those two particular individuals. And, as with the Stoic unique examples, it would be hard to formulate a general rule about when such a decision would be right and when wrong.

GANDHI ON PERFORMING ONE'S OWN *SVADHARMA*, NOT ANOTHER'S

Gandhi's most significant use of the idea of individual duty arose from the Gita's insistence that one must perform one's own duties, not another's. Women bound by a vow to one kind of work should not take up some other service.[46] One's *svadharma* is to look after one's neighbors and dependents, not to go rushing to some far corner of the world, which may only disturb distant people with some act of knight-errantry.[47] To Mirabehn, his devoted attendant whom he sent away to perfect her Hindi, he insisted that that was her *svadharma* and her main task. He could not advise what else to do on the side; there were several acceptable possibilities and the choice must be hers.[48]

IMPLICATIONS FOR RECRUITMENT TO HOME-SPUN CLOTH, NONCOOPERATION, NONVIOLENCE, WITHDRAWAL FROM POLITICS, AND THE STATUS OF DALITS

This insistence on not performing another's *svadharma* placed the most interesting restrictions on Gandhi's defense of, and recruitment to, his own policies. Against opponents he sometimes defended his preference for the tactic of noncooperation and for his home-spun cloth campaign, not by saying that these policies were right, but only by saying that they were his personal *svadharma*. Even more startlingly, he said about the campaign for home-spun cloth, not that the alternative of bloody revolutions was wrong,

45. Mahabharata 5.139–44, discussed by Aditya Adankar, "Karna's choice: courage and character in the face of an ethical dilemma," in T. S. Rukmani, ed., *The Mahabharata: Whatever Is Not Here Is Nowhere Else*, New Delhi 2005, ch. 9.

46. Gandhi, letter to Vasumati Pandit, 27 Oct 1932, *CW* vol. 51, pp. 305–6.

47. Gandhi, *Navajivan* 31 May 1931, translated from Gujarati by Pyarelal for *Young India* 18 June 1931, *CW*, vol. 46, p. 255. This duty to immediate neighbors was connected with *swadeshi*, self-reliance, and the campaign for home-spun cloth in the rules posted on Gandhi's room, on my 2009 visit to the Ahmedabad ashram.

48. Gandhi, letter to Mirabehn, 28 May 1927, *CW*, vol. 33, p. 382.

but merely that "bloody revolutions just do not appeal to me."[49] This personalization of his belief in nonviolence was more general, as emerged in chapter 4 above in connection with Gandhi's discussion of killing stray dogs. Broadening the discussion to nonviolence against animals and humans, he did not expect to be followed, except as a matter of tactics, by Muslims. They would say that their *dharma* was to beat a man who beats them, and they felt they could win independence from Britain that way. He would not advise Afghans on violence the same way as he advised Indians. Nor could the head of a household be expected to follow the nonviolent path of a recluse: the religious duty of allowing dogs to live even at the cost of his own life was not for him.[50] Equally, municipal councils included people of different religions. So they too could not be expected to introduce nonviolent measures to control animals.[51] When Gandhi left his Congress Party in 1940, upon their declining to issue an endorsement of nonviolence as a creed, he acknowledged, we saw, that while he had stuck to the "mission of [his] life," the Congress had equally been true to themselves. They were right not to endorse a conception of nonviolence as a creed, rather than a tactic, when they did not trust themselves to live up to that conception of nonviolence.[52] In effect they too had followed their *svadharma*. About engagement in politics in the sense of nonviolent resistance,[53] he thought that few could retain a nonviolent frame of mind if they engaged. They would be better off devoting themselves to constructive work such as the home-spun campaign. But in a speech about this to members of the Gandhi Seva Sangh, which had been set up for constructive work, he insisted that he could not tell who would succeed in remaining nonviolent within politics. Instead of recommending constructive work and a general withdrawal from politics, he refused to advise individuals what to do.[54]

Gandhi's strong belief in *svadharma* will surely have contributed to his reluctance to join the leader of the Dalits, Ambedkar, in criticizing the caste system as in itself responsible for their plight as excluded from any caste. He sought not to restructure the caste system, but rather to appeal to the

49. *CW*, vol. 33, 1927, p. 224 (letter to Hirala Amritlal, 8 Apr 1927); vol. 29 (from *Navajivan* 20 Dec 1929), pp. 334–35.

50. Gandhi in *Day to Day*, vol. 8, pp. 273, 276, 280.

51. *Day to Day* 8, p. 321.

52. "Both happy and unhappy," *Harijan* 29 June, 1940, repr. Iyer, *Essential Writings*, pp. 248–51.

53. The model for politics here was Sardar Patel.

54. Speech to Gandhi Seva Sangh, 22 Feb 1940, repr. Iyer, *Writings*, vol. 1, pp. 415–43.

duties to others that he saw as already implied within the ancient division into four varnas, or social classes, based on professional occupation.[55]

GANDHI ON INDIVIDUALS

Gandhi's interest in individual duty was connected with a more general belief in the individual. He thought that industrialization had reached its apotheosis in Russia and had robbed people of their individuality, making them cogs in a machine. Instead, one needed self-sufficient villages.[56] The state power of socialism also destroys individuality. Indeed, the violence of socialism was worse than the violence of private ownership, and the ideal solution would be for private owners to act voluntarily as trustees for the poor, though if they refused, the state might have to force them.[57] By contrast, he argued that the right kind of socialism was one that depended on individuals. "Ultimately the world is made of individuals," he wrote in 1945 to his successor Nehru, whose belief in socialism he did not share. "If there were no drops, there would be no ocean." "The sum and substance of what I want to say is that the individual person should have control over the things that are necessary for the sustenance of life."[58] This reference to the bare necessities of life was further clarified in a conversation eighteen months later with his great-niece, Manu.[59] The Lord Krishna preached socialism in the Gita, he said. One should possess only what one requires, and all men are entitled to an equal share of food, clothing, and housing. It does not require huge organizations. Any individual can set about realizing it. "We should minimise our needs, keeping in mind the poorest of the poor in India. One should earn just enough to support oneself and one's family. [. . .] Even if a single individual enforces this ideal in his life," he said, appealing, as often, to the force of individual example,[60] "he is bound to influence others." The conversation finishes by repeating the view that the wealthy should act as trustees of their wealth. Earlier he had sought to reassure the owners of estates (zamindars) that Nehru's talk of the nationalization of property need not frighten them, so long as they held their property in trust

55. I thank Cosim Sayid for raising this question.

56. Discussion with Maurice Frydman, *Harijan* 28 Jan 1939, repr. Iyer, *Writings*, vol. 3, p. 529.

57. Interview with Nirmal Kumar Bose, published later in *The Hindustan Times*, 17 Oct 1935, *CW*, vol. 59, pp. 316–20, repr. Iyer, *Writings*, vol. 3, p. 600.

58. Letter to Nehru, 5 Oct 1945, repr. Iyer, *Writings*, vol. 1, p. 286.

59. Talk with Manu Gandhi, camp at Patna, 15 Apr 1947, repr. Iyer, *Writings*, vol. 3, pp. 582–83.

60. See further on the force of individual example chapter 7.

for their tenants,[61] and he connected trusteeship with individuality. "The nation," he said, "cannot own property except by investing it in individuals," such, presumably, as themselves.

A year after the letter to Nehru, Gandhi gave a central role to the individual in the India he would like to see after Independence. In the structure composed of innumerable villages, life "will be an oceanic circle whose centre will be the individual always ready to perish for the village, the latter ready to perish for the circle of villages, till at last the whole becomes one life composed of individuals."[62] Here the individual, though central, will offer self-sacrifice for the wider circles. Margaret Chatterjee has noticed the comparison between Gandhi's oceanic circle and the circles in the discussion by the Stoic Hierocles of the duty to draw outer circles of people closer towards the circle embraced by family love.[63] She suggests that Gandhi may have seen the Stoic idea reflected in W. E. H. Lecky's *History of European Morals* of 1869, which he consulted. But Gandhi's call for self-sacrifice for the wider whole she found only in Adam Smith's adaptation of Stoic thought in his *Theory of Moral Sentiments* (6th ed., 1760).

THE STOICS ON INDIVIDUALS

To return to the Stoics, we have encountered in chapter 1 Seneca's idea that the individual is part of the wider community like the stones in an arch. This may seem, as in Gandhi, to subordinate the individual to the community. But it is compatible with what we have also encountered: the intense interest in individuals. The interest is required to make them watch whether indifferents appear alluring or alarming (chapter 1), to teach them the difference between a mere target and the aim that really matters (chapter 2), and between what is and what is not under their will's control, to help them create a self that no tyrant can enslave (chapter 3), and to inspire them to explore and develop their individual persona and duties (chapter 6).

In the next chapter I shall turn from the shared interest of Gandhi and the Stoics in individual duty to their more general hesitations about universal rules in morality.

61. Answers to zamindars, *The Pioneer*, 3 Aug 1934, repr. Iyer, *Writings*, vol. 3, pp. 556–59.

62. "Content of Independence," *Harijan* 21 July 1946, *CW*, vol. 91, p. 326, cited by Mehdi, "The Political Dimension of the Contemplative Life."

63. Hierocles in Stobaeus vol. 4, p. 671; Margaret Chatterjee, *Gandhi's Diagnostic Approach Rethought*, Delhi 2007, ch. 7, "The oceanic circle," pp. 148–74.

CHAPTER SEVEN

Hesitations about general rules in morality

The ideas of persona and *svadharma* mean that there are duties that apply only to some people. In the extreme cases, we saw, a duty might apply only to one person because of his unique history. The attempt to formulate a universal rule about such a duty would neither have the requisite concision nor be useful to any actually existing other individual. But there are other ways too in which rules may fail to be universal. Instead of failing to apply to all individuals, they may instead fail to apply to all circumstances, insofar as those are distinguishable.

Some of Gandhi's own decisions had a unique quality that would make it very difficult to bring them under a rule. His decision to inaugurate the Salt March against British taxation, or to recommend avoiding Jinnah's partition of India by offering the premiership of the whole to him, could not usefully be brought under any statable rule.

Gandhi's hesitations about universal rules of conduct had many different grounds.

UNATTAINABLE IDEALS BETTER FOR SPIRITUAL ASPIRATION THAN RULES ATTAINABLE BY ALL

Christ criticized the Pharisees, said Tolstoy, and was saddened by the rich man, both of whom did everything required of them by law. To follow the law is not yet to show charity, and the rich man was unable to sell all he had and give to the poor. Christ, in Tolstoy's view, offered not a set of achievable rules, but an unachievable ideal.[1] Gandhi followed Tolstoy in favoring unattainable ideals. He argued that a religious or spiritual ideal should not

1. Leo Tolstoy, "Afterword to The Kreutzer Sonata," 1890, translated by Robert Edwards

be a "cut-and-dry model" or "code of conduct [. . .] possible for all." Otherwise, there would be no room for "that constant striving, that ceaseless quest after the ideal that is the basis of all spiritual progress."[2] Gandhi's principle of nonviolence, we shall recall below, was recommended on the same ground as an unattainable ideal.

ENDORSEMENT OF RUSKIN'S ATTACK ON LAWS OF ECONOMICS AS INAPPLICABLE TO HUMAN BEINGS

Gandhi followed Ruskin, who had in *Unto this Last* (1860) attacked the laws of economic theory; Gandhi paraphrased it in 1908 under the title "*Sarvodaya*"—advancement of all. The economists' laws of supply and demand simply do not apply to humans, because human behavior is subject to feelings of warmth and affection that are not a matter of laws. Affection changes man's nature so that laws cannot measure its effect.

SOME ECONOMIC LAWS NOT *USEFUL* TO A POOR COUNTRY

Gandhi gave a different twist to the attack on economic laws in a speech to an economic society in 1916. He had two points to make. For poor countries like India, economic laws had to consider morality. Hence, even economic laws of universal application might be irrelevant to India.[3] Alongside many citations of Christ from the Gospel of St. Matthew, he declared: "Most of the economic laws which were consistent with moral laws were of universal application, but there might be in their restricted application some distinction and difference." He argued that an economist who did not investigate the laws of God and show how to distribute wealth so that there might not be poverty was a most unwelcome intrusion on Indian soil. Students of economics should reflect that what might be good for England and America need not necessarily be good for India. Indian conditions were in some respects essentially different, and he praised a speaker who had said that there was no economic problem that could be separated from the moral prob-

and repr. with revisions in Leo Tolstoy, *The Kreutzer Sonata and Other Stories*, Oxford 1998, pp. 163–77. Tolstoy cites Matthew 5:48, "Be ye therefore perfect . . . "

2. "Some more posers in *Ahimsa*," *Young India* 22 Nov 1928, repr. Iyer, *Writings*, vol. 2, p. 285.

3. Speech at Muir College Economic Society, Allahabad, 22 Dec 1916, *CW*, vol. 13, pp. 310–17, from *The Leader* 25 Dec 1916.

lem. That speaker was studying the real economics that was so essential for India, and reducing his studies inch by inch to practice. It was this reduction down from the universal to local practicalities that Gandhi considered the type of economics needed for India. In 1931 Gandhi gave an illustration of the need to vary the application of economic laws to the case of India: it is better for the freedom of the inhabitants of India's 700,000 villages that they manufacture their own clothing where they live.[4]

DIFFERENCES OF *SVADHARMA*: INDIVIDUAL DUTY

There was another context in which Gandhi rejected universalizing: in his repeated rejection of "Gandhism." He said, for example, "I love to hear the words: "down with Gandhism." An 'ism' deserves to be destroyed."[5] This may well have flowed from his belief that his values, his *svadharma*, could not be imposed on everyone.

Difference of *svadharma* was a most important reason why Gandhi hesitated to offer universal rules of conduct. I omit to discuss it further here only because it was the subject of chapter 6, and had already been illustrated for the case of nonviolence in chapter 4.

OUR LACK OF CERTAINTY AND INSISTENCE ON TRUTH

Akeel Bilgrami has taken up the subject of Gandhi's reasons for eschewing universalized moral rules and considered what his reasons might be: not our lack of certainty, but an interest in conscience and a preference for setting an example rather than expressing condemnation.[6] I should like to take up his insights.

As regards our uncertainty, Bilgrami says that Gandhi does not use the appeal to ignorance found in John Stuart Mill and, I would add, earlier in John Locke and before that during the English Civil War in Richard Overton on the side of the reformist Levellers, and in antiquity. The appeal is to our ignorance of what is right as a reason for not universalizing our moral

4. "Superstitions die hard," *Young India* 2 July 1931, repr. Iyer, *Writings*, vol. 3, p. 519.

5. "Question box," *Harijan* 16 March 1940; letter to Rameshwari Nehru, 7 June 1946; speech to Gandhi Seva Sangh, 22 Feb 1940, repr. Iyer, *Writings*, vol. 1, pp. 61, 64, 423.

6. Akeel Bilgrami, "Gandhi the philosopher," http://www.mkgandhi.org/articles/philgandhi.htm, originally published in *Economic and Political Weekly*, 38, 2003, 4159–4165.

opinions to the conduct of everyone in the same circumstances.[7] Bilgrami further argues that there would be a confusion involved in the argument that we must be diffident about our present opinions because (according to our present opinion) our past opinions have definitely sometimes been wrong. In any case, he adds, Gandhi was not diffident.

I think, however, that uncertainty about what was right for other people, combined with his insistence on confining oneself to the truth, did play an important role in Gandhi's attitude. I also think that Gandhi's belief in *svadharma*, personal duty, provided one reason among others for uncertainty about what would be right for everybody. In the case, cited in chapter 6, of his close attendant, Mirabehn, it was only her *svadharma* of learning Hindi on which he could pronounce, despite knowing her so well; about the rest he professed himself too ignorant to advise. But there are examples of ignorance extending also to the *svadharma* of others. One is provided by Gandhi's speeches to a society established for nonpolitical constructive work such as the promotion of home spinning, the Gandhi Seva Sangh.[8] He recommended that 84 out of its 243 members were qualified for politics and should therefore leave the society, among them Vallabhbhai, better known as Sardar Patel, the accomplished enforcer of Gandhi's and later of Nehru's political programs, But when questioned, he said he did not know how many would maintain their nonviolent commitment if they did politics. "I do not wish to give my view about even one individual doing it or not doing it. I do not have enough material about it. I do not know how far those who accept power observe non-violence and stand for truth. You would be put to test if you take part in politics of power. I cannot say to what extent you would pass the test. Vallabhbhai is conducting the experiment by remaining in politics. He would leave it when he finds that it is not proper for him to be there. The Sangh does not wish to take any responsibility in this matter. It is left to the conscience of each individual. Each should regard his own conscience as the authority. No outsider can take any decision in the

7. Richard Overton, "The Arraignment of Mr Persecution," 1645, quoted by H. N. Brailsford, *The Levellers and the English Revolution*, London 1961, pp. 55–56; John Locke in both *An Essay Concerning Toleration* of 1667 (p. 273 in the edition of J. R. and Philip Milton, Oxford, 2006) and the better known *Letter Concerning Toleration* of 1689; John Stuart Mill, *On Liberty*, ch. 1. For antiquity see Themistius (late 340s–384/5), in *Themistii orationes*, ed. H. Schenkel, Teubner vol. 1, Leipzig 1965, 67b–70c, Oration V, trans. Peter Heather and David Moncur, *Politics, Philosophy and Empire in the Fourth Century: Select Orations of Themistius*, Liverpool University Press, 2001, especially chap. 3.

8. Speech to Gandhi Seva Sangh, 21 and 22 Feb 1940, repr. Iyer, *Writings*, vol. 1, nos. 149–50, pp. 415–43, at 419, 433, 443.

matter. For instance, Vallabhbhai is engaged in political work. But I do not know his mind. I do not know Vallabhbhai's feelings, nor yours."

There is an appeal to ignorance here. It is like the response in Epictetus to the question whether to hold the chamber pot: "That is for you to bring into consideration, not for me. For you are the one who knows yourself."[9] Gandhi is not denying that we could frame universalizable rules about when it is right to engage in politics. We could say that no one should go into politics, if that would damage his nonviolence. The point is rather that that principle does not tell us what everyone should actually do. Since we cannot know everyone's character, we cannot draw conclusions about what they should do (about their *svadharma*, we could say). Instead, each must appeal to his own conscience. However, for that to be reliable, we shall see, a great deal of practice is needed in listening to its voice.[10]

We saw in the introduction that Gandhi endorsed the Jain belief in individuals having access only to partial truths, *anekântavâda*. This provided a more general reason for uncertainty. Combined with Gandhi's insistence on truth, it played a role in another context: Gandhi said that the fallibility of our judgment is a reason for not practicing violence, and for sacrificing only oneself, not others. He says something similar about punishment for the same reason. Talking to a group that had taken a vow of nonviolence, the Khudai Khidmatgars, he insists that the punishment of robbers is not for man "with judgement weak," but for God, who alone is the infallible judge.[11]

OUR CONSCIENCE ONLY SOMETIMES TELLS US WHAT OTHERS SHOULD DO

The appeal to conscience is explicit in Gandhi's speech to the Gandhi Seva Sangh. Since we cannot know the ability of each individual to remain nonviolent, we cannot tell them their *svadharma* either, and the individual must discover it from his conscience. But, Bilgrami points out, conscience is unlike a universalized rule, because it does not necessarily tell anyone what *others* should do. As he well says about Gandhi, "Morals is only about conscience, not at all about principles."

9. Epictetus, *Discourses* 1.2.11.

10. Chapter 8 below.

11. *Hind Swaraj*, pp. 90–91; "On the verge of it," *Young India* 21 May 1925, repr. Iyer, *Writings* 2, pp. 307–8; talk to Khudai Khidmatgars at Lakki, *Harijan* 19 Nov 1938, *eCW*, vol. 74, p. 164.

I think this is true to a large extent. But I would qualify it by saying that conscience can prescribe for others *indirectly*. For what it tells the individual may be that he or she should change the behavior of *others*. We shall find an example of this in a moment, because Gandhi's conscience did tell him that he should be opposing society's treatment of the class of "Untouchables," as he first called the Dalits, before he called them "Harijans." But we shall see that when Gandhi gave prescriptions to all humans, they tended to concern the right *attitude* of nonviolent love to all others. By contrast, his conclusions about the consequent *conduct* required were restricted. In the case of the Dalits, they were restricted to a particular society and its institutions.

RULES VERSUS SETTING AN EXAMPLE

This brings me to Bilgrami's further intriguing suggestion, that Gandhi holds back from universalized moral principles because they imply the unloving attitude of criticism of those who fail to comply. Instead, Gandhi sets other people an example. I agree that setting an example is one of Gandhi's important methods of changing attitudes. But I believe he has many methods. The threat of fasting is another, the appeal to his own conscience another, and I think that criticism is yet another. Gandhi criticized people severely, and in doing so he respected his nonviolent "law of love," so long as the criticism did not involve any hatred or ill will. He sought to change attitudes to the Dalits by *all* these methods, partly by the *example* of introducing Dalits to his ashram and later to the Harijan village that he created for them,[12] partly by *criticizing* his fellow Hindus as being no better in their humiliation of Dalits than the notorious British General Dyer, who had made Indians crawl in Amritsar in 1919.[13] The method of duress by *fasting* was used when he employed his multipurpose fast unto death as a threat so as to enforce on others his own remedy for Dalits in the Poona Pact of 1932.[14] He appealed to *conscience* and "the inner voice of conscience," in

12. I have described Gandhi's pride in his admission of the first ashram Dalit and a visit to his Harijan village in my *Opening Doors: The Untold Story of Cornelia Sorabji, Reformer, Lawyer and Champion of Women's Rights in India*, London and New Delhi 2010, ch. 21.

13. "The spinning-wheel movement," *Navajivan* 26 Feb 1921; speech at suppressed classes conference, *Young India* 27 Apr and 4 May 1921, *eCW*, vol. 22, p. 316, and vol. 23, p. 44.

14. Rajmohan Gandhi, *Mohandas*, pp. 370–73.

arguing that Dalits should be allowed into temples closed to them.[15] In this example *conscience* had implications not only for himself, but for what others should allow.

UNIVERSAL INJUNCTIONS CAN BE MADE ABOUT ATTITUDE MORE EASILY THAN ABOUT CONDUCT

Gandhi had another reason for caution about rules of nonviolent conduct, besides the duties imposed by mistaken conscience. For he thought it a complicated question what *action* was compatible with a nonviolent *attitude*. The need for the right *attitude* of nonviolence is universalizable, at least as a desirable aspiration from which we inevitably fall short. What *conduct* that attitude calls for can be discussed only case by case. Below, we will find the same result in the Stoics, that a general "formula" could be given about the need to see others as fellow humans, but more specific advice about conduct can only pick out a few examples. Even so, Gandhi may have gone further, as we saw in chapter 4, when he refused to insist even on an *attitude* of nonviolence for those who were committed to an opposite belief in the value of retaliation.

SOME UNIVERSAL INJUNCTIONS ARE ONLY APPARENT EXCEPTIONS

We could be misled when Gandhi calls his injunction against the use of force, encountered in chapter 4, an eternal principle without exceptions. In fact he goes on to say that the injunction is a counsel of perfection because it is better to have a lofty, though unattainable, aim: "Therefore when I say that the use of force is wrong in whatever degree and under whatever circumstances, I mean it in a relative sense. It is much better for me to say I have not sufficient non-violence in me, than to admit exceptions to an eternal principle. Moreover my refusal to admit exceptions spurs me to perfect myself in the technique of non-violence." He repeatedly gives advice on how to act if it is not within your power to refrain from using force. What is exceptionless is the principle about what would be perfect.

15. Rajmohan Gandhi, *Mohandas*, p. 309, citing Gandhi in the *Bombay Chronicle*, 16 Sep 1927, *CW*, vol. 40, p. 105.

Gandhi claimed that *satyagraha*, insistence on truth, as providing the force used in nonviolent resistance, was a law of universal application.[16] But we have seen that he did not mean that everyone should put it to that use, because, like the Stoics, he did not think that everyone had the right personality for everything. The universality of the law in this context will rather have had to do with its practice always having desirable effects. On the other hand, he did admittedly treat as a universal requirement one small part of the insistence on truth, when he said against Bertrand Russell, "Truth telling admits of no exceptions,"[17] a claim closer to Socrates than to the Stoics, who allowed lies in exceptional cases. Russell had said that he felt no worse for lying to the pursuing hunt about which way the fox had gone. Gandhi pointed out that he could simply have refused to answer the question. He may have thought that better alternatives were always available to lying, whereas humans did not always have alternatives to violence.

Gandhi again denied exceptions, when he was questioned about having offered euthanasia to a suffering and incurable calf. "But the question may very legitimately be put to me: would I apply to human beings the principle I have enunciated in connection with the calf? Would I like it to be applied in my own case? My reply is yes; the same law holds good in both the cases. The law of *yatha pinde thatha brahmande* ('as with one so with all') admits of no exceptions, or the killing of the calf was wrong and violent." But he goes on immediately to show how different normally are the case of a calf and a human. "In practice however we do not cut short the sufferings of our ailing dear ones by death because as a rule we have always means at our disposal to help them and because they have the capacity to decide for themselves." The point about humans, unlike calves, being able to make decisions is taken up in a continuation of the subject of the calf. If another person can express his wish, his life cannot "be taken against his will without violating the principle of *ahimsa*."[18]

LOCAL RULES FOR GANDHI OR HIS ASHRAM

Of course Gandhi imposed on himself and on members of his ashram many unbreakable rules such as celibacy and, in his own case, days of silence.

16. Answers to questions at Constructive Workers' Conference, Madras, *The Hindu* 26 Jan 1946; *Harijan* 31 March 1946, repr. Iyer, *Writings*, vol. 3, p. 575.

17. *Harijan* "Question box," 9 June 1946, repr. Iyer, *Writings*, vol. 2, p. 206.

18. "The fiery ordeal," *Young India* 4 Oct 1928, repr. Iyer, *Writings*, vol. 2, p. 271; "More about *Ahimsa*," *Young India* 1 Nov 1928, repr. Iyer, *Writings*, vol. 2, p. 280.

But these rules are clearly applicable only to himself, or to his accepted community.

THE STOICS

I come now to the Stoics. What we often find with them is that when they talk of a moral law or rule, it turns out not to specify informatively what conduct is required. When we do find more specific Stoic rules of conduct, they may either be mere examples rather than generalizations, or, if general, may be subject to an unspecified number of exceptions according to circumstances. Nonetheless, I must tread carefully, because it has been the subject of controversy whether the Stoics sought to cover ethics by a set of rules of conduct, with admirable scholars on either side of the debate.[19] I should be disappointed myself, if the Stoics gave such an important value to rules, because I think that rules can only be a subordinate aid in ethics, and an aid that can cover only a little of what one needs. This is not to deny that aids are useful in their place.

STOIC VIRTUOUS CONDUCT VERSUS DUTIES

To some extent rules can be formulated to express the Stoic actions sometimes called in English "appropriate actions" and sometimes "duties" (Greek *kathêkonta*, Latin *officia*). Performing duties, for the Stoics, is something much less than acting virtuously. Stoic virtue is a profound state of mind. It is not mere conformity to certain types of action nor even to action with the right motivation. In order to act virtuously, the Stoic has to perform

19. On one side are Brad Inwood, "Rules and reasoning in Stoic ethics," in Katerina Ierodiakonou, ed., *Topics in Stoic Philosophy*, Oxford 1999, ch. 4, pp. 95–127; Charles Brittain, "Rationality, rules and rights" *Apeiron* 34, 2001, 247–66; Katja Vogt, *Law, Reason and the Cosmic City*, Oxford 2008, ch. 4. On the other side, importance of rules: Gisela Striker," "Following nature: a study in Stoic ethics," *Oxford Studies in Ancient Philosophy* 9, 1991, pp. 1–73; David Sedley, "The Stoic-Platonist debate on *kathêkonta*," in Katerina Ierodiakonou, ed., *Topics in Stoic Philosophy*, Oxford 1999, pp. 128–52; Phillip Mitsis and J. de Filippo, in Paul Vander Waerdt, ed., *The Socratic Movement*, Ithaca, N.Y. 1994, pp. 252–71; Phillip Mitsis, "The Stoics and Aquinas on virtue and natural law," *Studia Philonica Annual*, 15, 2003, 35–53; Mitsis, "Moral rules and the aims of Stoic ethics," *Journal of Philosophy* 83, 1986, 556–58; Mitsis, "Natural law and natural right in post-Aristotelian philosophy," in *Aufstieg und Niedergang der römischen Welt*, part 2, vol. 36, no. 7, Berlin 1994, pp. 4812–4850; Mitsis, "Seneca on reason, rules and moral development," in Jacques Brunschwig and Martha Nussbaum, eds., *Passions and Perceptions*, Cambridge 1993, ch. 10, pp. 285–312; Mitsis, "The early Stoic theory of natural law," in K. Boudouris, ed., *Hellenistic Philosophy*, Athens 1993–94, vol. 2, pp. 130–40.

these same rightly motivated duties in a certain way.[20] But when we ask in what way, we are often given no more than an adverb such as "virtuously," "justly," or "prudently."[21] We can gather that duties performed virtuously will be performed with true understanding about the whole of life that cannot be diverted, however taxing the situation. But *rules* are not offered as capable of explaining the difference between virtuous and ordinary performance of duties. So I think it might be widely agreed that there is a limitation on the utility of rules right away, if they cannot explain virtue.

There is another problem too. If we look for Stoic duties that hold invariably, the only one we are given is living in accordance with virtue.[22] That means that we can formulate invariable rules only by appealing to the adverb "virtuously." This is not going to give us anything as informative as the Ten Commandments of the Jewish Law ("Thou shalt not kill," etc.).

STOIC NATURAL LAW AND "FORMULA" VERSUS PRECEPTS

It might be thought rules would be found in contexts where the Stoics speak of natural or divine law. But there is a difference between the Stoic concept of natural law and the concept of human legal systems. In human legal systems a law is often a rule. But when examples are given of the Stoic divine and natural law, they have an entirely different character. Cicero's *On Duties* reflects the work of the Stoic Panaetius and discusses his Stoic predecessors Antipater and Diogenes and his pupil Hecato. Five times in book 3, Cicero gives an example of a Stoic law, for which he uses four expressions: "law of nature" four times (*naturae lex*), "law of nativity" (to paraphrase "born with a law"—*lege natus*), "law of nations" twice (*ius gentium*) and "formula" three times (*formula*, also in Latin). On each of these occasions he gives the same example of a law. There are common bonds of humanity and certain behavior would break them. Antipater is made to put it more positively: the common interest of human society should be yours and vice versa.[23] Not only does Cicero take no interest in whether the "law" is phrased as a prescription or not, but the "law," valuable though it is, is not specific about what to do or not to do in the way that the rules of modern legal systems are, or again the Ten Commandments.

20. Cicero, *On Duties* 1.3.8, 3.14; Diogenes Laertius, *Lives* 7.108–10.

21. Cicero, *On Ends* 3.59; Sextus, *Against the Experts* 11.200–201; Stobaeus vol. 2, pp. 85,18–86,4 and 96,18–97,5.

22. Diogenes Laertius, *Lives* 7.109.

23. Cicero, *On Duties* 3.19–21, 3.23. 3.27–28, 3.52–53, 3.69.

It is telling that Seneca in the next century comes out with just the same example, when he looks for a *formula*. In two letters, 94 and 95, he discusses the value of precepts (*praecepta*) and of doctrines (*decreta*). He asks what precepts we should give: that we should refrain from shedding human blood, stretch out a hand to the shipwrecked, show the way to someone who is lost, share bread with the starving? These precepts are concrete enough. But they are far from comprehensive, and Seneca despairs of using precepts to say *everything* that is to be done or avoided. So instead he looks for a *formula* to cover *everything*. After describing the natural bonds of human society, he thinks the *formula* is best summed up in the verse of the comic playwright Terence: "I am a human; nothing human do I think to be alien from me."[24] This is comprehensive, but of course it no longer has the utility of being specific and concrete.

Some modern interpretations of the Stoics pass from their talk of a law to talk of *laws* in the plural.[25] But although that would be appropriate to human legal systems, we need to see if there is justification for moving to the plural in connection with Stoic natural law. So far what we have seen the Stoics offering as a natural law is simply one thing: the bonds of humanity. Human laws are numerous because they are specific. Stoic natural law seems so general that it can afford not to be composed of such a multiplicity of laws. If that is the case, then Stoic natural law looks more like the "law of love" that Gandhi took over from Tolstoy. That was not a set of laws, nor of rules, but an attitude of mind. At the very least, one is not going to need indefinitely many laws, in the way that Seneca feared one might need indefinitely many precepts.

As a matter of fact, Brad Inwood has collected from Seneca other examples of a, or of the (Latin does not distinguish), law of nature. It is nature's law, for example, that we should die, that we need only bare necessities, that we will meet difficulties, and then, as before, that we should not and need not be wicked to each other.[26] There are not many examples, and I am not sure that they represent different laws. It may be that nature is thought of as unitary and that these are so many aspects of its one law.

24. Seneca, *Letters* 95, 53.

25. See Gisela Striker's pioneering "Following nature: a study in Stoic ethics," *Oxford Studies in Ancient Philosophy* 9, 1991, pp. 1–73, at pp. 80 and 88, and the very fully argued Philip Mitsis, "Natural law and natural right in post-Aristotelian philosophy: the Stoics and their critics," *Aufstieg und Niedergang der Römischen Welt*, part 2, vol. 36, no. 7 Berlin 1994, pp. 4812–4850, at p. 4813.

26. Brad Inwood, "Rules and reasoning in Stoic ethics," in Katerina Ierodiakonou, ed., *Topics in Stoic Philosophy*, Oxford 1999, pp. 95–127, at p. 119 n. 73.

STOIC "DOCTRINES"

We have seen Seneca contrast the general "formula" about humanity with the more concrete, but particular, precept. This occurs in the course of two letters, 94 and 95, that also contrast *doctrines* (Latin *decreta*, Greek *dogmata*) with precepts and assess the utility of each for ethics. Doctrines are essentially required, and some interpretations have viewed these as moral principles, or determinate principles of conduct.[27] But I agree with those who think that some of them are drawn from Stoic doctrines about nature. In fact, doctrines from *all* the Stoic branches of philosophy are, I think, relevant to life, including doctrines about nature and psychology, about theology and about logic as well as doctrines about ethics. The Stoics think that we need to know what is natural: what goal (*telos*) it is natural to pursue in life, what other objectives it is natural to prefer or disprefer, and that it would be natural to feel kinship with all humans. At some stage—it is controversial when—we may need to know that nature and the natural have been arranged by a providential God. If we are to calm misguided emotions, we need to know their nature—that, unlike mere sensations, emotions depend on our thoughts—that is why reason can alter emotions. Our deliberations must also conform to *logic*. So doctrines of logic as well as of natural science are relevant to guiding conduct. From ethical doctrines we need to know that only virtuous character has supreme value in its own right, as well as how many virtues there are, how distinguished and how interdependent. None of these are exactly rules of conduct.

PREFERENCE FOR MENTORS OVER UNIVERSAL PRONOUNCEMENTS

Seneca denied that universal pronouncements (*in universum pronuntiare*) could necessarily be applied to particular practical issues about what to do,[28] and the Stoics were not the first to look for alternatives to general rules of conduct. The question had already arisen in Plato and Aristotle in connection with legislation. Plato raised this question in the *Statesman* and it was solved in different ways by him and by his pupil Aristotle. Plato argued that the prescriptions of the law were too simplified to take account of all the particularities of individual cases. But since the legislator cannot sit beside

27. Mitsis, "Natural law and natural right in post-Aristotelian philosophy," p. 4845; David Sedley, "The Stoic-Platonist debate on *kathêkonta*," in Katerina Ierodiakonou, ed., *Topics in Stoic Philosophy*, Oxford 1999, pp. 128–52, at p. 132.

28. Seneca, *Letters* 22.1–3, 70.11.

each individual throughout his life prescribing what is appropriate (295A-B), he makes do with the second-best shorthand of laws. But the legislator should be free to override his laws.[29] Aristotle instead offered the solution in his *Nicomachean Ethics* that judges should be given discretion in the application of laws.[30] He repeatedly argued that in ethics and politics you need a kind of *perceptivity* or eye of the soul, which he called *nous* or intellectual recognition, in order to appreciate the particularities of what is called for here and now.[31] It is based on having in mind as a target what ought to be aimed at in life.[32] It might be protested that such perceptivity would be fallible, but that is equally true of the laying down of rules. Aristotle is not tackling the problem of fallibility, but pointing to the well-known phenomenon that some people are perceptive. The person with this perceptivity is the arbiter of the right amount, the right time, the right objective,[33] and that is why book 6 chapter 1 introduces a book-length discussion of this kind of perceptivity. The implication is that if we are not perceptive ourselves, we should look to what such an arbiter would decide. But there is no suggestion that this arbiter must be a ruler or someone with official authority. One could presumably keep in mind a local arbiter who had the right perceptivity.

I see the Stoics as agreeing with this tradition, although Seneca names Epicurus, not Aristotle, as the source of it. Seneca states explicitly that we cannot pronounce in general terms (*in universum pronuntiare*) about certain subjects. Just as a doctor cannot prescribe unless he is on the spot to feel the pulse, so Seneca cannot tell his correspondent when and how to carry out his plan to retire. Nor can we make general statements about whether to commit suicide when an external force threatens us with death.[34] It is not surprising then that Seneca, citing Epicurus as originator of the idea, repeatedly advises you to have a philosopher as companion and mentor,[35] or to imagine an admired philosopher simply watching you.[36] Seneca, like Epictetus after him, also recommends imagining a past philosopher to serve

29. Plato, *Statesman* 294A–296A.

30. Aristotle, *Nicomachean Ethics* 5.10.

31. Aristotle, *Nicomachean Ethics* 2.9, 1109b20; 4.5, 1126b2; 6.8, 1142a26–30; 6.11, 1143a35-b5; 1143b13–14; 6.12, 1144a29–30; 6.13, 1144b6–17.

32. Aristotle, *Nicomachean Ethics* 6.1, 1138b22–25; 6.7, 1141b12–14.

33. Aristotle, *Nicomachean Ethics* 2.6, 1107a1–2.

34. Seneca, *Letters* 70.11, 22.1–3.

35. Seneca, *Letters* 6.5–6, 52.1–4.

36. Seneca, *Letters* 11.8–10, 25.5–6, 32.1, 83.1–2.

as a model and example (*exemplum*),[37] and he once combines the imagined watcher and mentor.[38] On the other side it has been urged that the Stoics do not refer to *exempla* before Panaetius in the later second century BC.[39] This is an interesting finding, but I think it is sufficiently explained if the Stoics wrote before Panaetius about the perfect Stoic sage who no longer needs anyone as an example. It does not imply that before Panaetius the Stoics, or Zeno in particular, thought that ethics requires universal rules instead of exemplars.

ZENO'S SYLLOGISMS

Zeno has a different peculiarity, which I do not, however, think relevant. He likes to present his theses in the form of brief syllogisms, which he put to interlocutors in the form of questions. All the surviving syllogisms of Zeno, and one by his immediate successor, Cleanthes, have been studied by Malcolm Schofield.[40] Most of the syllogisms are about theology, psychology, or nature, only two are about ethics, but none is presented as a rule of conduct, even if we might infer one. The syllogisms were attacked, all of them by the same man, Schofield suggests, Zeno's contemporary the dialectician Alexinus. Zeno's use of the genre is criticized by both Cicero and Seneca.[41] Seneca, though relating some Stoic syllogisms on virtue, comments that they are as yet very few.[42] The practice does not look like an attempt to produce a comprehensive code of conduct in the form of rules, and it does not seem in any case to have been pursued energetically after Alexinus' attack.

THEÔRÊMATA AS PHILOSOPHICAL DISTINCTIONS

There is, however, a more important concept in Stoic thought that has been cited on the other side, that of *theôrêmata*. These have been called "the-

37. Seneca, *Letters* 11.9–10, 95.72, 104.21–22; *On Leisure* 1.1; *On the Shortness of Life* 14.5; Epictetus, *Handbook* 33.12.

38. Seneca, *Letters* 11.9–10.

39. Sedley, "The Stoic-Platonist debate on *kathêkonta*," pp. 150–51.

40. Malcolm Schofield, "The syllogisms of Zeno of Citium," *Phronesis* 28, 1983, pp. 31–58; Schofield, *The Stoic Idea of the City*, Cambridge 1991, appendix F, "Cleanthes' syllogism," pp. 130–35.

41. Cicero, *On the Nature of the Gods* 2.10; Seneca, *Letters* 82.

42. Seneca, *Letters* 87.11.

orems, "principles of conduct," "principles and "rules."[43] They are introduced in at least two important contexts. One context is that of Epictetus' point that ethical preconceptions, for example about what is good and what advantageous, are hard to apply. It is for advice on applications that we resort to philosophers.[44] In an analogy, Epictetus says that we have a preconception of what is healthy, but there is no agreement about remedies, because the preconception is hard to apply. The source of the trouble is that these remedies have not benefited from a correct *theôrêma* such as he is going on to describe. We must first use a *theôrêma* to divide up (*diarthrôsis*) the subject matter before we can apply our preconception of good or advantageous. One division is amongst desire, impulse, and assent. If we take just desire, we must distinguish what it is in general possible to attain and what it is *for us* possible to attain. What it is possible for us to attain is what God wills. Unless we confine our wants to that, we shall be forever frustrated. Epictetus expresses his conclusion as a rule: "Wish nothing but what God wishes." But is his *theôrêma* here the rule, or the *philosophical distinctions*? I shall shortly give an example in which Epictetus *distinguishes* a rule from the philosophical distinctions on which it is based and explicitly calls it a rule (*kanôn*). But first I shall consider other passages that suggest to me that the *theôrêmata* are the philosophical distinctions that guide conduct whether or not the guidance takes the form of a rule.

The other passages speak of the four main virtues inherited by the Stoics from Plato: wisdom, courage, temperance, and justice.[45] These are pieces of knowledge, expertise, and wisdom (*epistêmê, tekhnê, phronêsis*),[46] with shared (*koina*) *theôrêmata*. Each is a structure (*sustêma*) of *theôrêmata*, and once again health[47] is contrasted with moral virtue as not being a structure of *theôrêmata*. For if you have virtue, you are *theôrêtikos* (you understand the theory, to paraphrase the good translation of Long and Sedley) of what is to be chosen, endured, withstood, or distributed—four actions corresponding to the four virtues. Each virtue involves primarily knowing what to do

43. Sedley, "The Stoic-Platonist debate on *kathêkonta*," p. 129; A. A. Long and D. N Sedley, *The Hellenistic Philosophers*, vol. 1, Cambridge 1987, p. 384; most fully discussed in two papers by Mitsis, "Natural law and natural right in post-Aristotelian philosophy," pp. 4823–24 with n.23, and "The Stoics and Aquinas on virtue and natural law," *Studia Philonica Annual* 15, 2003, 35–53.

44. Epictetus, *Discourses* 2.17.

45. Stobaeus vol. 2, pp. 62,15–17 and 63, 6–24; Diogenes Laertius, *Lives* 7.90, 7.125–26.

46. Stobaeus, vol. 2. p. 63, 6–24; Plutarch, *On Stoic Self-Contradictions* 1034C–E; *Anecdota Graeca Paris*, ed. Cramer, vol. 1, p. 171, in H. von Arnim, *Stoicorum Veterum Fragmenta*, vol. 3, no. 214.

47. Diogenes Laertius, *Lives* 7.90.

in its own area. Moderation, for example, requires theoretical understanding (*theôrein*) of impulses. But each virtue must know secondarily about the subject of the other three. This is presumably the context and meaning for the claim that the theoretical understandings (*theôrêmata*) are common (*koina*) to all four virtues. The word "common" does not here mean a *universal* principle of conduct, but that each virtue must involve knowing about the others. Moreover, each virtue must also involve knowing what other virtues it has as subdivisions. What we have seems to me a set of theoretical philosophical distinctions that help us to act virtuously in the four relevant ways. We do not have a set of universal rules of conduct.

THE RULE (*KANÔN, REGULA*)

In spite of my disagreement with the "universal principle" interpretation, there is something to which Epictetus actually applies the word "rule" (*kanôn*). The Latin equivalent, *regula*, is used by Cicero and Seneca.[48] Moreover, what Epictetus calls a rule is something that might well be inferred by somebody who had mastered the first example of a *theôrêma*. Epictetus in the relevant passage is training his students, and he tells them to ask about everything that impresses them whether it is under the control of their *prohairesis*. *Prohairesis* is a philosophical term, which, with oversimplification, I have in chapter 3 paraphrased as *will*. What is not under the control of the will, he tells his students, must be thrown out. They must not set their hearts on it. In this way, they may eventually learn to identify themselves simply with a rightly directed will and become invulnerable. Epictetus explicitly calls it a rule (*kanôn*) when he says, "If it is not under the control of your will, throw it away." It is very like the rule that was not called a rule, but that followed the first example of a *theôrêma*: "Wish nothing but what God wishes." For this was also introduced by the question: "Do you wish what is possible?"[49]

This is a very interesting rule, because it is determinate, and yet it has very wide scope, unlike Seneca's precepts, and Epictetus probably allows no exceptions. You must always regard these things as indifferent in the sense explained in chapters 1 through 3, which does not exclude viewing them as preferred. It is therefore very much the type of rule that should satisfy those who see Stoic rules of conduct as having a central place. But it is rather exceptional to find such a rule. It does not form part of a comprehensive code

48. Epictetus, *Discourses* 3.3.14–19; Cicero, *On Duties* 3.19–22; Seneca, *Letter,* 95.39.

49. Epictetus, *Discourses* 2.17.17, 2.17.22.

of conduct. Moreover, it depends on the prior grasp of distinctions or *theôrêmata*, namely philosophical theory or *theôrêma* about what *prohairesis* is, and about what is or is not under its control.

There may be implicit rules, but they are not explicit, connected with all three fields of study that Epictetus lists in his treatment of *theôrêmata* in *Discourses* 2.17.10–17. The field he discusses there is desires, but in 3.2 he says more about the other fields. They include *assenting*, which is especially important for emotions, since emotions are described as assents to the appearance that harm or benefit is at hand and to appearances about how to react. Seneca's account of how anger grows[50] could well suggest to us the rule that if you want to avoid anger, you had better question such appearances quickly. But it is interesting that Seneca does not himself find it useful to formulate such a rule. The remaining field is impulses (*hormai*), which have to do with duty (*kathêkon*) and acting with good reason as son, brother, etc. It has been pointed out to me that Epictetus has an implicit rule in his discussion of such duties in 2.10.[51] He even starts with an imperative addressed to everyone: "Examine who you are." But this imperative is not intelligible on its own without reading on into the discourse: you are first a human, next a son, next a brother, and each of these names suggests duties. Epictetus is exhorting us to consider our personae, in order to discover what our duties are. But once again, despite the initial imperative, he does not find a rule useful, but offers a whole discourse.

EXCEPTIONS FOR DIFFERENT CIRCUMSTANCES

A final reason for thinking that the Stoics are not seeking comprehensive rules of conduct is that they say that nearly all duties are circumstantial (*peristatika*). That is to say, they are duties only in normal circumstances, but the opposite may be your duty in exceptional circumstances. The Stoic sage may "*even*" eat human flesh.[52] The same applies to what is naturally preferred. Health is preferred only in normal circumstances, but in exceptional circumstances it may be appropriate to prefer sickness.[53] Admittedly, there are some duties that admit of no exceptions, but the only one specified, we saw, is living in accordance with virtue,[54] and there is no rule that tells you how to perform a duty in the virtuous person's way. The theory

50. Seneca, *On Anger* 2.2.1–2.4.2.
51. I thank Jordan Backstrom for the point.
52. Diogenes Laertius, *Lives* 7.121.
53. Epictetus, *Discourses* 2.6.9–10.
54. Diogenes Laertius, *Lives* 7.109.

of personae turned out in chapter 6 to require the suicide of Cato, but of no one else, so exceptional was he. When elsewhere I first broached the subject of rules of conduct, I collected a number of exceptional decisions from the Stoic texts.[55] Suicide is sometimes permissible. Sometimes a vow does not have to be kept and sometimes lies are allowed. What is borrowed need not necessarily be returned—an example from Plato. Parents are not always to be obeyed. A Stoic should not always engage in public life—chapter 10 below will consider the exceptions. It is sometimes better to mutilate oneself, or to give away one's property, and it can be better for one's foot to be muddy. Only in some cases is there any attempt to bring the exceptions under specific or determinate rules. In one of two treatments of suicide, but not the other, five circumstances are laid down for the Stoic to commit suicide.

CONCLUSION: ONE LAW, ONE RULE, MULTIPLE AIDS TO DECISION-MAKING

The discussion suggests that Stoicism has one principal natural law, "Do not break the bonds of human society," and one principle rule, "Wish only what is possible for you." Both prescribe, like Gandhi, an attitude of mind, rather than listing specific conduct to be undertaken or avoided.

Despite the shortage of comprehensive rules, Stoicism offers an exceptional number of aids to decision-making. The "rule"—wish only for what is possible—is intended to govern all desires. The law of nature or "formula" about human bonds guides moral attitudes. The specific precepts—share a crust of bread with the starving—guide conduct in selected cases. The "doctrines," which I have taken to be drawn from the Stoic system as a whole, are an essential background for Stoics. Of more immediate relevance to decision-making is the innovative theory of personae in the light of which decisions in life should be made.

55. Sorabji, *Self*, pp. 163–64, citing Diogenes Laertius, *Lives* 7.109; Cicero, *On Ends* 3.60–61; Olympiodorus, *Commentary on Plato's Phaedo* 1.8, ed. and trans. L. G. Westerink, *The Greek Commentaries on Plato's Phaedo*, vol. 1, Amsterdam 1976; Cicero, *On Duties* 3.92–95 and 1.70–71; Stobaeus vol. 2, p. 111; Philo, *On the Cherubim* 14–15; Plato's example from *Republic*, book 1, borrowed by the Stoics according to Philo, *On the Cherubim* 14–15; Musonius Rufus frag, 16 in Teubner ed., translated by Cora Lutz, *Yale Classical Studies* 10, 1947; Seneca, *Letters* 68; Diogenes Laertius, *Lives* 7.108–9; Epictetus, *Discourses* 2.6.9. To these should be added Cicero, *On Duties* 1.31–32.

CHAPTER EIGHT

Moral conscience

The idea of moral conscience proved central to Tolstoy's work on non-violence, which so much influenced Gandhi. The last chapter showed how Gandhi himself often appealed to moral conscience in preference to moral rules. The Stoics also made their own contribution to the concept of moral conscience But by the time the Stoic Seneca was talking about conscience in the first century CE, the relevant words had been in use for five centuries.[1] So the Stoics were only adding their contribution to a long-established subject. This is not always recognized. Some of the Latin-speaking Church Fathers, like Lactantius, focused on Cicero and Seneca because they wrote in Latin and may have given an impression that the Stoics actually introduced the concept. Rather, what they did was to introduce into an ongoing concept certain emphases of their own. I shall start by looking at the earlier origins they inherited.

SHARING KNOWLEDGE WITH ONESELF OF A DEFECT: FROM FIFTH CENTURY BCE PLAYWRIGHTS TO THE STOICS

In Greek playwrights of the fifth century BCE we find talk of sharing knowledge with oneself (*suneidenai heautôi*) of a defect or shortcoming, often but not always a moral one. When the defect is not moral, the idea is at a greater distance from the eventual concept of moral conscience. The idea

1. I have traced this in an address to the Oxford Patristics Conference of 2007, published as Richard Sorabji, "Graeco-Roman origins of the idea of moral conscience," *Studia Patristica*, 44, 2010, pp. 361–83, and in "Moral conscience: contributions to the idea in Plato and Platonism," in Vassilis Karasmanis and Arnold Hermann, eds., *The Presocratics and Plato: A Festschrift for Charles Kahn*, Las Vegas, 2011. The history of the concept up to modern times is the subject of a book in preparation, *Moral Conscience Through the Ages*.

of sharing with oneself suggests that one is split into two parts, a part that knows of the defect and a part that still needs to receive that information. It is commonly thought that the phrase must have the more obvious meaning of sharing knowledge with *another* person. But that tempting assumption seems to me wrong. The idea of sharing knowledge with *another* became widespread more slowly.

When we have the full phrase with the reference to sharing with *oneself*, then we can be sure that the self-shared knowledge is of a *defect* or shortcoming. When we have less than the full phrase, just sharing knowledge, as a verb or a noun, then the expression can have a wide range of other meanings that only the context will reveal. Of the fifth-century playwrights, Aristophanes used the full phrase, while Euripides used a shorter form, but, as it turns out, in the same sense.[2]

In Plato in the next century there are nine straightforward occurrences (plus one in Xenophon) and two of a more interesting mixed character in which Plato speaks of people sharing guilty knowledge with *another* person who shares knowledge of that secret with *himself*.[3]

Surprisingly, the full construction passed very easily from Greek into Latin, through the use of the Latin adjective *conscius* (sharing knowledge), because I can be said to share knowledge with myself (*mihi*) of a defect. The Latin comic playwright Plautus has the adjective *conscius* as early as the century after Plato, the third century BC, and includes a mixed self- and other-sharing of guilty knowledge.[4]

Epicurus, who founded his school in Athens just before the Stoics in 307 BCE, was accused of constructing a concept of conscience as fear of detection and punishment.[5] Whether conduct would ever be just without fear of detection had earlier been discussed by Plato, who used as a thought experiment the story of Gyges' ability to become invisible.[6] But Epicurus per-

2. Aristophanes, *Wasps*, lines 395–96; Aristophanes, *Knights* 184 (ironic, using "good" for "bad"); Aristophanes, *Women Celebrating Thesmophoria* 477; Euripides, *Medea* 495; Euripides, *Orestes* 999–1002.

3. Xenophon, *Socrates' Defence* 24; Plato, *Apology* 21B; 22D; *Symposium* 216 A; *Ion* 533C (re not being a good speaker on most subjects); *Republic* 331A, 607C–D; *Phaedrus* 235C; *Theaetetus* 206A; *Laws* 773B. For mixed self- and other-knowledge, see *Apology* 34B; *Laws* 870D.

4. Plautus, *Rudens*, line 1247.

5. Cicero, *On Ends* 2.16.35, 2.22.71; Seneca, *Letters* 97.15–16.

6. Plato, *Republic* 359D–360D, cited by Cicero, *On Duties* 3.19.78. See Shadi Bartsch, *The Mirror of the Self*, University of Chicago Press, Chicago 2006; Mark Alfano, "A Genealogy of the Conscience of the Consequentialists," M.A. diss, , CUNY Graduate Center, 2009, and, Alfano, "Gyges in the Panopticon: an empirical investigation of social distance heuristics," submitted for publication 2010.

formed a service by pointing to the *forward*-looking roles of conscience in *averting* wrongdoing or *reforming* past misconduct.

He also had a more benign recommendation, later endorsed by the Stoic Seneca, that we should imagine an admired philosopher watching our conduct to avert us from wrong.[7] Seneca and his fellow Stoic Epictetus, we saw earlier,[8] also suggested the variant of imagining an admired philosopher as a model (*exemplum*) to direct us aright. We should ask ourselves what our model would do.[9] The imagined watcher was not originally identified with conscience, but such an identification was to be made by Adam Smith in the eighteenth century, when he reinterpreted conscience as an imagined impartial spectator.[10]

The concept was used by the later Epicurean Philodemus[11] around 100 BCE, in works that have been dug out from the volcanic lava that buried his library 179 years later, after it was moved to Herculaneum in Italy. Philodemus talks of sharing knowledge with another and of sharing it with oneself. He does so in his treatise *On Frank Speech*, which concerns talking frankly to students partly in the context of *confession*. The students are to *confess* faults in the Epicurean residential school two hundred years after Epicurus. It is here that Philodemus talks of sharing guilty knowledge with oneself, at least if I am right to revive the change of one easily confused letter, to replace the inappropriate reference to swelling (*sunoidêsis* for *suneidêsis*) with a reference to conscience. If the professor *neglects* his student, what will be diminished is the student's sense of *conscience*, not a swelling. This is confirmed by the recurrence 4 lines later of the verb for sharing knowledge and a reference in another column of the same work to even the slaves sharing knowledge of something. Philodemus also already has a reference to *good* conscience, which became prominent later in Cicero and the Stoics, although he there uses a different and uniquely rare word for sharing knowledge (*sungnôsis*). Philodemus uses the concept again in his work *On Rhetoric* and it had indeed been used by lawyers and orators as early as the fourth century BCE.

7. Seneca, *Letters* 11.8–10, 25.5–6, 32.1, 83.1–2. See Bartsch, *Mirror*.

8. Chapter 7 above.

9. Seneca, *Letters* 11.9–10 (imagining both watcher and mentor), 95.72, 104.21–22; *On Leisure* 1.1; *On the Shortness of Life* 14.5; Epictetus, *Handbook* 33.12.

10. Adam Smith, *Theory of Moral Sentiments*, part 3, ch. 1.

11. Philodemus, *On Frank Speech (sometimes translated as On Frank Criticism)*, ed. Olivieri, fragment 67 and col. 12a, with the reading of C. J. Vooys; *On Death*, ed. Kuyper, col. 34, line 35; *On Rhetoric*, ed. Sudhaus 2, pp. 139–40, frag. 11, lines 1–8.

Cicero in the first century BCE was an orator and lawyer as well as devotee of philosophy, and he has over two hundred uses of terms such as *conscius* and *conscientia* in oratorical and legal contexts as well as many in philosophical contexts. In legal contexts, it is often relevant to be talking about a witness, an accomplice, or a confidant. Accordingly, in Cicero the reference to sharing guilty knowledge with *another* becomes very common. Cicero is unusual in not referring to the role of conscience in *averting* wrong action, and he is also rebuked by the Church father Lactantius for failing to recognize that repentance is useful for reform.[12]

One valuable contribution of the Stoics was indirect. Their idea that mistaken emotion—and more generally mistaken impulsion to action—might be avoided if we questioned appearances before assenting to them was not applied by them particularly to matters of conscience. In chapter 1 we saw it applied to matters of value concerning harm, benefit, and appropriate reaction. But it would encourage the questioning of conscience. Joseph Butler's definition of conscience as "an approbation of some principles or actions and disapprobation of others" has been thought to derive from the Stoic Epictetus, even though Epictetus was referring to the approbation and disapprobation of values other than those of conscience.[13]

In the first century CE, the Stoic Seneca emphasizes a *joyful* conscience, in his work *On Benefits*, about the proper relations between philanthropists and their beneficiaries. This took the idea of conscience in a different direction from that which Christianity was going to follow. The Christian emphasis was on a *troubled* conscience, apart from such special cases as the joyful conscience of martyrs. Conscience for the Stoics also tended to remain a private affair, not subjected to outside scrutiny as it could be by an Epicurean professor, or by the Christian Church. Furthermore, the infallibility of conscience, though seldom discussed before St. Paul denied it, was explicitly asserted by the Stoic Seneca.[14]

Despite these movements away from the future direction of Christianity, Stoicism played a role in the development of the Christian idea of conscience. This was because Christians turned to Greek and Roman Philosophy in order to fill out the important but sketchy picture bequeathed to them by their first writer on the subject, St. Paul, who was Seneca's almost exact contemporary in the first century CE.

12. Lactantius, *Divine Institutes* 6.24.2, preserving a fragment of Cicero's *Academica*.

13. Bishop Butler, *Fifteen Sermons preached at the Rolls Chapel*, 2nd ed. 1729, preface 19; cf. Epictetus, *Discourses* 1.1.1.

14. Seneca, *On the Shortness of Life* 10.3.

ST. PAUL'S INNOVATIONS AND CHRISTIANITY

The most important innovation by St. Paul was his connecting conscience (*suneidêsis*) with the *law* written in our hearts—a law referred to in Jewish Scripture.[15] Although Paul did not *identify* conscience with the law in our hearts, the connection with law had the effect of widening the idea of conscience by letting it draw on a *general* knowledge of right and wrong, for its knowledge of *personal* defect or merit. The general knowledge of right also gave conscience a stronger role in *directing* people to right as well as *diverting* them from wrong. It was an important distinction that Paul made between conscience and the law in our hearts, because we still feel that conscience rebukes us or directs us in the light of values that we already have, rather than instructing us in those values for the first time.

A second important innovation was Paul's insistence that conscience was fallible.[16] He also no longer included under the Greek term the idea of awareness of merit, or of nonmoral defects, or awareness of the faults of others. Paul's insistence on the fallibility of conscience made room for the view that we have a duty continually to question our conscience.

CHRISTIAN IMPORTATION OF STOIC IDEAS

There were a number of Christians after Paul who filled out their picture of conscience by borrowing ideas found in Stoic philosophy. Origen, in the third century CE, writing in Greek, associated the law written in men's hearts with the Stoics' "common conceptions," or human preconceptions of good and evil.[17] He also, like Seneca, picked up the practice of interrogating oneself each night on whether one had spent the day aright, although he did not use the Greek word for conscience, and, he drew not from Seneca, but like Seneca from the Pythagoreans, who enunciated the idea in their *Golden Verses*. Moreover, whereas Seneca was trying to progress in the direction of virtue and tended to be rather self-congratulatory, Origen connected the self-interrogation with shame, compunction, and repentance.[18]

The Christian Lactantius, writing in Latin about conscience in the century after Origen, praised both Seneca for saying that it is no use keeping

15. Letter to the Romans 2:15; compare Isaiah 51:7a, Jeremiah (not in the English Bible) 38:33.

16. Letter 1 to the Corinthians 4:4, 8:7–13.

17. Origen, *Against Celsus* 1.4.

18. Seneca, *On Anger* 3.36; Epictetus, *Discourses* 4.6.35; Origen fragment on Psalms 4 from René Cadiou, *Commentaires inédits des Psaumes*, Paris 1936, p. 74; *Selection on the Psalms* IV 9, *PG*, vol. 12, 1144B–1145B, drawing on the *Golden Verses*, lines 40–44.

our conscience closed, because we lie open to God, and Cicero for speaking in similar terms.[19] But he made some changes: first he equated the divine law, which Cicero had ascribed to the Stoic Zeno, not like the Stoics with preserving the bonds of human society, but with making the sacrifice of a pure *conscience* (*conscientia*).[20] Then he introduced the idea that God will remit sins (*remittere, obliterare, condonare, labem abolere*), where remission is unlike forgiveness, in that it erases sins from the ledger, instead of continuing to acknowledge them.[21] This is more appropriate than forgiveness to a God, whom Lactantius elsewhere sees, in his *On the Wrath of God*, as not moved by passion in any ordinary sense. It is no accident that in our passage Lactantius borrows the Stoic word for mercy or clemency, *clementia*, to describe God's remission of sins. The Stoic Seneca recommended mercy to the tyrant Nero, by addressing to him an essay *On Clemency*, but he would not have recommended *pity*, which the Stoics saw, unlike mercy, as an emotion.

NON-STOIC INFLUENCE: SOCRATES' GUARDIAN SPIRIT AND CONSCIENCE

There were also nonStoic influences from Greek philosophy on the Christian concept of conscience, and the one most relevant to Gandhi was an influence stemming from the account of Socrates given by Plato and Xenophon. They describe the belief of Socrates, their hero from the preceding century—the fifth, in his guardian spirit (*daimonion*). The guardian spirit was described as a voice, and it warned Socrates against misguided actions. It is not merely a grammatical point that the spirit spoke negatively, telling Socrates not to leave, rather than to stay. Rather, it spoke against misguided actions to which Socrates had formed an inclination. Furthermore, Socrates treated its warnings as indubitable, as Xenophon makes particularly clear.[22] Socrates was also represented as believing a guardian spirit to be a child of a god.[23] In the first century CE, Epictetus held that God has appointed a guardian spirit (*daimôn*) for each of us to watch our deeds.[24] In the second century

19. Lactantius, *Divine Institutes* 6.24.12–17, 18–20.

20. Lactantius, *Divine Institutes* 6.24.29; ascription to Zeno, Cicero, *On the Nature of the Gods* 1.14.36.

21. Lactantius, *Divine Institutes* 6.24.1–10. I owe the distinction of remission to discussion with David Konstan, as elaborated in his book, *Before Forgiveness*, Cambridge 2010.

22. Plato, *Apology* 31D–32A; *Phaedrus* 242B–C; Xenophon, *Recollections of Socrates* 1.3.4.

23. Plato, *Apology* 27D.

24. Epictetus, *Discourses* 1.14.11–15.

CE the Platonist Albinus, wrote in Latin his *On the Daimôn of Socrates* that a *daimôn* was provided in place of conscience (*vice conscientiae*). Nearly a thousand years after the execution of Socrates in 399 BC, another Platonist philosopher, Olympiodorus, the last pagan philosophy professor in Alexandria, was addressing students who were now all Christians. In self-defense he said that when he spoke of a guardian spirit, they should understand conscience. The two were equated.[25]

The Platonist Plutarch in the first century CE discussed the question how the voice communicated with Socrates.[26] The theory he presented turned on the idea of understanding a message (*noêsis logou*). It is like the understanding (*sunesis*) one has in dreams, and actually there is no voice. The message (*logos*) of the guardian spirit contacts the thinker by means of the content of what is indicated and thought (by means of *to dêloumenon and noêthen*). Changing the simile, Plutarch said that it is like a reflection. There are not even verbs or nouns. The air is transformed by what is thought and itself becomes a message (*logos*). The message passes right through ordinary people, but finds an echo in people who have the right kind of psychological stability.

This theory was repeated in a Latin version by Calcidius, a Christian commentator on Plato's *Timaeus* in the fourth to fifth century CE. It is as in dreams: there is no voice, but the meaning (*significatio*) imitates the work done by voice.[27]

Once again the earlier philosophical discussions may have affected one of the most influential Christians. At any rate, Augustine in the fifth century CE could have read his fellow Christian Latin-speaker Calcidius, when he discussed a related Christian question. How does God speak to men? Not by using sound, but not by sight as in dreams either. Instead, he said, very like the Platonists, that God speaks by means of truth itself to anyone who can hear with the mind, instead of the body.[28]

GANDHI ON CONSCIENCE AS INDUBITABLE

I shall now turn from Stoic and Platonist contributions to the idea of conscience and look at Gandhi's. We saw in chapter 4 that Tolstoy discussed conscience in *The Kingdom of God Is Within You*, where there are more

25. Apuleius, *On the Daemon of Socrates* 16; Olympiodorus, *Commentary on Plato's First Alcibiades* 22,14–23,7.

26. Plutarch, *On the Guardian Spirit of Socrates* 588B–589D.

27. Calcidius, *Commentary on the Timaeus*, ch. 255, p. 288.

28. Augustine, *City of God* 11.2. I thank David Robertson for the reference.

than fifty references. His theme was that violence goes against conscience in so uncomfortable a way that the insistence of conscience on nonviolence will in the end inevitably win in the Christian world. In that work, which particularly influenced Gandhi, Tolstoy expressed no doubts about the indubitability of conscience.

Gandhi too treats the sayings of his conscience as indubitable, despite the Christian tradition stemming from Paul about the fallibility of our understanding of conscience. In this he could have felt confirmed by Plato's *Apology*, which he first came across in 1907[29] and later paraphrased in Gujarati. In that dialogue Socrates treats the warnings of his guardian spirit as indubitable and as coming from the child of a god. Gandhi views the voice of conscience as the voice of God, something that St. Paul never said, and although the voice does not confine itself to warnings, it is otherwise treated, like Socrates' guardian spirit, as indubitable.

Nonetheless, Plato's *Apology* will not have been the original source of Gandhi's belief in the indubitability of the inner voice. Rather, it was part and parcel of his attitude to faith described in the introduction above. Reason must be followed in its sphere, but it is not infallible, because it can so easily be overcome by superior logic. Faith by contrast has a sphere of its own, and in that sphere it is infallible.

Gandhi's unquestioning attitude towards his conscience is illustrated by the two occasions when his leading associate Rajagopalachari wrote, and in the second case crossed half of India, to warn him that his conscience had misinformed him in telling him to conduct a fast. One of these fasts was in 1924, the other in 1933. In 1924 Gandhi replied, "Somehow or other I *feel* the absolute correctness of the step even though I cannot demonstrate it to your satisfaction. I know how difficult it must be for you and others to accommodate yourselves to these sudden changes. But how shall I help myself? [. . .] Is it not better that I should do that rather than I should suppress the clear voice within?"[30]

After the second fast in 1933, Gandhi wrote: "I can say this—that not the unanimous verdict of the whole world against me could shake me from the belief that what I heard was the true voice of God. [. . .] For me the voice was more real than my own existence. It has never failed me, and, for that

29. Rajmohan Gandhi, *Mohandas*, p. 130. D. G. Tendulkar, *Mahatma*, records Gandhi as having read *The Defence and Death of Socrates* (*The Apology* with another extract) translated by H. Cary, London 1905.

30. Letter to Rajagopalachari, 15 Sep 1924, Iyer, *Writings*, vol. 2, pp. 128–29.

matter, anyone else."[31] The previous year he had written that the voice overrode intellect and reason.[32] This fitted with his not being able to argue his case convincingly to Rajagopalachari. It also reflected similar experience among the early Fathers of the Christian Church. St. Jerome in the fourth to fifth centuries understood what he called "the spark of conscience" to be a higher faculty than reason.[33] Looking back in 1939 on Rajagopalachari's second intervention in 1933, Gandhi wrote: "When I took the 21 days' purificatory fast in the Yeravada jail in 1933 and proclaimed that it was in answer to a call from God, Rajagopalachari came all the way from Madras to dissuade me. He felt sure that I was deluding myself. [. . .] I continue to think that I fasted in answer to the still small voice within."[34]

But in self-defense he felt obliged to enter some qualifications after the 1933 fast, such as he had already hinted at as early as 1909, when he said, "No man can claim that he is absolutely in the right or that a particular thing is wrong because he thinks so."[35] But here the words "because he thinks so" may be ruling out one ground for certainty, rather than ruling out certainty itself. In the reflection quoted from just after the 1933 fast, he added a clearer qualification: "And everyone who wills can hear the Voice. It is within everyone. But like everything else, it requires definite and previous preparation." In the retrospective passage of 1939, referring to Rajagopalachari's remonstrance, his warning was more emphatic: "I say this to warn you how unwise it may be to believe that you are always listening to God. [. . .] It is better that listening is also based on solid rock. This listening in presupposes the fitness to listen, and the fitness is acquired after constant and patient striving and waiting on God." There were other contexts too in which Gandhi entered caveats. Taken in sequence through the years 1924 to 1947, he said that conscience is not found in the young, nor in savages. It is acquired by laborious training and is the ripe fruit of strictest discipline. It can reside only in a delicately tuned breast.[36] It is not found in the cannibal. You need training and discipline to listen and there are honest

31. Gandhi, *Harijan* 8 July 1933, repr. Iyer, *Writings*, vol. 2, p. 132.

32. Gandhi, letter to Bhuskute, 25 May 1932, Iyer, *Writings*, vol. 2, p. 130.

33. Jerome, *Commentary on Ezechiel* 1.1. *PG*, vol. 25, col. 22.

34. Gandhi, discussion with members of Oxford group, *Harijan* 7 Oct 1939, repr. Iyer, *Writings*, vol. 2, no. 101, p. 136.

35. *Hind Swaraj*, ch. 17, p. 91.

36. Gandhi, *Young India* 21 Aug 1924, repr. Iyer, *Writings*, vol. 2, p. 125.

differences of opinion.[37] We may be deceived in thinking that we are listening to God.[38] Conscience needs to be awakened, and not everyone has done that.[39] Finally, speaking of truth and nonviolence, he entered the following caveat, which I have italicized, "*So far as I know my own conscience* I have myself striven through thought, word and deed to reach the ideal."[40]

Gandhi would have been perfectly consistent if he had thought that one must be wrong sometimes, while never thinking "I am wrong this time." But he has gone beyond that by suggesting how much preparation it takes to be sure that you are listening to the voice of God. This puts him in a much weaker position. For one thing, why is he so confident that his listening has been good enough? For another, how can he be so confident in telling others that they should consult their conscience to decide what their *svadharma* calls for?[41]

MISTAKEN CONSCIENCE BINDING—A DOUBLE-BIND

When Gandhi said, "Is it not better that I should do that rather than I should suppress the clear voice within?" he was appealing to a principle that was endorsed by a Christian more influential even than Augustine. St. Thomas Aquinas said in the thirteenth century that conscience is binding, even if it is mistaken.[42] Gandhi had already enunciated the principle in a passage just cited from 1909: "No man can claim that he is absolutely in the right or that a particular thing is wrong because he thinks so, but it is wrong for him so long as that is his deliberate judgment. It is therefore meet that he should not do what he knows to be wrong."[43]

Did Gandhi—like Thomas Aquinas—accept that mistaken conscience puts one in a *double*-bind, because both obeying and disobeying a mistaken conscience will be wrong? I have said in chapter 4 that Gandhi was conscious of the predicament of double-bind in the use of violence for protecting others. Killing a rabid dog or using tear gas to prevent rape or mayhem

37. Gandhi, "Religion of volunteers," *Young India* 23 Sep 1926, repr. Iyer, *Writings*, vol. 2, p. 126.

38. Gandhi, talk with Moral Rearmament visitors, 28 Sep 1939, in Gopalkrishna Gandhi, *Essential Writings*, p. 444.

39. Gandhi "note to Gope Gurbuxani, 4 March 1945, Iyer, *Writings*, vol. 2, p. 128.

40. Gandhi, talk with Englishmen at Patna, 25 Apr 1947, Iyer, *Writings*, vol. 2, p. 293.

41. I thank Mohamed Mehdi for these questions.

42. Thomas Aquinas, *Summa Theologiae* Ia IIae Question19, article 5; *On Truth* Question 17, article 4.

43. *Hind Swaraj*, ch. 17, p. 91.

put one in a position of sinning, whether one acted or not, although in each case one sin was preferable to the other.

GANDHI'S CONSCIENCE AS THE VOICE OF GOD, BUT GUIDING US ON THE BASIS OF VALUES NOT ALL ACQUIRED FROM GOD

Gandhi was convinced that conscience was the voice of God. But it guided him on the basis of values that he already had. He did not claim, like St. Paul, that all those values were also implanted by God. In fact, he said that his belief in nonviolence was acquired by reading Tolstoy. He never considered the worry that affected many English philosophers after John Locke in 1690 that "doctrines that have been derived from no better original than the superstition of a nurse, or the authority of an old woman, may, by length of time and consent of neighbours, grow up to the dignity of principles in religion or morality."[44] In fact, Gandhi's case provides a corrective to Locke. For it shows that even those who grant that our principles do not come from God do not have to leap to the opposite conclusion that they come from the superstition of a nurse or authority of an old woman. Gandhi's principles of nonviolence came to him from a reflective reading of Tolstoy in a context where he was, like Tolstoy, immersed in a culture of violence.

GANDHI ON HOW THE VOICE OF CONSCIENCE COMMUNICATES

With so much interest in the Voice, it is not surprising that Gandhi shared the interest of ancient Platonists and Christians in how the Voice communicated. Gandhi described that in his account of deciding to undertake his 1933 fast. "For me the voice of God, of Conscience, of Truth, or the Inner Voice or the 'still small Voice' mean one and the same thing. I saw no form. I have never tried, for I have always believed God to be without form. [. . .] What I did hear was like a Voice from afar and yet quite near. It was as unmistakable as some human voice definitely speaking to me, and irresistible. I was not dreaming at the time I heard the Voice. The hearing of the Voice was preceded by a terrific struggle within me. Suddenly the Voice came upon me. I listened, made certain that it was the Voice, and the struggle ceased. I was calm."[45]

44. John Locke, *Essay Concerning Human Understanding*, book 1, ch. 3, sec. 22.
45. Gandhi *Harijan* 8 July 1933, Iyer, *Writings*, vol. 2, pp. 131–32.

GANDHI AGAINST MASS CONSCIENCE

Gandhi's conception of conscience connected with his individualism. It was not that the dictates of conscience were always about something particular like a particular fast. Occasionally they were about something general like how the so-called Untouchables should be treated. But he insisted, "There is no such thing therefore as mass conscience as distinguished from the consciences of individuals."[46] He would have rejected Hobbes' claim that the law is the public conscience and must be followed rather than private consciences, which are nothing but private opinions.[47] He would also have been suspicious of Durkheim's talk of collective conscience. But Gandhi's own reasons are clear. He has just been describing how one needs training, discipline, and a delicately tuned breast to listen; a child, in his view, would not be ready. It matters too that he thinks, unlike Locke and Freud, that conscience is the voice of God speaking to one about one's problems. There is something personal and direct about these communications. However, he should have allowed that making sure one is listening correctly can sometimes be a collective matter. In the seventeenth century, after the restoration of the English monarchy, the Quakers sought a compromise.[48] The policy of everyone following his or her own conscience had weakened such revolutionaries as the Levellers—conscience was a central term for them. But the Quakers would not go to the opposite extreme of accepting the authority of priests. The compromise was to follow the sense of small group meetings of Quakers.

CONSCIENCE PRESCRIBES TO INDIVIDUALS, AND ONLY SECONDARILY, IF AT ALL, TO OTHERS

This brings me back to chapter 7. Conscience speaks to the individual. It does not, like a universalized rule, prescribe what everyone else should do in the same circumstances, but it does sometimes tell the individual to oppose what others are doing.

46. Gandhi, *Young India* 21 Aug 1924, Iyer, *Writings*, vol. 2, p. 125.

47. Thomas Hobbes, *Leviathan*, ch. 29, 7

48. Christopher Hill, *The World Turned Upside Down*, London 1972, Penguin edition 1975, pp. 252, 256.

CHAPTER NINE

Restrictions on private property in Gandhi, Christianity, Plato, and the Stoics

CHRIST AND CHRISTIANITY

Gandhi compared his restrictions on private property to those of Christ. In the Sermon on the Mount Christ had told his listeners, "You cannot serve God and Mammon [the god of avarice]." You should not hoard, nor should you ask about tomorrow, "What shall we eat?" "What shall we drink?" but you should seek first the kingdom of God, after which the other things would be yours as well.[1] On another occasion, Christ said that he had nowhere to lay his head.[2]

On certain missions he told his disciples to take no provisions or money with them.[3] The twelve disciples themselves apparently did some sharing, since there are two references to a common purse.[4] In addition, in a situation of emergency he urged those of the twelve who had a purse to take it and others to sell their cloak, so that they could buy swords for self-defense.[5] Their cloaks, then, and their purses, for those who had them, implied some private property, and minimal though it presumably was, it could be used to buy a sword.

Christ's message was not only for his immediate followers. The story is also told of the rich man who had obeyed all the biblical commandments and asked Christ what he should do to secure eternal life. When Christ said, "Sell what you possess and give to the poor," he went away, saddened, and Christ said, "It is easier for a camel to go through the eye of a needle than

1. Gospel of Matthew 6:24–33; the fullest report of the Sermon on the Mount is in Matthew 5:1 to 7:28.

2. Matthew 8:20.

3. Matthew 10:8–10, 19:21–29.

4. Gospel of John 12:6, 13:29.

5. Matthew 10:9, Luke 22:35–36.

for a rich man to enter the kingdom of God." His disciple Peter claimed that the twelve disciples had left everything and followed Christ, and Christ replied that those would have eternal life who had left houses, lands, or family for his sake.[6] He expected his followers to prefer him to their families,[7] and he recognized them as mother and brothers, in preference to his own.[8]

After Christ's death his disciples, now called apostles, introduced new types of restrictions on private property, different from the earlier minimization that appealed to Gandhi. The church that they created in Jerusalem appears to have concentrated on *sharing* property. Wealthy members sold their land and laid the money at the feet of the Apostles. Moreover, the Acts of the Apostles comments with satisfaction that there was not a needy person among them.[9] No interest is expressed in minimization for its own sake, although hostility is expressed to a man who secretly held back some of the sale, without sharing. When separately confronted, he and his wife are said each to have fallen down dead.

Neither shared nor private property, on one view, had been options originally after the creation of the world. On this view, the dominion that God granted to mankind, according to the Book of Genesis 1:26, was only for common *use*,[10] not for any kind of ownership. When, as Genesis 13:9 says, Abraham and Lot agreed to divide up the land, then there was ownership, but it was due to the law of nations, not to natural law.[11]

In later Christianity, it was not thought practical for all Christians to minimize or even share their property. This became an ideal at most for certain groups. Monks and other religious communities sometimes attempted the harder austerities, ordinary priests sometimes the lesser ones, but laypeople not necessarily either. Furthermore, among those who were inspired by minimization, entirely different approaches might be adopted. Franciscans (followers of St, Francis, 1181–1226 CE) were one of the four main mendicant orders. They were required to beg for alms if their work went unpaid. So also outside the Catholic Church the Waldensians (followers of Peter Valdez, a group founded around 1170 and treated as heretics) would collect alms to support the "perfected" members who substituted for priests. But

6. Matthew 19:16–30, Mark 10:17–31, Luke 18:18–30.

7. Matthew 10:35–37.

8. Matthew 12:46.

9. Acts of the Apostles 2:35, 4:32–5:10.

10. The idea of common *use* is found in the third century CE in Ulpian, *Digest* 1.1.5.

11. See Daniel Deckers, *Gerechtigkeit und Recht*, Freiburg 1991, discussing Vitoria's commentary on Aquinas, *Summa Theologiae*.

among Franciscans, alms for individuals did not solve the problem that the maintenance of monks and the aspiration to learning called for monasteries, libraries, granaries, and provisions. The Franciscans justified this not on the basis of the property being *shared*. Instead, they went back to the idea of *use* as against ownership, and claimed to have only the *use* of the property, not *ownership* of any kind. They claimed the property belonged not to them, but to the Pope as head of the whole Catholic Church.

Gandhi was closer to the original teaching of Christ than was the later Christian Church, in which the passages about wealth quoted by Gandhi were accepted at face value only by a minority tradition. As the Christian community spread far beyond Jerusalem, a majority had to be accommodated that accepted wealth. The spread of Christianity to non-Jews (Gentiles) was interpreted as having necessitated a relaxation of the ideal for laymen, and on some views for priests or even monks. Further justification was sought through controversies about the lessons to be drawn from the story of Christ, his disciples, and the early Church.[12]

One controversy centered on the story of the rich man and the eye of the needle. As early as the late second century CE, Clement of Alexandria in his *Who Is the Rich Man Who Can Be Saved?* reinterpreted the story of the rich man and the eye of the needle in a Stoic style as requiring only that the rich man be not *attached* to his wealth. Others suggested that what was intended might have been not a camel (*kamêlos*), but a ship's rope (*kamilos*), if that would help. Another view, presented to me in childhood, was that "Eye of a Needle" was merely the name of a narrow gate. Such reinterpretations were mentioned and ridiculed in the fifth century by an anonymous follower of the British monk Pelagius, since the Pelagians sought to reintroduce the ideal of poverty, but Augustine opposed them. The commoner view became merely that the rich should help the poor, and not all required as much of the wealthy as John Chrysostom, whom we saw making the rich man merely a *steward* of his master's money.

Another key point of controversy was the wealth created in the Church in Rome by the munificence of the Roman emperor Constantine in the early fourth century CE. Some came to see this as a betrayal of the ideal of poverty or sharing, some as producing new conditions that excused the shift away from those ideals.

12. See Gordon Leff, *Heresy in the later Middle Ages*, 2 vols., Manchester 1967; Peter Garnsey, *Thinking about Property*, Cambridge 2007. A brief, but useful overview is given by Doyne Dawson, "Primitive church, concept of," in *Dictionary of the Middle Ages*, vol. 10, Scribners, New York 1988, pp. 121–23. Ch. 6 of Dawson's *Cities of the Gods*, Oxford 1992, covers some of the premedieval texts.

Eventually the advocates of minimization could be seen as opposing the wealth of the Roman ecclesiastical authorities. The experience of the Franciscans illustrates the problem. When they claimed to have only the *use* of their buildings and provisions, not any kind of *ownership*, this was endorsed by one pope. But it was eventually scuttled in 1323 by another pope, John XXII. Provisions, he objected, were not merely used, but used up. As for the tradition of Christ's time, he cited the communal money box and declared it a punishable heresy to say that Christ and his disciples had neither private nor communal property.

Other Christians who advocated the *minimization* of property refused, unlike the Franciscans, to recognize the authority of the Roman Church, and their leaders were often persecuted.[13] After the Protestant Reformation, new Christian groups practiced the alternative option of *sharing* property, but also suffered persecution. Of these the Dukhobors (soul-wrestlers) in Russia, Protestant dissenters from the Orthodox Church, were actively supported by Tolstoy.

GANDHI ON CHRIST'S TEACHING

Gandhi found Christ's teaching on wealth and poverty very congenial, and quoted it at length in at least two addresses. One was a speech already mentioned[14] that he gave to the Muir College Economic Society, Allahabad. The other was a whole series of lectures in 1926 on St. Matthew's Gospel, chapters 1–6.

In his address to the Allahabad economic society Gandhi quoted Christ's reference to Mammon, his saying, "Take no thought for the morrow," and the story of the rich man with its moral about a camel passing through the eye of a needle. He also cited the injunction to seek first the kingdom of God, after which everything else would be added. In his 1926 talks he commented on Matthew 5:3, "Blessed are the poor in spirit," and interpreted it in terms of material poverty.[15]

In another invocation of Christ's teaching, a letter of 1930, Gandhi echoed the phrase, "Give us this day our daily bread" from the Lord's Prayer,

13. For the persecution of other groups advocating minimisation, and for the advocacy by early reformers of poverty for priests, see Gordon Leff, *Heresy*.

14. Chapter 7 above. Speech at Muir College Economic Society Allahabad, 22 Dec 1916, *CW*, vol. 13, pp. 310–17.

15. Bible teaching: lectures on the Gospel of St. Matthew 1–6, July–Oct 1926, in *Day to Day*, vol. 8, p. 266, cf. 286, 327.

taught by Christ in the course of the Sermon on the Mount, and Christ's injunction not to hoard against tomorrow's needs.[16] "Nonpossession," he wrote, "is allied to nonstealing. A thing not originally stolen must nevertheless be classified as stolen property if we possess it without needing it. Possession implies provision for the future. A seeker after truth, a follower of the law of love, cannot hold anything against tomorrow. God never stores for the morrow; He never creates more than what is strictly needed for the moment. If, therefore, we repose faith in His providence, we should be assured that He will give us every day our daily bread, meaning everything we require. [. . .] The rich have a superfluous store of things which they do not need, and which are therefore neglected and wasted; while millions starve to death for want of sustenance. [. . .] We find that in the Ashram we possess many things the necessity for which cannot be proved, and we thus tempt our neighbours to steal."[17]

SUBSISTENCE LIVING IN THE NONVIOLENT ASHRAM

The last letter concerned subsistence living in Gandhi's ashram. Poverty had been one of the prerequisites that he laid down for practicing nonviolent resistance in his *Hind Swaraj* of 1909.[18] But in the letter just quoted, he considered property incompatible not only with nonviolent *resistance*, but also with following the "law of love" in general, that is, with the ideal of a nonviolent *attitude*, practiced in his ashram. Besides the *minimization* of property, the ashram involved a certain amount of *shared* property, for example kitchen stores,[19] and of course the produce of the farm when they had it. But that was for practical reasons; it was the minimization that was his ideal. He was speaking of another of his successive ashrams when he said it was "the fundamental law of Nature, without exception, that Nature produces enough for our wants from day to day, and if only everybody took enough for himself and nothing more, there would be no pauperism in this world."[20] Speaking of an ashram again, he said that no human being could observe nonpossession to perfection—even the body was a possession. So

16. Matthew 6:7–13, Luke 11:2–4.

17. Gandhi, letter to Narandas Gandhi from Yeravada jail, Pune, 26 Aug 1930, repr. Iyer, *Writings*, vol. 3, p. 473.

18. *Hind Swaraj*, p. 97, discussed in chapter 1 above.

19. Letter to Narandas Gandhi, 19 Aug 1930, repr. Iyer, *Writings*, vol. 2, p. 471.

20. Speech on ashram vows at the YMCA, Madras, *The Hindu* 16 Feb 1916, repr. Iyer, *Writings*, vol. 2, p. 527.

nonpossession had to be a mental attitude, a willingness to "cultivate the spirit of detachment and give up one possession after another," including the body. "The loss of nothing whatever should worry us at all. [. . .] It is a good thing if we get food to eat and clothes to wear; it is also a good thing if we don't."[21] Gandhi would have liked these attitudes of indifference to spread to the whole population, but he proposed "to start with myself in showing that one could live satisfied with basic needs,"[22] and he applied the ideal next to his ashram.

As regards giving up the idea of one's *body* as one's own, he was as emphatic as the Stoic Epictetus:[23] "I must not possess anything on this earth as my property, not even this body, because this body also is a possession." If I think my body mine, I will still be violent. Perfect nonviolence and love can be exercised only by being prepared to renounce the body in death for the service of humans.[24] He thought that the law of nonviolence was unknowingly obeyed whenever a mother died for her child.[25] This renunciation was part of the "voluntary poverty," which was unlike the poverty of those whose needs were neglected. To a group of Franciscans who held a conference on voluntary poverty, he said that it left one never in want.[26]

Along with the minimization of one's *own* property in the ashrams went respect for the property of *others*. There had been thieves from outside and inside the ashram. But Gandhi recommended three steps to put a stop to thieving. One was to diminish possessions, so as not to tempt others. The second was to reform the surrounding villages, and the third was to extend the ashram's ministry in such a way that everyone would learn to look upon the settlement as their own.[27] He hoped that as the law of nonviolence spread, and with it the minimization of possessions, the stage would be reached when "lawful possession will command universal and voluntary respect. [. . .] Such possession [. . .] will not be an insolent demonstration of the inequalities that surround us everywhere."[28]

21. Gandhi, *Ashram Observances in Action*, Ahmedabad 1955, from the ms. of 1932, repr. Iyer, *Writings*, vol. 2, p. 587.

22. Answers to questions at constructive workers' conference, *The Hindu* 26 Jan 1946, *Harijan* 31 March 1946, repr. Iyer, *Writings*, vol. 3, p. 575.

23. See Chapter Three above discussing Epictetus on freedom.

24. Gandhi, speech at ashram on Ramanavami Day, 1 Apr 1928, *CW*, vol. 36, p. 165; interview with Nirmal Kumar Bose, *The Hindustan Times* 17 Oct 1935, repr. Iyer, *Writings*, vol. 3, p. 598; and letter to Narandas Gandhi, 26 Aug 1930, repr. Iyer, *Writings*, vol. 3, p. 474.

25. "The Eternal Problem," Question Box, *Harijan* 22 Feb 1942.

26. Speech at Guildhouse Church, 23 Sep 1931, *CW*, vol. 48, pp. 50–58, at 54.

27. Gandhi, *Ashram Observances in Action*, Ahmedabad 1955, from the ms. of 1932, repr. Iyer, *Writings*, vol. 2, p. 581.

28. "The Eternal Problem," Question Box, *Harijan* 22 Feb 1942.

IDEAL OF VILLAGE SUBSISTENCE AGAINST THE "CIVILIZATION" OF INDUSTRIAL CITIES

Gandhi had an ideal for the future of India as a whole. He had been impressed early on by three writers who encouraged him to prefer the life of bare subsistence in the villages to the materialism of the cities. He admired both Tolstoy[29] and Thoreau.[30] But above all he was struck by Ruskin's *Unto This Last* of 1860. This was surprising in that Ruskin was advocating neither minimized nor communal property. Nor did he share Gandhi's wish to do away with industry and commerce as encouraging acquisitive materialism. In fact, Ruskin was proposing a more practical model than either Tolstoy or Gandhi, and one that is said to have borne fruit in influencing the introduction of the welfare state by the Atlee government in Britain after the Second World War. Nonetheless, Gandhi named Ruskin as the third greatest influence after Tolstoy among men who had influenced his life.[31] Gandhi paraphrased *Unto This Last* in Gujarati with his own preface and conclusion. An English translation of his paraphrase appeared in *Indian Opinion* in 1909.

Ruskin's title, *Unto This Last*, we saw,[32] was taken from Christ's parable that endorsed giving the same wage to the workman who arrived in the vineyard *last*. This has been taken to embody the ideal of rewarding each according to his *need*. As Gandhi glossed Ruskin, the laws of economic theory, for example the laws of supply and demand, tell individuals how to get rich at the expense of others, with a consequent lowering of total prosperity and happiness, and a flight from village farms to city factories. Much later Gandhi was still advocating "to each according to his need," and declaring that the only type of socialism he endorsed was "even unto this last."[33] But

29. Chapter 5 above. Gandhi admired Tolstoy for living like a peasant and, we saw, shared Tolstoy's belief that the law of love, which included property-sharing, would inevitably prevail worldwide one day. Tolstoy attempted to give away his own wealth. Gandhi, "Count Tolstoy," *Indian Opinion*, 2 Sep 1905, repr. Iyer, *Writings*, vol. 1, no. 53, p. 107.

30. Gandhi first read Thoreau's essay on civil disobedience in 1907 and translated part of it for *Indian Opinion*, but he went on to read Thoreau's *Walden* and other essays which advocated rustic life: letter to Henry Salt, 12 Oct 1929, repr. Iyer, *Essential Writings*, no. 26, pp. 70–71.

31. Gandhi, speech of 10 Sep 1928 on the anniversary of Tolstoy's birth, *Navajivan* 16 Sep 1928, repr. Iyer, *Writings*, vol. 1, no. 59.

32. See introduction above, and, for a speech praising Ruskin's attack on the laws of economic theory, chapter 7.

33. Answers to questions at constructive workers' conference, *The Hindu* 26 Jan 1946, *Harijan* 31 March 1946, repr. Iyer, *Writings*, vol. 3, p. 573; interview with Louis Fischer, 17 July 1946, repr. Iyer, *Writings*, vol. 3, p. 577.

when he finished the conclusion to his paraphrase with the words, "This is the substance of Ruskin's book," he was in fact giving his own view.

In Gandhi's account of recent Western "civilization" as materialism, he was also influenced by Edward Carpenter's book of 1889, *Civilisation: Its Cause and Cure*. Gandhi wanted to get rid of the idea that Western civilization was a gift to India. On the contrary, the West would be better off without it.[34] One should have just enough for one's needs; it was wrong to have a bank balance.[35] What was required was a return from cities to villages, and to an oceanic circle of villages, uncrushed by external power.[36] Cities had unjustly exploited villages, and should serve them instead.[37] He associated cities with materialism, acquisitiveness, and technology. Industry was Mammon. In Russia it had removed individuality. In India it meant control of villages by a few, and should be replaced by cottage industry.[38]

Gandhi disagreed, we saw, with his chosen successor Nehru[39] in opposing socialism, along with communism, Bolshevism, and state control in general, the ground being that state power, like all power, is violent.[40] For the same reason, he did not believe in expropriating the money of the wealthy.[41] Instead, he advocated the wealthy voluntarily becoming *trustees* of their wealth primarily for the benefit of others.[42] This idea can also be

34. Letter to Henry Polak, 14 Oct 1909, letter to Lord Ampthill, 30 Oct 1909, letter to Maganlal Gandhi, 2 Apr 1910, repr. Iyer, *Writings*, vol. 1, pp. 293, 332, 336–37.

35. Talk with Manu Gandhi, camp at Patna, 15 Apr 1947, repr. Iyer, *Writings*, vol. 3, pp. 582–83.

36. E.g., *Hind Swaraj*, p. 69; letter to Lord Ampthill, 30 Oct 1909, repr. Iyer, *Writings*, vol. 1, p. 332; letter to Jawaharlal Nehru, 5 Oct 1945, repr. Iyer, *Writings*, vol. 1, p. 286; interview, 28 July 1946, *CW* vol. 85, pp. 32–34, repr. as "Gandhi's political vision: the pyramid vs the oceanic circle," in Anthony J. Parel, ed., *Hind Swaraj and Other Writings*, p. 189; "Snares of Satan," *Young India*, 6 Aug 6 1925, repr. Iyer, *Writings*, vol. 1, pp. 316–17.

37. Talk with Manu Gandhi, 18 Apr 1947, repr. Iyer, *Writings*, vol. 3, p. 532; interview with P. Ramachandra Rao, *The Hindu* 23 June 1945, repr. Iyer, *Writings*, vol. 3, p. 603.

38. "Snares of Satan," *Young India* 6 Aug 1925, repr. Iyer, *Writings*, vol. 1, pp. 316–17; two discussions with Maurice Frydman, *Harijan* 29 Aug 1936 and 28 Jan 1939 ; "Alternative to industrialism," *Harijan* 1 Sep 1946, repr. Iyer, *Writings*, vol. 3, pp. 532.

39. See chapter 6 and letter to Jawaharlal Nehru, 5 Oct 1945, repr. Iyer, *Writings*, vol. 1, p. 286; interview with an Egyptian, *Harijan* 13 Feb 1937, repr. Iyer, *Writings*, vol. 3, p. 567.

40. Talk with Manu Gandhi, camp at Patna, 15 Apr 1947, repr. Iyer, *Writings*, vol. 3, pp. 582–83; question and answer, 24 Jan 1946, repr. Iyer, *Writings*, vol. 3, p. 574; interview to Nirmal Kumar Bose, 9–10 Nov 1934, *Hindustan Times* 17 Oct 1935, *CW*, vol. 59, pp. 318–19; "My notes," *Young India* 15 Nov 1928, repr. Iyer, *Writings*, vol. 3, p. 554; "Question box," *Harijan* 1 June 1947, repr. Iyer, *Writings*, vol. 3, p. 586.

41. "Alternative to industrialism," *Harijan* 1 Sep 1946, repr. Iyer, *Writings*, vol. 3, pp. 532; "My notes," *Young India* 15 Nov 1928; "Answers to zamindars," *The Pioneer* 3 Aug 1934, repr. Iyer, *Writings*, vol. 3, p. 556.

42. There is a reference to well-placed persons being trustees of the poor as early as 1908 in *Indian Opinion* for 15 Feb, though the context is different. See also letter to G. D. Birla, 22 March

found in early Christianity in the stewardship for the poor in the Christians, John Chrysostom and Ambrose.[43] Nonetheless, if private owners refused to act as trustees, confiscation by the state would become necessary, carried out with the minimum of violence, and with or without compensation.[44] He extended to those in the resistance movement who were rich his insistence on an attitude of indifference to wealth. He put it by saying in his *Hind Swaraj* of 1909, "Those who have money are not expected to throw it away, but they *are* expected to be indifferent about it."[45]

PLATO'S RESTRICTIONS

The *Republic* of Plato (427–348 BCE) is not mentioned by Gandhi, but in it Plato, like Gandhi, imagined an ideal society that sought to eliminate luxury and family favoritism, at least among the rulers. He put his ideas into the mouth of Socrates. His city-state, partly modeled on Sparta, would be ruled by a class of warriors. To prevent the luxury that he deplored,[46] they would not own land, nor houses, nor private property beyond the barest necessity, nor store rooms closed to their neighbors. They would live communally in public property, with communal meals supplied. The regime was one of compulsory *sharing*, but not of strict *minimization*, since they would impose a levy on the agricultural classes to supply them with the needs appropriate to warriors, so that they would have neither surplus nor shortage.[47]

Plato's second, more hesitant proposal was that none of his warrior rulers would have exclusive possession of any woman or children, since this was a form of private property, as shown by talk of wife and children as being "mine." Instead, women (the perspective is male) and children would

1925, *CW*, vol. 26, p. 364; speech at Muir College Economic Society, Allahabad, 22 Dec 1916, *CW*, vol. 13, p. 317; Bible teaching: lectures on the Gospel of St. Matthew 1–6, July–Oct 1926, in *Day to Day*, vol. 8, p. 266 ; *Autobiography*, part 4, ch. 4, p. 245; interview to Nirmal Kumar Bose, 9–10 Nov 1934, *Hindustan Times* 17 Oct 1935, *CW*, vol. 59, pp. 318–19; interview with an Egyptian, *Harijan* 13 Feb 1937, repr. Iyer, *Writings*, vol. 3, p. 567; "Answers to zamindars," *The Pioneer* 3 Aug 1934, repr. Iyer, *Writings*, vol. 3, 556; introduction to *Varnavyavastha*, *Harijan* 28 Sep 1934, repr. Iyer, *Writings*, vol. 3, 564; answers to questions at constructive workers' conference, Madras, *The Hindu* 26 Jan 1946, and *Harijan* 31 March 1946, repr. Iyer, *Writings*, vol. 3, pp. 574–76; talk with Manu Gandhi, Patna, 15 Apr 1947, repr. Iyer, *Writings*, vol. 3, p. 582–83; "Question box," *Harijan* 1 June 1947, repr. Iyer, *Writings*, vol. 3, p. 586.

43. Chapter 5 above.

44. Interview to Nirmal Kumar Bose, 9–10 Nov 1934, *CW*, vol. 59, 316–20.

45. *Hind Swaraj*, p. 97.

46. Plato, *Republic* 372D, 399E.

47. Plato, *Republic* 416D–417B.

be *shared*, though not at will, since there would be considerable state supervision of sexual relations for eugenic purposes. Births would be supervised to conceal which children belonged to which parents.[48] As a result, everyone in the warrior class would call everyone else children or brothers or sisters or mother or father, according to age. The aim was to make everyone speak in unison, using the word "mine" not of different relatives, but of everyone in the group. This would in turn make everyone pleased or pained at the same events. Hence the city would be as unitary (*mia*) as an individual person who is pained or pleased at what happens to any bodily part. Plato then brought back in at 464B the earlier proposals about private property, and considered that the two sets of proposals would achieve the same purpose of unification. The earlier restriction on private property would contribute to unity by preventing hatred and plotting.[49] Plato thought that this resolved something that also concerned Gandhi. If no wife or child is exclusively mine, I will not try to drag things off into my family house, but will be concerned equally for the whole community. Plato believed that the sharing would also achieve another aim that Gandhi would espouse: lawsuits would virtually disappear, at least among the warrior class. For they tend to arise from exclusive possession of money, children, and families, whereas now the warriors will have everything in common—except their own bodies. Plato here underestimated as much as Gandhi the importance of family relations.

In his *Critias*, Plato represented his arrangements for the military class as having been actually implemented in a golden past.[50] In his last work, *The Laws*, he referred briefly to somewhat similar arrangements in even more striking terms: the eyes, ears, and hands of the citizens—possibly still the ruling warrior class only—seem to see, hear, and act in common.[51] Nothing could be further from Gandhi's individualism. But Plato now concentrated instead on a more practical second-best type of society, one in which private property was restricted in a still more interesting way. Instead of Guardians bereft of private property, one now had a guaranteed minimum unit of property, but after four increments any further surplus would be handed over to the state. Thus the richest would be at most five times as rich as

48. Plato, *Republic* 459D–464E.

49. Plato, *Republic* 417B.

50. Plato, *Critias* 110C–D.

51. Plato, *Laws* 739B–D. Garnsey points out that citizenship might have come to be restricted here to Guardians. Garnsey, *Thinking About Property*, p. 15.

the poorest. For present-day England, I have heard that the disparities have reached 400-fold, and are 273-fold in one part of London alone.[52] Plato's richest would surely be more content, since no one could become wealthier than themselves.

Recommendations like those of Plato's *Republic* had been lampooned twenty years earlier by the comic playwright Aristophanes.[53] But the most devastating criticism was provided by Aristotle arguing in his *Politics* why Plato's was not a possible way of producing unity.[54]

Gandhi would have been appalled at the violence of the state's redistribution of property, a redistribution to the ruling class, and at the greater violence, secrecy, and mendacity of the program for mating and births. He was already opposed to modern socialism as violent in its redistribution of property and as mistrusting of individuals. On the other hand, he might have approved Plato's objection to money, children, and families as being the main source of litigation.

THE STOICS' CYNIC HERITAGE

The Stoics, like Gandhi, considered an ideal society as well as actual society, but they did not, like Gandhi, attempt to create ideal communities, even on the scale of his ashram, which consisted of 277 people in 1928.[55] Like Gandhi, they gave a place to the minimization of property, both in their ideal city of the wise, and as a possible aspiration for individuals in actual cities.[56] Zeno will have drawn his interest in minimization from the Cynics: his teacher, Crates, and his teacher's teacher, Diogenes of Sinope.

Diogenes, a contemporary of Plato and Aristotle in the mid-fourth century BCE, himself wrote a *Republic*, now lost. He there claimed, if we can believe the fragmentary reports, that coinage should be replaced by

52. Plato, *Laws* 744E–745A; Aristotle, *Politics* 1265b21–3. I thank John Dillon for the comparison.

53. Aristophanes in his *Ecclesiazusae* of 393 BCE, where women were represented as taking over and introducing similar measures.

54. The unity of a city, Aristotle said in *Politics* 2.1–6, depends not on similarity, but on reciprocity of *dissimilar* services, which makes a city more self-sufficient than an individual. "Mine" said of children by Plato's warriors would mean not "belonging to me," but belonging to the collectivity, which makes for less agreement, less care, and less love. As regards land, he preferred that possession should be private, but that the legislator should make people willing to share its use. The unity that Plato seeks ought to be gained instead through education.

55. "Satyagraha Ashram," *Young India* 14 June 1928, repr. Iyer, *Writings*, vol. 2, p. 549.

56. I shall omit from consideration the Stoic idea of a cosmic city including gods as well as humans, because this is not relevant to private property.

knucklebones.[57] As knucklebones are available to anybody, especially butchers—I have seen a whole pathway made of them—they would not serve, as does coinage, to maintain disparities of wealth. According to legend, Diogenes did not want unnecessary private possessions, which is why he lived in a wine jar instead of a house, folded his cloak double and slept in it, and threw away his cup and his bowl after he saw a child managing without,[58] keeping only his leather food pouch.[59] He lived by begging, and when found begging from a statue, said that he did so in order to practice being refused.[60] Not surprisingly, he did without slaves after losing his only one.[61] He repeated Pythagoras' saying that friends have all things in common,[62] and rejected the idea of families as private property, advocating instead free love by mutual consent, and holding sons in common.[63] Moving freely between Athens and Corinth, he denied that he belonged to any particular one city, rather than being a citizen of the world (*kosmoplitês*).[64] The motives for his proposals included his love of freedom (*eleutheria*)[65] and his preference for the natural over the conventional.[66] Although not all these ideas necessarily come from Diogenes' *Republic*, they look like a deliberate riposte to the state control in the *Republic* of Plato.

It is not clear that Diogenes could have intended to describe a city composed exclusively of beggars, without anyone to beg from, or of people owing no allegiance to any city, and yet, as others have pointed out, the holding of sons in common and the resistance to currency seem to presuppose some connection with life in a city. The situation may be clearer with Diogenes' follower, Crates.

It was said that Crates sold his valuables, distributed the money to fellow-citizens, was persuaded by Diogenes to throw money into the sea, and arranged that his sons should get no money if they became philosophers, because in that case they would not need it.[67] He declared that much prosperity (*polla olbia*) was prey to vanity,[68] and that justly acquired possessions

57. Philodemus, *On the Stoics*, col. 16 (Dorandi).
58. Diogenes Laertius, *Lives* 6.22–23, 6.37.
59. Diogenes Laertius, *Lives* 6.33, 6.37.
60. Diogenes Laertius, *Lives* 6.49.
61. Seneca, *On Tranquility* 8.7.
62. Diogenes Laertius, *Lives* 6.37, 6.72.
63. Diogenes Laertius, *Lives* 6.72.
64. Diogenes Laertius, *Lives* 6.38, 6.63.
65. Diogenes Laertius, *Lives* 6.69, 6.71.
66. Diogenes Laertius, *Lives* 6.38, 6.71
67. Diogenes Laertius, *Lives* 6.87–88
68. Diogenes Laertius, *Lives* 6.86.

were like the wealth of a beetle or ant.[69] He said that his country was Ignominy and Poverty, which could not be assailed by fortune. In other words, his country was a way of life. It contained not one tower or roof, but was as wide as the earth.[70] On one view, Crates was discussing an ideal earthly city, which he called "Foodpouch." The relevant lines start: "There is a city, Foodpouch." But it has been ingeniously suggested that instead he is talking about his food-pouch and comparing it to an ideal city,[71] albeit ideal for an individual Cynic living in an ordinary city in which he still had to beg for food. What Crates said of his city or food-pouch is that it owned nothing (*ouden ekhousa*) and contained no parasitic fools and again its people did not possess weapons to gain money or fame, but were content with thyme, garlic, figs, and loaves. If he is referring to the attitude and life of an individual Cynic in an imperfect city, satisfied with a beggar's pouch, it might be objected that begging is parasitic in one sense. But he will have meant that it does not depend on fawning at the table of a particular chosen superior.

Another supposed student of Diogenes in the fourth century B.C. was Onesicritus, mentioned in chapter 4, who accompanied Alexander the Great to India, and reported with approval on the arrangements of a Cynic style in the land of King Musicanus of Sind.[72]

ZENO, FOUNDER OF STOICISM, 300 BCE, AND CHRYSIPPUS, HEAD 232–206 BCE: MINIMIZATION OF OWNERSHIP IN THE IDEAL CITY

Zeno, the founder in 300 BCE, and Chrysippus, the third head of the Stoic school in Athens, treated property differently in the context of an ideal city and of actual cities. Zeno was the third person, after Plato and Diogenes, to write a *Republic*. Chrysippus wrote *On Republic* (or *On Government, peri politeias*), in which he discussed the *Republic* of Diogenes and apparently of Zeno. Zeno's seems to have described an ideal city for the wise. Of the

69. Crates in Giannantoni, *Socratis et Socraticorum Reliquiae*, 2nd ed., Naples 1990, vol. 2, VH Crates frag. 84, lines 20–21, from Julian, *Orations* 7.9, 213A–214A.

70. Diogenes Laertius, *Lives* 6.93, 6.98.

71. Diogenes Laertius, *Lives* 6.85. The reinterpretation of "Foodpouch" is that of John Sellars, "Stoic cosmopolitanism and Zeno's republic," *History of Political Thought* 28, 2007, 1–29.

72. There were no slaves, there were communal meals, there was no use of gold and silver, and resort to law courts was restricted to cases of murder or defamation. Contracts depended instead on the individual's judgment of who could be trusted: Strabo, *Geographica* 15.1.34, 15.1.54; M. H. Fisch, "Alexander and the Stoics," part IV, *American Journal of Philology*, 58, pp. 129–44, esp. 133.

six topics that have been identified from the few surviving fragments, three bear on property and the family.[73] First, he advocated for his wise citizens the abolition of coinage whether for exchange or for travel abroad, which would presumably impede the accumulation of wealth. Second, he allowed sex by consent of any man with any woman. The second reform, he said, by removing possessive relations, would get rid of the jealousy arising from adultery and would create fatherly affection for all children alike,[74] though a neighboring passage encourages having children as a result of *gamein* (usually understood as marriage).[75] Third, he rejected three of the central institutions of Greek city life: law courts, temples, and gymnasia.[76] This bears on our subject, because law courts were exactly what Plato had hoped to make unnecessary by abolishing the major sources of litigation: money, children, and families, three kinds of possession. I think we can infer, fourth, another feature of Zeno's republic. Zeno was said, like the ideal Cynic of Epictetus later on, to have had no slaves,[77] and slavery would be hard to square with the concord in his republic.

Chrysippus is said to have agreed with Zeno in advocating free love, but only among the wise, with resulting paternal affection for *all* children alike, and evidently no private possession of families.[78]

It was only the good and the wise who could live up to the provisions of the ideal city. The free love that holds in Zeno's *Republic* is described as holding among the *wise*.[79] And only the good could be citizens in such a city, since Zeno said that only the good are citizens, friends, and kin. Others are enemies and alien to each other.[80] In this respect, Zeno's republic of *wise* people was at best viable, like Plato's republic of *just* people under wise rulers, only for idealized citizens.

The city is best taken literally as a community of people living together, although there might be more than one city. Once again, this is implied, as

73. Malcolm Schofield, "Zeno of Citium's anti-utopianism," ch. 3 of his *Saving the City*, London 1999, recognizes (i) eugenics and having children, (ii) education for virtue, (iii) free love, (iv) abolishing temples, law courts, and gymnasia, (v) abolishing coinage, and (vi) women and men wearing the same sort of clothes and performing the same exercises naked. He assumes (vii) common meals.

74. Diogenes Laertius, *Lives* 7.131.

75. Diogenes Laertius, *Lives* 7.121.

76. Diogenes Laertius, *Lives* 7.32–33 and 131.

77. Seneca, *Consolation to Helvia* 12.4.

78. Diogenes Laertius, *Lives* 7.131.

79. Diogenes Laertius, *Lives* 7.32–33 and 131.

80. Diogenes Laertius, *Lives* 7.32.

others have pointed out,[81] by the provisions for sexual relations and the care of children along with the abolition of coinage and of temples, law courts, and gymnasia from "cities" in the plural. The citizens will not have been isolated wise individuals scattered across the earth or within a city of the nonwise. Nor will they have been a cohesive group of wise people within a city of the nonwise, since that would not free them from law courts. In the next chapter[82] I will reject the idea that they would form a single world-wide community, an idea that has been based on a far-fetched, and over-interpreted, chapter of Plutarch.

FROM CHRYSIPPUS TO DIOGENES OF BABYLON AND ANTIPATER IN THE SECOND CENTURY BCE: PRIVATE PROPERTY A *PREFERRED* INDIFFERENT IN ACTUAL CITIES

As regards private property in actual cities, Zeno paved the way for the idea that private property is a "preferred indifferent" in the sense described in chapters 1 through 3. In other words, though indifferent, it was normally right and your duty to prefer it. The introduction of the terms "indifferent" and "preferred indifferent" is ascribed to Zeno himself.[83] We know that he would have to class private property as indifferent, because only virtue and vice have the status of being actually good or bad. But Chrysippus is the first Stoic to make it clear that private property is both indifferent and preferred. Thus on the one hand, it is said to be mad to think nothing of wealth and not to hold on to it. But on the other hand, to a good man, losing his fortune (*ousia*) is said to be like losing a mere drachma.[84] As for marriage and raising children, this is what the wise man will do, according to Zeno,[85] presumably in the actual city, even though it too is an indifferent.[86]

The classification of private property in actual cities as a preferred indifferent allowed for opposite emphases. In the century after Chrysippus, the second century BCE, four successive Stoics (the first three being heads of the school in Athens) emphasized the *preferability* of private property. They were Diogenes of Babylon, Antipater, Panaetius, and Hecato, each the teacher of the one cited next. Cicero presents the first two debating whether

81. Malcolm Schofield, *The Stoic Idea of the City*, Cambridge 1991.

82. See the comments reported there of Phillip Mitsis on Plutarch, *On the Fortune or Virtue of Alexander the Great* 329A–D.

83. Stobaeus, vol. 2, pp. 57,18–20, 84,22.

84. Plutarch, *On Stoic Self-contradictions* 1047E–1048B.

85. Diogenes Laertius, *Lives of Eminent Philosophers* 7.121.

86. *SVF*, 3.163, 3.164.

the seller of a house should disclose rot to the prospective buyer. The naysayer, Diogenes, meets Antipater's appeal to the bonds of human society by replying that those bonds had better not mean there is nothing which is one's own (*nihil suum cuiusque sit*).[87] The preferability of private property is not questioned here, although Epictetus would return in the first century CE to stressing its indifference, while Seneca earlier in that century was to oscillate between the two emphases.

THE PLEA THAT PRIVATE PROPERTY IS ALSO COMMON: FROM CHRYSIPPUS' THEATER SEAT TO PANAETIUS AND HECATO IN THE SECOND CENTURY BCE

Those who emphasized the preferability of private property tried to soften their attitude by allowing that private property was in some sense common as well. But the concession turns out to be a rather weak one. Chrysippus was the first to plead that private property was also common and to give the analogy of a theater seat. As Cicero tells us, he says that a theater seat is common property, but on the other hand, once someone has occupied (*occupare*) a seat for a show, it can rightly be said to be his (*eius*). In the same way in a city or in the cosmos justice does not oppose each having his own (*suum quidque cuiusque sit*).[88] The analogy of the theater seat here does not give other people much access to private property. But we shall see it used differently by Seneca and differently again by Epictetus.

Cicero also appeals to private property being common in a work in which he claims principally (*potissimum*) to be following Panaetius, and following him a great deal (*multum*): his *On Duties*. But he says that in the third and last book of *On Duties* he has less guidance from Panaetius. Cicero, perhaps reflecting Panaetius, acknowledges that nothing is *by nature* private property (*privata nulla naturâ*), and that things are *by nature common* property (*naturâ communia*). But the emphasis is nonetheless on privacy. For he gives a long list of ways in which things can legitimately become private property: long occupancy of what was empty, conquest, law, bargain, purchase, or allotment, as in the allotments made to veteran soldiers. Once they are private property, the boot is on the other foot. Because each has acquired his own, he should hold on to what by nature had once been common, and anybody who seeks to get it will be violating the rights (*ius*)

87. Cicero, *On Duties* 3.51–55.
88. Cicero, *On Ends* 3.67.

of human society.[89] On Cicero's account, what belongs in common should be used as common, but what is private should be used as one's own.[90] But what does belong in common? He allows that nature has produced some things for the common use of men, and the common bond must be preserved, but the example given is not one of property but the duty of showing a lost stranger the way, since it costs us nothing. As for what is assigned (as private property) by civil law, it is to be kept hold of in the manner the law prescribes.[91] In book 3, perhaps still following Panaetius, Cicero repeats his earlier dire warning even more strongly, saying that to take something from another is more contrary to nature than death. It destroys the natural society of the human race.[92] Cicero may or may not still be following Panaetius in his strongest statement of all in book 2: states and cities were established chiefly so that people could hold onto their possessions.[93] Here the plea of natural commonness does little to offset the rights of the property holder.

Whether or not Cicero's views were all encouraged by Panaetius, the commitment to private property of his pupil Hecato is at least as great. He defends private property by saying that we wish to amass it not just for ourselves, but for our children, relatives, and friends, and above all for our country because the riches of individuals are the riches of the state, since the state benefits.[94] It has rightly been said that this is another attempt to represent private property as somehow *common*,[95] and this time I think the intended implication is not so much that private rights nonetheless remain intact, but that somehow common rights have not been *completely* excluded.

Hecato also raised questions about slaves that imply that they are no more than property, when he continued the Stoic debates about expediency and morality, always, according to Cicero, favoring expediency. Expediency prevailed in the question whether the good man should still feed his slaves when grain prices are high, and whether one should throw overboard an expensive horse or a cheap young slave to prevent one's ship sinking in a storm.[96]

89. Cicero, *On Duties* 1.21.

90. Cicero, *On Duties* 1.20.

91. Cicero, *On Duties* 1.51.

92. Cicero, *On Duties* 3.21–22.

93. Cicero, *On Duties* 2.73.

94. Cicero, *On Duties* 3.63. Phillip Mitsis emphasizes the professed concern for the state as another version of the claim that private property is common. Mitsis, "The Stoics on property and politics," *Southern Journal of Philosophy* 43, 2005, pp. 230–49.

95. Mitsis, "The Stoics on property and politics."

96. Cicero, *On Duties* 3.89.

THE STOICS POSIDONIUS 135–51 BCE AND SENECA FIRST CENTURY CE: COMMON PROPERTY IN A PAST GOLDEN AGE

So far not much has been shown to follow from the appeals to things being by nature *common* in Panaetius, and before him in Chrysippus with his common theater seat, as well as after him in Hecato's idea of private property being for one's children and country. But Posidonius was a Stoic of independence and originality, who headed the Stoic school not in Athens, but on the island of Rhodes, and who greatly expanded the range of topics discussed by Stoics. We learn from Seneca that Posidonius spoke of a past Golden Age when humans lived in caves, cliffs, and hollow trees with no need of houses, and all their resources available for common use. They were governed by the wise, and nobody was poor until avarice fragmented society and caused poverty. A new group of wise men was then needed to create technology.[97] Seneca agrees that the early age was an age without poverty and that poverty came in because of avarice. But he does not agree that it was wise men who discovered the technology to gain luxury. He thinks that true wisdom is rather to be found in Diogenes the Cynic, who showed us that we do not need luxury. He describes with disdain pipes for spraying perfumes to a height and mobile ceiling panels displaying different patterns as each new course is served. Nor does he agree that early humans were wise, so much as innocent of how to sin.

Before Posidonius the idea of a Golden Age without private property can be found in a number of sources.[98] But Posidonius paid particularly close attention to Plato. He might therefore have been interested that Plato's propertyless society of warriors, although not a primitive society, was said by Plato in the *Critias* to have been instituted in a (gold-free) Golden Age.[99] The idea that private property and gold were absent from primitive society may also have been in Epicurus, since it is put by his expositor Lucretius in the first century BCE, although the primitive past is not described as golden.[100]

97. Posidonius' view is recorded and commented on in Seneca, *Letters* 90, see esp. paragraphs 3, 5–18, 36–46.

98. E.g., Hesiod, *Works and Days*, and the Aristotelian Dicaearchus, recorded in the later work of Porphyry, *On Abstinence from Killing Animals* 4.2.1–4.

99. Plato, *Critias* 110 C-D.

100. Lucretius, *On the Nature of Things* 5.1113.

SENECA, 4 BCE TO 65 CE: INDIFFERENCE, BUT OSCILLATION BETWEEN MINIMIZATION AND PREFERENCE

In the first century CE, we find a Stoic who stressed the value of poverty against wealth, Attalus, the teacher of Seneca; Seneca himself remained, despite his wealth, attracted by this view. He approved of Posidonius' age of innocence, we have seen, in one way, but his greater admiration for Cynicism is extended to a more recent Cynic, Demetrius, who refused a huge sum of money from the Emperor Caligula; Seneca thinks that Demetrius would refuse a gift, however large, if he were not allowed to give it away to others.[101] What matters is not how much land you own, but whether you know how to share it with a brother, or how to remain cheerful if a neighbor shaves a bit off your ancestral land. You are only a tenant on ancestral land. Lawyers say that public land cannot be acquired by mere use of it (*usus*). The ancestral land that you call your own is public, and indeed belongs to the whole human race.[102] Here Seneca picks up the theme that land is common. In almost Gandhian mode he once advocates *minimization* and says that the best amount of private property to have is just above the borderline of poverty.[103] These remarks do not deny the right to private property, but Seneca's main message so far belittles its importance.

Seneca, however, was himself a wealthy man as tutor to the future emperor Nero. He twice lost much of his wealth, first when exiled from 41 to 42 CE for alleged adultery, and later in 64 CE, when Rome needed rebuilding after the fire and after two years of attempts he succeeded in giving away part of his wealth, in the vain hope of averting the emperor's hostility.[104]

As a wealthy man, Seneca was moved in one work to reply to criticisms of Stoic wealth, criticisms such as he had himself suffered. The defense is not compatible with the minimization in his other text. But in *On the Happy Life*, he finds wealth not only legitimate, but even instrumentally good for promoting virtue. He would give wealth away to people who were good, or whom he could thereby help to make good. He even argues that wealth is capable of a greater range of virtues than poverty. The poor can show fortitude, but the rich can also display moderation, liberality, diligence, orderliness, and magnificence.[105] There is also a brief passage in one

101. Seneca, *On Benefits* 7.11.1, also 7.8.3.

102. Seneca, *Letters* 88.10–12.

103. Seneca, *On Tranquillity* 8.8.

104. On Seneca and wealth see Miriam Griffin, *Seneca: A Philosopher in Politics*, Oxford 1976, ch. 9, "Seneca *praedives*," pp. 286–314.

105. Seneca, *On the Happy Life* 22.1, 23.

of the letters in which Seneca further speaks as if, although a good character is enough to make a person happy, one will not be maximally happy (*beatissimus*) if pressed by too many dis-preferred circumstances.[106]

Seneca makes use of the idea of land being *common*, first with the insistence that one is merely a *tenant* on inherited land. The sharing here is presumably only with ancestors and descendants. It becomes clear that common property gives you much less than private when Seneca appeals to the theater analogy. He does so in an entirely different context. An objection had been made to the Stoic view that the wise person possesses everything, and that friends have everything in common. In that case, the objection ran, how can one give to a wise person, or a friend give to a friend, something that is not already owned by the recipient?[107] In reply, Seneca appeals again to the analogy of a theater seat, in this case the seats reserved for knights. His point is that occupying something common is unlike private possession, in that it gives you only very *restricted* rights. This is what leaves room for giving a gift into the *private* ownership of a friend or wise man, because *common* ownership gave him few rights. Admittedly, you would have the right to stay in your seat for a performance or to cede it, and if you ceded the commonly owned seat, you would have made a genuine gift to your friend at least for that one performance. Nonetheless, a commonly owned seat cannot be taken if it is occupied. Nor can the occupant sell, let, or live in it. Similarly, although friends have all things in common, one cannot use what a friend owns privately against his will, nor does merely common ownership of something allow one to sell, consume, or alter it.[108]

THE STOIC EPICTETUS 50 TO 125/130 CE: RESPECT FOR OTHERS' PROPERTY BUT MINIMIZATION ADMIRED AND ATTACHMENT DISPARAGED

The Stoic Epictetus also made use of the theater analogy, but used it in the opposite way, to emphasize the rights of the property holder. One cannot take someone else's wife any more than one can throw someone out of his theater seat, however much it may be true that women are by nature common property (i.e., originally available, like the theater seat, to others).[109]

But while respecting the property of *others*, Epictetus recommends minimizing what one calls one's own. He compares calling my body "mine"

106. Seneca, *Letters* 92.16.

107. Seneca, *On Benefits* 7.4.1

108. Seneca, *On Benefits* 7.12.2–6.

109. Epictetus, *Discourses* 2.4.9–11.

with calling "mine" the bed in an inn.[110] Here he switches to treating the possession of something common in the opposite way as giving you little.

As already mentioned, Epictetus expresses great admiration for an idealized Cynic way of life. He describes the ideal Cynic as owning neither house, city, possessions, nor slaves (*aoikos, apolis, aktêmôn, adoulos*), nor wife or children.[111] Epictetus also criticizes the use of "one's own" as applied to a vast range of things we are said to have. As seen in chapter 3, they include our farm, our slaves, our clothes, our house, our horses, even our bodies. The only thing under our control is our tendency of giving or withholding the assent of our reason to the right things or the wrong things, for short our *prohairesis*.[112]

Epictetus' denial that my body, or anything other than my capacity for assent is mine is opposite to the view of a younger Stoic of the second century BCE, Hierocles. According to Hierocles, in the natural Stoic process of *oikeiôsis*, that is, of coming to treat things as one's own, it would be natural and right for each of us to extend the attachment we feel for our nearest in ever widening circles outwards, until we could think not just of our own family as ours, but of all mankind.

THE STOIC HIEROCLES, SECOND CENTURY CE: PROCESS OF ATTACHMENT TO PROPERTY NATURAL

It has been pointed out that Hierocles tells us something new, that there are three types of natural *oikeiôsis*. It is natural to become attached to one's own person, to other people, and to *property*.[113] Attachment to property, then, is natural. Although this may startle, it fits with what had been reported two centuries further back as the standard Stoic view. In the natural process of becoming attached, *oikeiôsis*, the first thing at which one aims is preservation of one's own person and what conduces to it, both of which have a certain value.[114] This would seem to allow value to property as conducive to self-preservation. But if so, even here the Stoics seem to enter a qualification, because we are next told that the natural process ought to

110. Epictetus, *Discourses* 1.24.14.

111. Epictetus, *Discourses* 3.22.45–47.

112. Epictetus, *Discourses* 4.1.83, 4.4.29, 1.1.10–12; *Handbook* 1. This is emphasized by A. A. Long, "Stoic philosophers on persons, property ownership and community," in Richard Sorabji, ed., *Aristotle and After*, supplement 68 to the *Bulletin of the Institute of Classical Studies*, 1997, ch. 2, pp. 13–32.

113. Hierocles, *Elements of Ethics*, col. 9, lines 3–10, cited by Long, "Stoic philosophers on persons, property ownership and community," at p. 38.

114. Cicero, *On Ends* 3.16–20.

lead us to transcend the initial aim as we become adult and to aim at virtue instead, which is the only true good.[115] This in turn would be qualified, however, since virtue itself could turn out to involve the right use of property if one had it.

STOICS ON SLAVERY

Slaves are a form of property that provided a test case for Stoicism. To their credit some of them, including probably Chrysippus, denied that any slavery was natural. This is in a passage whose second half can be associated with Chrysippus and whose first half rejects Aristotle's view that some slavery is natural: "no human is a slave by nature; irrational animals take the place of slaves." The comment on animals is ascribed to Chrysippus by Cicero.[116] The only earlier denials of the naturalness of slavery were in the fourth century BCE by the sophist Alcidamas, whom Aristotle cites as having appealed to natural law, by the comic playwright Philemon, and, in the case of slavery through conquest, by certain unnamed lawyers.[117] Some Stoics, speaking from the point of view of the master, added that possession of slaves (*despoteia*) was bad.[118] Yet no Stoic is recorded as having recommended the abolition of slavery. Some, like Hecato, may not have changed their attitude at all.[119] But a number of intermediate steps could be taken. I have said that Zeno, like the Cynics, had no slaves. I inferred that his ideal republic would contain none. Epictetus, the ex-slave, admired the ideal Cynic who, albeit for his own sake, had none. I imagine that Epictetus had none himself. Others wanted a very different attitude to slaves, and not only for the sake of the master. Chrysippus makes only a small start, thinking of a slave as a perpetual hired laborer.[120] But Seneca writes a whole letter on humane treatment of slaves, in which he says that the man you call your slave arose from the same seeds as you, enjoys the same sky, breathes, lives, and dies like you.[121] This conclusion ought to have been drawn by Stoics from their theory of *oikeiôsis*, which makes it natural and just to extend to all humans the attachment one feels for one's nearest. It was also the subject

115. Cicero, *On Ends* 3.21–22.

116. Philo, *On the Special Laws* 2.69; Cicero, *On Ends* 3.67.

117. Aristotle, *Rhetoric* 1.13, with scholion; Philemon fragment 6, Kock; compare lawyers mentioned by Aristotle, *Politics* 1.6, 1255a 3–12.

118. Diogenes Laertius, *Lives* 7.122.

119. For Hecato see above.

120. Seneca, *On Benefits* 3.22; cf. Cicero, *On Duties* 1.41.

121. Seneca, *Letters* 47, citation from 47.10

of Seneca's most general precept (*praeceptum*), and the law of nature or of nations (*lex naturae, ius gentium*) and the rule (*formula*) that Cicero based on Stoicism that one must always act towards others as members of the human community.[122] Seneca returns elsewhere to the subject of humane treatment, albeit for the sake of the master's virtue.[123] And he takes up at length a question raised by Hecato, whether a slave can confer a benefit on a master, which he answers with an emphatic "yes," arguing, among other things, that masters control the body, not the mind, of a slave.[124] Other Stoics recommended that slaves should study philosophy.[125]

Why did not Seneca get rid of his slaves? This connects with the Stoic idea that you must live not only according to your human nature as a rational being, which would call for humanity, but also according to your individual *persona*, including the position into which you have been born or acquired by chance. Seneca was born of high rank, became a senator, and was appointed tutor to the future emperor. The right way to live is not the same for everybody. The disinterest in abolition may also connect with the Stoic idea, although that was most of all emphasized later by Epictetus, that you must distinguish between what is in your power and what is not. Epictetus was unusual in thinking that very little was in your power. Certainly, a general abolition of slavery did not seem to be in anybody's power, but Zeno will have thought of his own refusal of slaves as well within his power, and this was the way in which Stoic opposition to slavery could express itself.

We may compare how the Stoics opposed gladiatorial shows, albeit chiefly because of the effect on the spectator, without, however, recommending abolition. Staying away from the games would be parallel to owning no slaves oneself.

TAKING STOCK: THE CONSISTENCY OF STOIC ATTITUDES

I think it can now be made clear that Stoic attitudes to private property, although so varied, followed a consistent path. The Stoics held that different things are appropriate in different *circumstances* (*peristaseis*).[126] It therefore makes a vital difference whether you are considering existing society, or an

122. Seneca, *Letters* 95.53; Cicero, *On Duties* 3.19–21, 23, 27, 69.

123. Seneca, *On the Happy Life* 24.3.

124. Seneca, *On Benefits* 3. 18.1–28.6.

125. Reported by Lactantius, *Divine Institutes* 3.25.

126. E.g. Epictetus, *Discourses* 2.6.9–10; Diogenes Laertius, *Lives* 7.109; cf. Sextus, *Against the Experts* 11, 64–66.

ideal society, and if an ideal society, whether it is a society of wise humans living together in a single city, an aspiration I have ascribed to Zeno, or a very primitive society of cave dwellers who could not have much property, like Posidonius'. Minimization might reasonably be approved in different degrees in the last two societies, but dis-preferred in current society.

But what do the Stoics think when we come to current society? Insofar as minimization was still celebrated, intermittently by Seneca and more consistently by Epictetus, this was partly from admiration of the Cynics, and in Epictetus for the sake of freedom from attachments. But more commonly, Chrysippus' use of Zeno's category "preferred indifferent" allowed different Stoics to offer different emphases. There was a surge in one direction in the second century BCE, when the four Stoics cited put all their emphasis on wealth being *preferred*, without actually denying that it was indifferent. They toyed—merely toyed, I think—with the defense that in some sense private property was still by nature common, and Hierocles added a case for *nature* favoring private property. However, Seneca sometimes and Epictetus always put their stress on the need to view private property as *indifferent*, although Seneca wavered insofar as he also wanted to defend his wealth. All this leaves the Stoics, apart from Seneca's oscillations, basically consistent. But emphases are important and their extent is made all the plainer when we notice that Gandhi could have agreed only with some of the emphases: the minimization of private ownership, even of one's own body, respect for the property of others, the indifference of one's own, but not its preferability.

Gandhi and the Stoics are less close to each other on this topic than on others. But seeing the different ways in which they were each ready to accept property restrictions throws light, I think, on the ideas themselves, because the range of ways in which restrictions can be seen as acceptable is much greater than one might at first have imagined.

CHAPTER TEN

Isaiah Berlin's Stoic revolution: depoliticization

In chapter 2 I offered two explanations of how the Stoics and Gandhi would try to remain detached in pursuit of political goals. Gandhi subordinated them to spiritual goals. The Stoics took as their goal aiming aright, not hitting the target. Isaiah Berlin's view, by contrast, detached the Stoics from political goals altogether. More than one of his arguments was precisely that their emotional detachment made political choice and engagement pointless. Although he had many other arguments, these ones alone make it worth examining his case. The case is important too because, although Gandhi achieved a certain detachment about politics, he was most famous of all as a politician. Berlin's picture of the Stoics would make them totally unlike him. Berlin makes the issues sharp and exciting, as no one else can. He wrote:

> The three crises in Western political theory, when at least one central category was transformed beyond redemption, so that all subsequent thought was altered, occurred in the 4th century BCE, during the Renaissance and towards the end of the 18th century in Germany.[1]

In reverse order, he was referring to Romanticism, Machiavelli, and the Cypriot founder of Stoicism in Athens in 300 BCE, Zeno of Citium. Who but Isaiah Berlin could have made such a bold and imaginative statement? The first of his three transformers of Western political thought, Zeno, has

1. See chapter 3, n. 12 for full references to the first Storrs lecture of 1962, eventually reprinted by Henry Hardy as editor of Isaiah Berlin, *Liberty*, under the title "The birth of Greek individualism: a turning-point in the history of political thought," at pp. 287–321 (the page numbers used here).

only fragments of his writing surviving, and is usually nowadays the subject of close scholarly scrutiny. Berlin brings him to life with a shock.

BERLIN: INDIVIDUAL MORAL VALUES AND THE INNER LIFE REPLACE POLITICAL THEORY

Berlin claimed that the view of Socrates, his disciple Plato, and Plato's student Aristotle was swept away within twenty years of Aristotle's death. They had regarded a human as "an intrinsically social being" (p. 293), and human "fulfilment as necessarily social and public." As a result, "personal ethics [was] deduced from social morality, ethics [was] a branch of politics, the whole [preceded] the parts" (302, 310). But with the Stoics it was as if political philosophy "had suddenly vanished away" (302, 310, 318, 319).

The alleged change was above all due to Zeno, the founder of Stoicism in Athens in 300 BCE. There were a few others, notably Epicurus, founder of a rival school, but the Stoics were more influential (306) and are dwelt on at greater length. Thanks, then, especially to Zeno, people came to see "the value of the State [as] consisting in what it contributes to the individual satisfactions of its individual members" (301). "Individual salvation, individual happiness, individual taste, individual character emerge as the central goal, the centre of interest and value. [. . .] The State [. . .] is not the central function of [a man's] life" (319). We find after this date "genuine individualism, the doctrine that there are personal values—pleasure, or knowledge, or friendship, or virtue, or self-expression in art or life—to which political social arrangements should be subordinate" (299). "Society is fundamentally a hindrance to self-sufficiency." We must "regulate public affairs in accordance with the rules of private morality" (310). Social institutions are "means," not ends (317).

Berlin adds to his interpretation some theses about the "inner life." In the new period we have "in place of the outer life, the inner life. [. . .] The highest of all values is peace of soul, individual salvation" (303). "The only genuine life is the inner life. [. . .] The only portion of himself that is within [a man's] control is his inner consciousness" (317–18).

BERLIN: POLITICS ITSELF ABANDONED

Not only political theory, but according to Berlin, politics itself was abandoned by the Stoics. It had become a "squalid" and "degrading" occupation (310, 319). Some kind of depoliticization in the Hellenistic age—roughly the 300 years after Aristotle—was earlier maintained by Hegel, preserved in the classic guide to Greek philosophy by Zeller, and subsequently repeated both before and after Berlin for the case of the Stoics, but not necessarily in the strong form that he offers.[2]

BERLIN'S MODIFICATIONS TO HIS THEORY

Berlin defends his picture by including and excluding certain thinkers. After describing Stoicism as "in principle [. . .] anti-political" (309), he excludes from his account the later Stoics of the period of Roman hegemony as producing a "specious revival of political philosophy" (318). He does not say why it is specious. Further, as indicated, he combines with Zeno as cofounder of individualism the thinker who founded the rival school in Athens seven years earlier in 307 BCE, Epicurus. Berlin's discussion of Epicurus is briefer (303–6), but he can say of his attitude: "Public life is a snare and a delusion, and you should participate in it only if [. . .] it offers some kind of opiate to you" (305). The Stoics are normally contrasted with the Epicureans as regarding public life as a prima facie duty. But Berlin is not the first to have tried to reduce the contrast. Seneca pointed out that both sides admitted exceptions: Epicurus said that the wise person will not engage in political life, "unless something intervenes (*intervenire*)." The Stoics said that he will, "unless something prevents (*impedire*) it." But, Seneca goes on to argue, anything that prevents the Stoic doing good in the State *could* be seen as preventing him from doing politics at all.[3]

Berlin introduces another necessary modification. There were a few earlier "predecessors of the new individualism" (312–15 at 314): before Socrates in the fifth-century BCE, the sophist Antiphon and, following Socrates, Antisthenes and Aristippus. After that, in the fourth century BCE, the two Cynics, Diogenes of Sinope and Crates, espoused "full-blown individualism," but were regarded as eccentric. Berlin does not stress that aspect of Cynic influence that I have treated as most important, the idea that most things are *indifferent*. It is this idea, I argued in chapters 1 and 3, taken over, named, and refined by Zeno, that made possible two things that Berlin

2. A list is provided by Miriam Griffin, whose reply to Hegel's depoliticization thesis is confined, as its title indicates, to "Political thought in the age of Nero," *Neronia VI, Rome à l'époque néronienne*, Collection Latomus 268, 2002, 325–37. In the 1892 English translation of the relevant part of E. Zeller by O. J. Reichel, *Stoics, Epicureans and Sceptics*, see pp. 322–26. Cf also the careful statements about the Stoics in Peter Brunt, "Stoicism and the Principate," *Papers of the British School at Rome*, 43, 1975, 7–35; Julia Annas, *The Morality of Happiness*, Oxford 1993, pp. 306–11.

3. Seneca, *On Leisure* 3.2–4.

does mention: Stoic detachment (303) and Stoic freedom (318). I argued in chapter 3 that Zeno made a major contribution to European thought about freedom, but it was not a contribution that Berlin would approve.

FOUR RIVAL CONSIDERATIONS: (1) THE STOICS CALL FOR POLITICAL ENGAGEMENT, WITH EXCEPTIONS EXPLOITED CHIEFLY BY SENECA

I will now outline a view to set against Berlin's. His idea that politics was considered by the Stoics squalid and degrading is hard to fit with the later Stoic view that roles such as Athenian demesman, or Areopagite, or Roman senator help to constitute your persona and so determine your duties. More than that, the point is explicit from the beginning that the wise Stoic will normally engage in politics. It was Zeno, the founder of Stoicism, so Seneca tells us, who declared: "The wise man will engage in State affairs (*res publica*), unless something prevents him."[4] Moreover, as Berlin acknowledges (309), two of Zeno's pupils went to act as political advisers, one at least of them sent by Zeno himself.[5] After Zeno, the Stoics continued to hold that the Stoic should normally engage in public life (*politeuesthai*).[6] What is repeatedly said about the Greek Stoics of the first two centuries — Zeno, Cleanthes, Chrysippus, Diogenes, Antipater—is that although they preached this, they did not follow their own advice.[7] At least, then, they thought participation was normally right, not degrading. Nor was it merely permissible, as Berlin implies when he takes the Stoics to say only that the Stoic *may* serve the state, if nothing stops him.[8] The need to participate is usually put in terms of what the *wise* man (*sophos, sapiens*) or the man of understanding (*noun ekhôn*) does. The Stoic heads at most aspired to wisdom, and none of them would claim to have achieved it, but the point

4. Seneca, *On Leisure* 3.2.

5. Zeno sent his Cypriot pupil Persaeus as an ethical adviser to the Macedonian ruler of Athens, and his pupil Sphaerus played some role on the side of the poorer in land redistributions under King Cleomenes III in Sparta.

6. Stobaeus vol. 2, pp. 94.8–11, 2.109.15–18, 2.111.5–9; vol. 4, p. 192,10–13; Diogenes Laertius, *Lives* 7.121; Cicero, *On Ends* 3.68; *On Duties* 1.28–29; Plutarch, *On Stoic Self-contradictions* 1034 B.

7. Plutarch, *On Stoic Self-contradictions* 1033 B-E; Seneca, *On Tranquillity* 1.10; *On Leisure* 6.5.

8. I thank Phillip Mitsis for pointing out Berlin's wording. Miriam Griffin, *Seneca: A Philosopher in Politics*, 2nd ed., Oxford 1991, regards as special pleading and contrary to his normal view Seneca's argument in his *On Leisure* that the Stoic can always be excused from political participation.

is not confined to the wise. Engaging in public life is said in general to be more equitable (*aequius*).[9] Berlin argues that participation is not, as it had been for others, the central function of his life. (319) But I do not believe it was the central function of life for philosophers in Plato's *Republic* 519–20, or in Aristotle's *Nicomachean Ethics* 10.8, which both give a role alongside politics to time for philosophising and the exercise of virtues in private.

As the Roman Republic failed and the empire succeeded, there may have been more frequent resort to Zeno's concession, "unless something prevents him." Cato, despite his own political participation, is said to have advised his son not to engage in public life after Julius Caesar seized power.[10] But Seneca in the first century of the Roman Empire was the main exception. For a period he plunged more than any Stoic into politics. But he may all along have been inclined to oscillate on withdrawal from public life. At any rate, in *On Tranquillity* he offers to help a disciple, Serenus, imagined as oscillating between engaging in public life and disengaging.[11] Moreover, the classic work of Miriam Griffin[12] makes clear that, even as a young man, he made a late start, delaying his entry into the Roman Senate. After entry, his participation was interrupted when he was exiled by Emperor Gaius from 41 to 49 CE for alleged adultery with the emperor's sister. But when he returned, he hoped to exercise a Stoic influence as tutor to the twelve-year-old future emperor Nero and from Nero's succession in 54 CE, through acting as his adviser and speechwriter, even while he also sought leisure to write for himself. When he failed to influence Nero by his discourse *On Clemency* of around 56, and had been compromised in Nero's defense of his act of matricide in 59, his subsequent attempts to withdraw were understandable. For his own safety, he asked Nero in 62 for permission to retire and hand over his wealth, but Nero refused. He withdrew as far as he could and his wealth was accepted in 64 after the great fire of Rome. In 64–65, the time of his famous *Letters* to Lucilius, Seneca was suspected of participating in the Pisonian conspiracy, and Nero required his suicide. Given this history, it is in some cases not surprising that Seneca recommended withdrawal from public life, during or after a life of service, or from the beginning.[13] Even so,

9. Cicero, *On Duties* 1.28–29.

10. Plutarch, *Life of Cato the Younger* 66.3.

11. Seneca, *On Tranquillity* 1. 8–10

12. I here follow Griffin, *Seneca: A Philosopher in Politics*, ch. 10, "The philosopher on political participation."

13. He did so to his father-in-law Paulinus in *On the Shortness of Life* (48–55 CE), to Serenus in *On Tranquillity* (before 62 CE), to his addressee in the imperfectly surviving *On Leisure* (before 62 CE, if addressed to Serenus), and to his real or fictive correspondent Lucilius in the *Letters* of 64–65.

the decision on withdrawal depended in Seneca, as in other Stoics of the time—Athenodorus and Epictetus—on one's particular circumstances and persona.[14] *On Leisure* looks like an exception and seems to be making an uncharacteristically extreme case for withdrawal.[15] Yet, despite his selective advocacy of withdrawal from public life, Seneca always has to give arguments for favoring the course that Zeno had treated as an exception.

Seneca's occasional isolationism remained unusual, and Epictetus the ex-slave reverted to the more usual Stoic emphasis. He proclaimed against an Epicurean that he ought to hold office and make just judgments. He also thought that even under Nero and Vespasian the defiance of an Agrippinus or a Helvidius Priscus, son-in-law of Thrasea Paetus, was worthwhile and could make an emperor back down. The exception he allowed was for the ideal Cynic, whose total adoption of a persona that Epictetus admired justified him in withdrawing from public life.[16] Also in line with orthodoxy was the still later view of Marcus Aurelius as emperor that he must serve the palace as his stepmother, even though philosophy was his mother.[17]

(2) CONSTITUTIONAL PHILOSOPHY NOT THE NORM

The political philosophy that Berlin finds missing from Stoicism is said (303) to be about the city, the education of citizens to perform their tasks within it, bad and good constitutions, the need for hierarchies or their dangers, the value of small organized communities and of extrovert social life, how to train specialists in governing men, the appropriate reward of unequal gifts, and the different gifts valued by different constitutions. It might be added to Berlin's case that there is only one isolated reference to a Stoic preference for a "best" constitution.[18] But in reply to his complaint, it needs to be said that Plato and Aristotle were the exceptions in developing this branch of political philosophy. It is not to be found in Socrates. Plato often puts his own ideas into Socrates' mouth in his dramatic dialogues, especially in the ones that are thought to be written later. But on the standard view, the real Socrates took for discussion from Berlin's list at most education, and that

14. Seneca, *On Tranquillity* 3.1–8 (Athenodorus), 6.1–4, 7.2; *On Leisure* 1.4, 3.3–4; Epictetus, *Discourses* 1.2. 12–24.

15. Griffin argues that Seneca does not endorse the view mentioned just before the text breaks off at chapter 8, that a wise man should *always* withdraw because in any existing state he and the state can never endure (*pati*) each other.

16. Epictetus, *Discourses* 3.7.21, 1.2.12–24, 3.22.83–85

17. Marcus Aurelius, *Meditations* 6.12, cited above.

18. Diogenes Laertius, *Lives* 7.131.

was an education that led the youth to be sceptical about current political values, rather than fitting them for service within that value system. In fact, Plato makes Socrates say that his guardian spirit warned him not to engage in politics, and that ordinary politics is incompatible with philosophy.[19] The Stoics can be seen as going back to the Socrates, who did not anticipate Plato's interest in constitutions. Berlin cites a putative exception (296). Socrates is represented in the early dialogue *Crito*[20] as arguing that he must not escape from prison, because he is obligated to obey the laws of Athens, both because he owes his birth to those laws and because, by never leaving, he has shown himself content with them. This claim of obligation is a political one. But it is not an assessment of whether the laws of Athens are good laws and so it does not belong on the list of political topics that Berlin finds present in Plato and abandoned by the Stoics (303). It is rather a statement of Socrates' personal debts. To put it in Stoic terms, it maintains that Socrates' past allegiance to Athens formed part of his persona and created an obligation.

Some of the issues in political philosophy that interested Plato and Aristotle were later to be discussed by Cicero in *On Laws* and *On a Republic* and some were discussed earlier by those philosophers, such as Protagoras, who were asked to write laws for the many colonies that were sent out from bigger Greek cities from the sixth century BCE onward. The colonizing tradition will have interested Plato and both he and Aristotle advised rulers. There will be another explanation of his resumption of interest in forms of government if we can believe the evidence of the disputed *Seventh Letter* controversially ascribed to him. According to this, he was invited to join the government of the thirty tyrants in 404, but was disillusioned by them and by the ensuing democracy which executed Socrates in 399 and in this mood, he made the first of three trips to Sicily, where he was sooner or later to seek to influence the tyrant of Syracuse.

(3) STOICS FOLLOW PLATO'S NEW SOCRATIC CONCEPTION OF MORAL AND SOCIAL POLITICS

In any case, Plato expressed a new conception of politics, when in his *Gorgias*, he made Socrates, who had played a minimalist role in Athenian politics, say that he was the only true politician, seeking, as he did, to make

19. Plato, *Apology* 31C–32A; *Republic* 496A–C. I thank Tad Brennan for the second reference.

20. Plato, *Crito* 50A–54D.

people good and just.[21] If, unlike Socrates, Plato went on in his *Republic* to study constitutions, the difference from Stoic or Gandhian politics could still be lessened, if the interest in constitutions was subordinate to the "true politician's" aim of making men just, and designed to show what constitution would secure that.

The Stoic Zeno avoided studying constitutions for a different reason from that of Socrates. He turned in his own *Republic* to an ideal city in which Socrates' aim had been achieved and the citizens were already wise and just, so that he was not looking for a constitution to bring that result about. In fact, like Socrates in the *Gorgias*, he would look not to a constitution to effect this, but for change at the level of *individuals*.

Although Stoic interest was particularly in *individual* morality. it nonetheless often focused on the individual's obligations in *society*, as pointed out for the age of Nero by Miriam Griffin.[22] The Stoics considered the duties that one's *social* role or "persona" imposed. Thus, Seneca discussed the duties imposed by wealth on benefactors and recipients.[23] Marcus Aurelius considered this too, and presented an entirely opposite view, that instead of secret consciousness of benefaction, the benefactor should forget his action.[24]

Social too is the Stoic insistence on the naturalness of *oikeiôsis*, of extending mutual attachment and fellowship among all humans. Although Berlin describes the theory as biological and moral, not political (320), he acknowledges that it was to have tremendous political implications. It provided an alternative to the rival Epicurean view of individual humans as naturally hostile competitors who entered into political arrangements solely for their own protection by way of a contract. Moreover, the idea would surely influence aspirations for an ideal city. In a city of Stoic sages, fellow-feeling of all for all would be the expectation.

Social again were the beliefs about the extent of private property and the possession of slaves, which could be different in ideal republics and in

21. Plato, *Gorgias* 521A, 521D, cf. 504E, 513E–514B, 517B–C, 527D–E. The *Gorgias* along with Seneca are the two comparisons with Gandhi offered by Mohamed Mehdi in "The Political Dimension of the Contemplative Life: Engagement and disengagement in Plato, Seneca and Gandhi."

22. Miriam Griffin, "Political thought in the age of Nero," *Neronia VI, Rome à l'époque néronienne*, Collection Latomus 268, 2002, 325–37.

23. Seneca, *On Benefits*, discussed by Miriam Griffin, "Seneca's pedagogic strategy: *Letters* and *de beneficiis*," in Richard Sorabji and Robert W. Sharples, eds., *Greek and Roman Philosophy* 100 *BC–*200 *AD, Supplement to the Bulletin of the Institute of Classical Studies*, 94, 2007, vol. 1, pp. 89–113.

24. Marcus Aurelius, *Meditations* 5.6, 9.41.5.

actual societies. I argued in chapter 9 that interest in these property arrangements continued uninterrupted in Stoicism.

(4) STOIC ENGAGEMENT IN CONVENTIONAL POLITICS AFTER ZENO

After Zeno, two of whose students engaged in conventional politics, there is admittedly a dearth of known examples of engagement until the later Roman Republic. But this cannot have been because of what Zeno taught his pupils. Of course, people had to be of the right social status to engage in conventional politics. There was little prospect of a slave doing so.[25] In the Roman Republic, we may not know the motives of the Stoic C. Blossius, who supported Tiberius Gracchus' schemes for land redistribution to the poor in 133 BCE. But many of the Romans who embraced philosophy were aristocrats and so were expected to play political roles.[26] Indeed, in times of tyranny and empire, they, like Gandhi, provided some of the leading political resistance.

Particularly important was the younger Cato (95–46 BCE). According to Plutarch's *Life* of him, which drew, probably via an intermediary, on an account by Cato's contemporary Munatius Rufus, Cato as senator was the first and the last person at work each day in the Senate and as quaestor in the Treasury, where he enforced honest payments. He also took the post of praetor, and he uncompromisingly withstood, sometimes with success, attempts by the future triumvirate, Pompey, Crassus, and Caesar, to subvert the constitution and take power for themselves. At the same time, he refused to take illegal advantage of them when he would have been able to. He rejected lucrative roles that others sought. According to Plutarch, when forced to undertake a mission to Cyprus that others considered lucrative, he carried out the task, despite intractable conditions, with scrupulous accounting and no profit for himself or his friends, bringing back to the Roman state more profit than came from all of Pompey's conquests put together. When Caesar won the Civil War and advanced on the city of Utica in 46 BCE, Cato first saw to the wishes of those trapped in the city, and only when no more could be done, committed suicide as a guarantee of individual freedom.

25. A leading Stoic under the Roman Empire, Epictetus, started as a slave, just as the first Greek Cynic, Diogenes, had for a time been enslaved.

26. See David Sedley, "The Ethics of Brutus and Cassius," *Journal of Roman Studies* 87, 1997, pp. 41–53.

When the Roman Republic was replaced by the Empire, Seneca in the next century as tutor, then speech-writer, to a Roman emperor, tried and failed to inculcate Stoic values into him. Subsequent Stoic aristocrats held office, as Stoicism required, but only offered moral resistance to the emperor. However, that was not because of a change in Stoicism, but because of a change in what was possible under an empire. The Stoic Epictetus describes two Stoic senators who defied emperors, Quintus Paconius Agrippinus and Helvidius Priscus,[27] Helvidius appealing to his role as a senator. Helvidius' father-in-law, the Stoic Senator Thrasea Paetus, from whose *Life* of Cato the Younger Plutarch drew, had also stood up conspicuously to the emperor. When he was condemned and committed suicide in 66, the year after Seneca's death, Griffin points out,[28] his adherence to Stoicism was actually one of the charges brought against him. Stoicism was thus officially recognized as political. Resistance to the emperor might seem to be all that was left. But history is full of surprises, and in the next century, the Roman emperor himself was a practicing Stoic, Marcus Aurelius. So politics was still a Stoic duty, and a duty no longer simply for the emperor's subjects, but for the emperor himself.

BERLIN MISLED BY THREE TYPES OF EVIDENCE?

I shall finish by looking at the three types of evidence that I believe misled Berlin, and by considering his special thesis about the Stoic stress on the *individual* and his *inner life*.

(i) In offering evidence, Berlin refers to what he calls the Stoics' "total detachment," and describes as being opposed to "political commitment" (303). If the Stoics are totally detached, they can surely live with any political constitution. They have learned how to remain serene, whatever the political situation. So why should they bother about it?

Part of the answer to this first argument involves returning to the idea of *preferred* indifferents. The emotional detachment that the Stoics recommend, though very real, cannot be described as "total." Among many important qualifications, Zeno distinguished among the objectives he described as "indifferent." Some, we saw in chapters 1 through 3, were considered natural objectives and normally to be *preferred*, such as health and life, while others were normally to be dis-preferred, like sickness and death. Wealth was later described by Chrysippus as an indifferent to be preferred in actual

27. Epictetus, *Discourses* 1.2. 12–24. See also chapter 6 above.

28. Griffin, *Seneca*, pp. 360–66.

societies, as we saw in chapter 9. It was only in the ideal republic that there would be no coinage. Moreover, we have seen, Antipater, head of the Stoic school in the mid-second century BCE, maintaining that it was your duty to do everything in your power (*pan to kath' hauton*) to obtain the naturally preferred objectives[29]—for yourself and others. The emotional detachment came in only retrospectively, if, through no fault of your own, you failed to secure them. This qualified detachment, then, would not exclude preferring some political goals rather than others, and pursuing them energetically. The detachment need not be, as Berlin says, "in place of" political commitment (303), but was perfectly compatible with such commitment.

Berlin appeals a second time to emotional detachment (308) to infer political disinterest. He says of Stoic wise people, "They can live in any city; it doesn't matter where, for being passionless they will feel no special attachment to any body of men." But this seems to misconstrue the way in which the Stoic sage is passionless. He (or she, it must be understood) is passionless because he regards the right things as indifferent. But this is not to deny that he has the right preferences and dis-preferences. Because exile, war, or fire so often removed people from their cities, the Stoic sage must be prepared without passion to lose his or her home city. But this is not the sage's preference. The home city will normally be preferred. One could not normally expect to have any political role in a foreign city, unless sent there in a privileged capacity, such as adviser to a ruler, or as governor of a Roman province. If one could acquire a political role, it would be easier to have a good effect in some cities than in others. It is not true that "it doesn't matter where."

(ii) The second piece of evidence used by Berlin is a text of Plutarch. The Stoics, Berlin says, have no loyalty to small organic communities, because they believe in "a world without national or city frontiers" (303). He seems to be referring to Zeno's ideal republic, and equating it with a worldwide "city" of all humans whatsoever, with the further twist that *all* humans are envisaged as having become wise. That Berlin envisages all humans as having become wise is shown by his taking the reference to be to "a world filled with wise men" to whom "society is fundamentally a hindrance" (310). That Berlin is thinking of all humans is also shown by his particular use of the Plutarch passage, a passage which claims to give the main point of Zeno's *Republic*, and asserts that it was Alexander the Great who put Zeno's theory into effect (although not, presumably, by making all humans

29. Stobaeus vol. 2, p. 76.9–15; Clement of Alexandria, *Stromateis* 2.21; Cicero, *On Ends* 3.22, 5.20; Plutarch, *On Common Notions* 1070F–1071E, 1072E–F.

wise). Berlin takes the middle of the (now much disputed) report on Zeno and gives a translation that, with my few interspersed glosses, clearly separated, runs as follows (308):

> We should not live by [*kata*: in accordance with] cities or demes [subunits of citizens], severally divided according to our own ideas of what is just, but should consider that all men are demesmen and fellow citizens; there should be one life [*bios*] ' and one world [*kosmos*], just as of a herd feeding together, nurtured by a common pasture.[30]

Berlin's editor rightly adds that the Greek word for "pasture" also means "law."

Since Berlin wrote, different translations have been suggested and the entire reliability of the passage has been questioned. But I follow Phillip Mitsis[31] in supposing that, however far-fetched Plutarch's comparison with Alexander, the report on Zeno can be accepted if Zeno's original point stressed the one divine law of nature in opposition to the varied laws of demes or cities. He is said by Cicero to have believed in a divine law of nature that commands what is right and forbids the opposite.[32] Zeno may then originally have banned not living in separate *cities*, but living in accordance with (*kata*) their separate *laws*, rather than in accordance with the one divine law of nature. This could be made still clearer without Berlin's comma after "demes."

The part of Berlin's description that matters is the claim that members of Zeno's republic found society a hindrance. I have already said in this chapter that I think that the Stoics, so far from being against society in the actual world of small communities, had strong social interests. As for Zeno's ideal republic, interpretation is bound to be speculative, but in chapter 9 I favored the case for taking it to be a set of reasonably small communities of the wise. To draw the conclusion that society was regarded as a hindrance, we would have to trust Plutarch's passage about one form of life and justice and interpret it in a particularly strong sense as rejecting any society.

(iii) Berlin's third type of evidence is Zeno's iconoclasm. He cites as anti-society the proposals in Zeno's ideal republic for the central institutions of Greek society (308): Zeno's ideal republic would have no law courts, tem-

30. Plutarch, *On the fortune or virtue of Alexander the Great* 329a–b.

31. I have benefited from the unpublished interpretation of Phillip Mitsis in his "Hellenistic political theory" delivered in a joint symposium with me held at the plenary panel of the annual meeting of the Society for Ancient Greek Philosophy at Fordham University, 16 October 2009.

32. Cicero, *On the Nature of the Gods* 1.14.36.

ples, gymnasia (which kept youths fit for military service), or coinage,[33] and there were questions about private property.

It is true that Zeno's ideal was revolutionary. But that does not mean that he and Chrysippus, who thought armed forces useless, were against society. The idea about the conventional institutions of coinage, law courts, and perhaps marriage and separate families was presumably that the wise would not need these provisions. In Berlin's terms, their ideal society may have been anarchistic, but this was because it followed not a plethora of human laws, but the divine law of human fellowship. We are handicapped by the fact that many of the fragmentary records were preserved by opponents who wanted to emphasize the shocking rejection of these conventions, not to record the life envisaged without them.

Berlin cites in the same breath again (308–9) the reports that Zeno's ideal republic gave free license in matters of conventional Greek morality, allowing eating the limbs of dead parents, free love, and incest.[34] This was presumably a revision of Plato's forcibly state-controlled award of sexual partners, and secrecy about parenthood, which made incest hard to avoid, in his earlier book of the same title, *Republic*. Zeno's proposal was instead choice of partner according to individual taste, to use Berlin's expression (319). But does this mean that individual taste had actually become the central goal, and that society had been rejected? The Stoics carefully stated their central goal (*telos*), as following nature, and connected it with virtue. The rejection of conventional relations to lovers and children does not imply an absence of society. A common alternative interpretation is that Zeno was against following conventional morality in society regardless of circumstances, but favored natural, instead of conventional, law. However, we are once again handicapped by hostile sources.

IS THE INNER LIFE A NEW STOIC INTEREST?

To turn finally to Berlin's antithesis of political participation with the *individual* and his *inner life*, I am not persuaded by his view that stress on the inner life is a new Stoic interest. In one way, Socrates, Plato, and Aristotle had all been stressing the importance of seeking *virtue*, seen as an inner state of the soul. But inner *peace of mind*, by contrast, was something

33. Diogenes Laertius, *Lives* 7.33, and other sources collected in *SVF*, 1.264–65. I leave on one side the rejection of temples and gymnasia, since suggested motivations are conjectural.

34. The Cynics had already challenged state institutions and conventional morality before Zeno. See the useful catalogue in Marie-Odile Goulet-Cazé, *Les Kynica du stoïcisme*, Hermes Einzelschriften 89, Stuttgart 2003, pp. 57–58.

different from inner virtue. It had on the one hand been sought much earlier in the fifth century BCE by Democritus, but was on the other hand for Plato and Aristotle a product of virtuous character, rather than something to be directly sought. The Stoics accepted some of each view: peace of mind could be taught up to a point even to non-Stoics,[35] but would be fully provided only by virtue.

Control of the inner life is something different again, and the Stoic Seneca, so far from thinking it universally possible, pointed out that not everything inner can be controlled not, for example, twinges of sensation. It is only rational *judgments* that can be controlled by reflection. But that area of inner control is important, since it can give peace of mind by eradicating emotional attitudes.[36]

HAS THE HORIZON SHRUNK TO THE INDIVIDUAL OR EXPANDED TO A COSMIC COMMUNITY?

There is one more claim of Berlin's to discuss. Is his word "individualism" the right one to describe Stoic values? I have been disagreeing with his ascription to the Stoics of a particular kind of individualism. It is a self-oriented kind that regards politics as of interest only insofar as it furthers the values of the individual. The individual's values which are prioritised are described by Berlin as "personal values" and "private morality" (299, 310). "Personal ethics," he says, "are no longer derived from social morality, [. . .] the whole no longer precedes the parts" (302). But the Stoics tended to see their view the other way round. Seneca says in the first century CE that we should not privilege our own interests, but should think of ourselves merely as parts of a larger whole, like stones in an arch, *Letters* 95, 53. The larger whole of which he is thinking is not the small society of Plato and Aristotle, but the whole human race. This is to think differently from Berlin. Seneca sees himself as appealing not to something *smaller* than before, *personal* values, *private* morality, but to something larger.

This enlarged horizon arises at several points in Stoic ethics. Berlin himself ascribes to Zeno aspiration for a world-wide republic. Berlin is right that the naturalness of *oikeiôsis*, of extending a feeling of attachment to all human beings, is not a political idea in a conventional sense. But it is not on the face of it an idea that narrows down to the individual, but one that

35. The Stoic Chrysippus, reported by Origen, *Against Celsus* 1.64, 8.61.

36. Seneca, *On Anger* 2.2–2.3.

expands to all mankind. There is a still wider conception in Stoicism, first explicitly ascribed not to Zeno, but to the third head, Chrysippus: the idea of a cosmic city, including not only wise humans, but also gods.[37]

Least of all would the Stoics recognize Berlin's view that something as narrow as individual *taste* (319) had emerged as the central goal. Many tastes are artificial, and even the Stoics' Cynic predecessors were intent on replacing the artificial by the natural. Taste, moreover, can be a matter of whim. But Zeno's personal morality fell under the very strict constraints of following the law of God and taking virtue as his goal. Virtue is typically exercised in relation to others. So is God's law. I argued in chapter 7 that divine law in Stoic texts is most commonly expressed as the requirement to respect the bonds of human society. This is the same requirement as was offered by Seneca as the most general moral "formula" available in the passage where he said that we are parts of a whole like stones in an arch.[38] The morality that the Stoics follow is not so much "personal" or "private" as already public in the sense of involving concern for other humans.

OTHER KINDS OF ATTENTION TO THE INDIVIDUAL

This is not to deny that the Stoics might be individualists in other ways. Attention to the individual takes different forms.[39] Seneca's idea that we are parts of a whole and must not privilege our own interests might seem the very antithesis of individualism. But it brings in the individual in an unexpected way. Seneca's preference for whole over part fits with the fact that the suffering of the individual had long been regarded by the Stoics as a matter of "indifference." But the thesis of the "indifference" of individual suffering had called for a lot of attention to individuals to help them absorb the indifference of their suffering.[40] I have already hinted in chapter 1 at the huge inner reflection required in order to reevaluate what matters. This depends on what sort of being you wish to be, and it involves the individual's "inner life."

My point has been not to deny the Stoic inner life, but to insist that it dovetails with social, and with ordinary political, activity. The very idea of *me* or *self* calls for inner reflection. But it can be used in different ways for political and social relations. Epictetus famously protects the true Stoic

37. Philodemus, *On Piety*, col. vii.12–viii.4, Heinrichs.

38. Seneca, *Letters* 95.53.

39. So Richard Sorabji, *Self*, pp. 157, 167.

40. See also my introduction to Richard Sorabji and R. W. Sharples, eds., *Greek and Roman Philosophy 100 BC–200 AD*, Bulletin of the Institute of Classical Studies, suppl. 94, 2007, p. 6.

from suffering, by reducing the individual's sense of "me" to his *prohairesis* (his commitment to the right valuations). His *prohairesis*, unlike his body, is exempt from domination by a political master. Epictetus then uses the reduced sense of "me" to defy a political tyrant ("you can chain my leg, but not me").[41] Yet Epictetus' Stoic successor Hierocles can use the idea of self in an opposite way: your inner self, the mind (*dianoia*), is surrounded by objects of concern in concentric circles. Your concern for circles of other human beings, however distant, should draw them closer to the innermost circle that is your own body, and hence closer to your inner self, which is the center point.[42] Social feeling should bring others closer to your inner self.

In chapter 6 I recognized in Stoicism reasons for attention to the individual that were different again: the search for one's individual persona, the need to resist the emotive appearance of indifferents and to distinguish between one's target and one's aim. In addition, I argued, when discussing human rights in chapter 5, that the Stoic stress on character gave some importance to the individual, because the individual's virtuous endeavor was treated as more important than its effects in society at large. None of these forms of attention to the individual had anything to do with privileging the individual's tastes or interests.

THE CYNICS AND INDIFFERENCE

Although Berlin recognizes a role for Zeno's Cynic predecessors, it is the role of abandoning politics. I think this is not what Zeno took over from his Cynic teacher. Rather, what he adopted was the idea of the *indifference* of conventional objectives, although it took Zeno to articulate and name that concept and to qualify it.

41. Epictetus, *Discourses* 1.1.23. See chapter 3 above.

42. Hierocles, *Elements of Ethics*, in Stobaeus vol. 4, p. 671, 7–16, which I have interpreted in *Self*, Oxford and Chicago 2006, pp. 43–44, 194. Even your body, though outside the *inner* self, may not be outside the self altogether, as Epictetus recommends it should be, when he denies that his leg is part of himself. See Seneca's *Letters* 121.16, for the idea that a new-born infant feels concern for a "me" or "ego" that consists at that stage in a constitution that is mostly physical. In Plutarch, *On Stoic Self-contradictions* 1038B, more ambiguously, the Stoic Chrysippus is said to hold that as newborn children we are attached to ourselves *and* our (bodily) parts (*oikeioumetha pros hautous kai ta merê*). In another fragment of Hierocles' same work, talk about self-perception (*sunaisthêsis*) in animals is about their awareness of their own *bodily* parts and their use, Hierocles, *Elements of Ethics*, ed. A. A. Long, *Corpus dei papiri filosofici greci e latini* 1, Florence 1992, col. 2, lines 3 and 38.

RESUMÉ: THE STOICS AND GANDHI

I have disagreed with Isaiah Berlin. If the Stoics did not opt out of politics, they cannot be contrasted on that score with Gandhi the politician. Nonetheless, I have found Berlin's insight into the novelty of the period particularly stimulating. His suggestions draw attention to the fact that something new did happen at the time of Zeno of Citium. Looking back, I can suggest that the two most important themes uniting the Stoics with Gandhi have been those of indifference and of the special place of the individual, which led to caution about universal rules of conduct. This chapter has focused almost exclusively on the Stoics. In the next chapter I shall take a retrospective look at Gandhi.

CHAPTER ELEVEN

Gandhi's philosophical credentials, his lapses, and his distance from other philosophers

GANDHI'S PHILOSOPHICAL CREDENTIALS

I shall return in retrospect to three of the questions I raised in the introduction. The first is about Gandhi's philosophical credentials. I said in chapter 2 that Gandhi was first and foremost a spiritual and moral leader, and only after that a politician. Where does his philosophical role fit in? I would put it second because I think it was important to him that his spiritual and moral views be explained, not merely pronounced, and the form that his explanations repeatedly took was philosophical. I described in the introduction two ways in which the form was philosophical. *First,* Gandhi did more than any philosopher I know of to subject his ideas to criticism through his daily and weekly writing, much of it nationwide. *Second,* he often gave reasons of a philosophical kind. For respect among different religions one reason was the impossibility of any of them describing God, the indescribable, but the prospect of many providing some approach to insight. We are now in a position to consider some further ways in which his ideas were philosophically expressed. A *third* and *fourth* emerge from the topics we have seen him discussing. They are not only (third) well-known examples of philosophical topics, traditionally handled by philosophers.[1] But fourth, in many cases, I believe, he discusses them with philosophical acumen, and in some with originality. Seven topics will serve as reminders.

As regards *rights and duties,* he relates them in a way quite different from that which has become familiar in the West. I gain *my* right to respect from my family, he says, only if *I* first perform *my* duties to them. The expected reference to *their* duties is not forthcoming. Moreover, Gandhi had

1. This would apply not only to the topics to be cited, but also to civil disobedience, noncooperation, the ethics of wealth, and many others.

his own reason for preferring a Charter of Human Duties to a Charter of Human Rights—insistence on one's own rights leads to violence, as insistence on one's own duties does not. (Insistence on the duties of *others* he hoped to conduct nonviolently).

Gandhi distinguished two kinds of *freedom*, political and personal self-rule, matching a Stoic distinction between nonsubordination and being one's own agent. He also insisted that one becomes irresistible (a kind of freedom) as one reduces oneself—one's wants—to zero. This is the freedom that Isaiah Berlin dismissed in the Stoic version as "sour grapes." But it is an important kind of freedom, as Berlin later recognized, and Gandhi's reminder should make us expand the number of kinds under discussion beyond the two on which Berlin focused—not that Berlin made the mistake of thinking that his were the only two.

It is fascinating to see Gandhi's requirements for *nonviolence* being strengthened in 1926 under the pressure of intense criticism. He was not a pacifist and he did not rule out all killing. But under pressure he had to add to Tolstoy's criterion of nonviolence—the absence of ill will and presence of good will—the further requirement that killing must be for the sake of the killed, if it is to avoid being violent. Nonetheless, even some violent killing, though evil, was to be countenanced for a number of different reasons: it might be the less bad course in a moral double-bind. Or again, it might be inevitable given our imperfection, but still to be regarded as evil, since a counsel of unattainable perfection was the only way to raise our standards. Yet again, a refusal to support the government's war effort could be justified only by a general policy of noncooperation that refused the government's benefits as well.

Most important were considerations of *svadharma*, differences of individual duty. Violence might be the least bad course in some people because they did not believe in Gandhi's nonviolence, or because they had taken on obligations of protecting others. Difference of belief, of duties taken on, and also of character and ability, were taken as creating different duties. This was, I believe, right and important. It enabled him to be selective, encouraging to nonviolent resistance only those suited by temperament for it, supplying roles in other "constructive" work to those unsuited, and leaving many to decide for themselves.

Gandhi, rightly in my view, usually hesitated to offer universal rules of conduct for everyone, except as an unattainable counsel of perfection (nonviolence), or where there was an alternative to what he forbade (lying). He might be readier to insist on the right *attitude* of nonviolence or truthfulness than to dictate what conduct that would require in different cases. But even with the *attitude* of nonviolence, which alone he thought right, he did not wish to impose it on those with opposite convictions, much as he might hope to convert them.

Better than universal rules, he thought, was the appeal of each person to his or her *conscience*. Here, as in the discussion of nonviolence, he rightly saw the possibility of a moral double-bind. If your conscience was mistaken, you would be in the wrong whether you followed it or not, but it was less bad to follow it. His strong conviction in almost every case of conscience that he was right was compatible with his recognizing that he must surely be wrong in some cases or other. But it was harder to square with his further recognition that listening to conscience is a difficult art.

Conviction was relevant also to his giving separate spheres to *faith* and reason. Telling was his response to an overrationalistic doctor that it would call for faith to take his medicines. Telling too was his insistence that reason could never be infallible because it could always be overthrown by superior reason. His belief that religious faith might become infallible was due to his connecting it with the very different activity of coming closer to God.

So far I have connected the philosophical character of Gandhi's ideas with four things: the exceptional subjection of them to criticism, the appeal to philosophical reasons, the appropriateness to philosophy of the topics, and the quality of the discussion. But there is a fifth aspect of good philosophy. It provides a *viewpoint* and makes you *see* things in a different way. Philosophy is not all argument. The viewpoints need not be based on argument. But arguments will be needed for defending, clarifying, and expanding the viewpoints, and this is just what Gandhi provided.

A *sixth* feature belongs only to *some* philosophy: that the viewpoints may be *organized*. This is very marked in Aristotle and the Stoics, very much less present in Plato's depiction of Socrates, while Plato himself might be seen as intermediate. In Gandhi I see his ideas as clustered around at least six pillars: nonviolence as love; insistence on truth; *moksha* or spiritual liberation; emotional detachment; the importance of the individual; and the importance of individual differences.

A *seventh* philosophical feature of Gandhi's work is the *interconnectedness within ethics* of different topics. We have seen that his views on emotional detachment raised problems about the treatment of family and the engagement in politics. We have also seen that the emotional detachment gave Gandhi a kind of freedom, and that this freedom was in turn necessary for practicing nonviolent resistance. The freedom, and hence the nonviolent resistance, depended, he thought, on celibacy and severely restricted property. Belief in nonviolence was a major reason for emphasizing duties over rights. Universal love or good will, though prized for itself, was also an important instrument in the political success of nonviolent resistance. In this role, it connected with the insistence on truth. The good will, combined with self-sacrifice, was intended to "open the ears" of opponents and lead them to a truthful dialogue. The insistence on truth was also required for learning to listen to the voice of conscience. The recognition that one does not know all the truth about others was a reason for telling others to consult their own consciences about their duties. Ignorance of the truth was also a reason for avoiding violent methods of reform and for other cautions—caution about calling on others to sacrifice themselves, or about punishing others for breaches rather than atoning for misdirecting them. Ignorance was again one of the reasons for hesitating to offer genuinely universal moral rules, although this was also based on belief in the individual and in individual differences.

So far all the examples have been drawn from ethics. But an *eighth* mark of philosophy is the *interconnection of issues across the whole of philosophy*. It is very difficult to write ethical philosophy without taking a view on matters other than ethics: on the nature of the world, of our knowledge of it and of the human mind. Gandhi is no exception. He treats this wider range of subjects, and this interconnectedness across philosophy is a further philosophical feature of his work. He has views on fallibility and infallibility, on physical and spiritual causation (redemption of others through prayer, persuasion through personal chastity), on human psychological capacities, on the soul, on past and future lives, and on God.

GANDHI'S LAPSES FROM HIS IDEALS

Another issue I raised in the introduction was how far Gandhi lived up to his ideals. Some of the ideals themselves are unappealing to many of us, for example those concerning the sacrifice of family and the testing of celibacy. But as regards the ideals we may admire, there were surely lapses in living up to them. So far I have said only that he lived up to his ideals to a surprising extent. That is not the impression that one would derive from a summary of his actions and the situations in which he acted. My view on his comparative consistency depended on looking beyond actions and situations to his *ideals*, which would not necessarily appear on the surface at the moment he was acting. They were worked out in more reflective moments through voluminous discussions. They were often very unexpected and developed in subtle ways. I have repeatedly argued that, when his underlying philosophy is taken into account, he was not the inconsistent politician that he appeared to many of his political opponents. To recall but one example, it should not be thought inconsistent of Gandhi to impose his own ideals only on some people, not on others. His ban on violent self-defense was a counsel of perfection. It could not always be attained; it should not be imposed on those in different situations from his own, or with different capacities, or even on those who did not agree with it. His belief in *svadharma*, differences of individual duty, would preclude this. Exploring the philosophy reveals more of the consistency in his life.

But now I would add a further consideration. I have mentioned in passing some examples of Gandhi's possible lapses, and there are others, of which much has sometimes been made. I have elsewhere described a case of wishful thinking, when a major supporter, Mr. Birla, was forced to correct Gandhi's denial that his campaign against machine-made cloth had caused violence. It had led to cloth burning at Mr. Birla's own factories.[2] In that case, his expectations of nonviolence, if correctly reported, were entirely unrealistic. It maybe asked whether the violence provoked by his Quit India campaign was not easily foreseeable,[3] and whether his Poona Pact, agreed in the context of his otherwise fasting to death, was the result of coercion rather than of true dialogue. A recent case study has treated as coercion Gandhi's insistence on his wife relinquishing her gold necklace.[4] I have mentioned also his criticizing himself for anger, and, unsurprisingly, he had periods of despondency. Some of these examples, if confirmed, might reveal a pattern to his lapses: coercion, self-deception about nonviolence, certain types of mood. Some of the lapses were serious. But it needs to be considered how much can be made of them in the context of Gandhi as a whole. The further point that needs to be made is that he adopted his values in the first place as goals somewhat too high to reach, in order deliberately to raise his sights. That is the context in which his lapses should be considered. The Stoic school could have benefited if it had taken seriously this ex-

2. Richard Sorabji, *Opening Doors: The Untold Story of Cornelia Sorabji*, London and Delhi, 2010, pp. 343–47.

3. For confessions of a violent attitude even among his closest followers, see Thakkar and Mehta, *Understanding Gandhi*, pp. 370, 455–56. For a striking interpretation of his intention in Quit India I am indebted to Tapan Raychaudhuri and his moving account in *The World in Our Time*, HarperCollins, Noida, India, 2001, p. 139: with Gandhi in prison, a regional committee authorized the destruction of government property—railway lines and post offices—so long as there was no violence against persons.

4. Vinit Haksar, *Rights, Communities and Disobedience*, 2nd ed., Delhi 2001, pp. 190–98.

planation of the failure to realize its ideals. But the early members stressed too much the equal viciousness of all that fell short of perfection.

While still discussing Gandhi's ideals—and I shall return to them—I should acknowledge again that I have concentrated on the Western analogues and influences, because these are the ones I know better. But inevitably Indian influences have also emerged. There was the Bhagavadgita, *brahmacharya* with its celibacy and the expectation of consequent spiritual power, reincarnation, *moksha* or spiritual liberation, the indescribable Brahman, Harishchandra's willingness to sacrifice his dearest, and the Jain doctrine of *anekântavâda*, or multiple partial perspectives on the truth. I do not know whether to call his insistence on truth (*satyagraha*) an Indian product or something of his own.

GANDHI'S PHILOSOPHICAL METHOD AS DISTANCING HIM FROM MOST OTHER PHILOSOPHERS

I want to finish with a point that again relates to the introduction. The evidence I first cited there for Gandhi's philosophical credentials was his subjection of his views to criticism. I said that he took this further than any philosopher I had encountered. But when one considers the details of how he sought criticism, a startling difference emerges from other philosophers. I am indebted to Bhikhu Parekh for pointing out to me this difference. The very same method of seeking criticism that Gandhi used for refining his ethical policies not only helped to confirm his philosophical credentials, but also, paradoxically distanced him from most other philosophers.

Gandhi refined his ethical policies by *experimenting* in problematic situations. Not only that, but his experiments were *public* and *shared*. We have encountered examples in his views on killing dangerous animals. He asked his ashram to discuss how to deal in an ethical way with the monkeys that were stealing their crops, and then he acted on the agreed policy. That was an experiment, but it did not stop with bringing in the members of his ashram. He then published the experimental results to his vast readership, so that they too were invited to comment. When he announced to that readership his support for the killing of stray dogs, their criticisms were vehement, and he published them with thoughtful answers in which his views were expanded in order to deal with the newly encountered issue. We can see him, in the light of the public discussion, adding an extra criterion of nonviolence as an additional safeguard—without retracting his original criterion. Such an expansion of his thought, incidentally, is not an inconsistency in any undesirable sense, but a proper stage in approximation to the truth.[5] What is now of interest is that the approximation was the result of *public* discussion of an *actual* situation.

It is important to see at what stage Gandhi involved the public. They were not the source of his nonviolent ideals. He acquired those ideals not from the public, but from reading Tolstoy, who wrote in the ancient Christian tradition. His experiments and appeals to the public served the purpose not of *acquiring* his nonviolent ideals, but of learning how to *apply* them. He did not involve the public at the stage when he was reading Tolstoy. He first involved them by publishing Tolstoy, and *teaching* them the values that he endorsed. He involved them again much later—and we can see why it made sense for him to do so—when he ran into difficult decisions about *applying* Tolstoyan values. He wanted to learn by refining his conclusions, but he also still wanted to teach and to refine the attitudes of the public. This was one more example of his insistence on truth (*satyagraha*).

This may help us to see whether any other philosophers were like Gandhi. The value of debate for discovering the truth would have been common ground with Socrates, Plato, and Aristotle, although their debates were with single individuals or with members of a philosophical school, rather than with the general public. The importance of engaging in public life was also common ground with the Stoics. But what parallels were there for refining the ethical policies of oneself and others on the basis of experiments or decisions on real-life situations? We might think of the Cynic school in which the founder of Stoicism, Zeno, first studied. Diogenes the Cynic experimented by living in an empty wine jar instead of a house, and his protégé Crates, the teacher of Zeno, experimented, according to tradition, by throwing his money into the sea. They were both experimenting in living naturally instead of artificially. Moreover Diogenes' eccentricities were the talk of Athens, and the subject of public criticism. One difference, however, from Gandhi is that Diogenes did not expect to learn anything from the public, but criticized their conventional ways with sharp and witty repartee. His belief in living a natural life did not come from them, and neither did their criticism refine the application of his views. His hope was rather to teach them something. The Roman philosophers can also be seen as experimenting in real-life situations. The aristocratic assassins of the tyrant Julius Caesar, Brutus and Cassius, had to square the tyrannicide with their various philosophical views, even if Brutus should be reassigned from the Stoic to

5. Even for his change in support for British war efforts, he provided a persuasive rationale: see chapter 4.

the Platonist tradition.[6] As the Roman Republic crumbled and was replaced by empire, the very public insistence on rectitude of Cato the Stoic and of later Stoics involved experimental confrontation with rulers in real-life situations, and was cited in order to teach others. But the public experimentation was not used by these Stoics to refine the application of their values. The experimentation constituted an application on which they decided for themselves without reference to the public.

Gandhi, then, seems to have been offering something unique, and this confirms what might have been expected. In speaking of his "experiments on ancient values" and of the exceptional extent of his search for criticism, I was thinking of him as having something unusual to offer. It has now become clearer why and at what point he engaged in experiments, and why and at what point he invited public criticism, not only in order to teach, but also in order to learn how to refine the views he already had.

6. So David Sedley, "The Ethics of Brutus and Cassius," *Journal of Roman Studies* 87, 1997, pp. 41–53.

SELECT BIBLIOGRAPHY

GANDHI: PRIMARY SOURCES

Works of Gandhi

The Collected Works of Mahatma Gandhi. These are available in two 100-volume series, one electronic and searchable, but with disputed differences of content, and different volume and page numbers. I have cited, where I could, the original printed version (cited as *CW*), Navajivan Publishing, Ahmedabad, 1955; an inexpensive new edition (with different pagination) is due out. The electronic edition (cited as *eCW*) is available on a CD ROM, which is hard to obtain, and is also currently on line at http://www.gandhiserve.org/cwmg/cwmg.html, which makes it for the time being more accessible.

M. K. Gandhi, *Ashram Observances in Action*, Ahmedabad 1955, from ms. of 1932.

M. K. Gandhi, *An Autobiography, or The Story of My Experiments with Truth* (cited as *Autobiography*), translated from 2 vols. of Gujarati by Mahadev Desai, Ahmedabad 1927 and 1929, Harmondsworth 1982.

M. K. Gandhi, *Discourses on the "Gita,"* Feb–Nov 1926, *CW*, vol. 32, also published as M. K. Gandhi, *The Bhagavadgita*, Orient Paperbacks, Delhi 1980.

M. K. Gandhi, *The Gita according to Gandhi*, translated by Mahadev Desai, from Gandhi's Gujarati translation of the *Bhagavadgita*, Ahmedabad 1946.

M. K. Gandhi, *Hind Swaraj* (*Indian Home Rule*) Gujarati 1909, English 1910; in *Hind Swaraj and Other Writings* (cited as *Hind Swaraj*), ed. Anthony J. Parel, Cambridge 1997.

M. K. Gandhi, "Is this humanity?,"1926, in Mahadev Desai, *Day to Day with Gandhi*, vol. 8.

M. K. Gandhi, *Sarvodaya* (Advancement of all), 9 articles in *Indian Opinion*, 16 April–18 July 1908, repr. in Iyer, *Writings*, vol. 3, pp. 410–32.

M. K. Gandhi, *Satyagraha in South Africa*, Ahmedabad 1928, 2nd ed. 1950.

M. K. Gandhi, "Story of a *satyagrahi*," in *Indian Opinion*, 1908, reprinted in *CW*, vol. 8, between pp. 173 and 229.

Mahatma Gandhi, *Non-violent Resistance* (*Satyagraha*), New York 1961 (an anthology).

Harijan, one of Gandhi's English language newspapers from 1933.

Young India, one of Gandhi's English language newspapers from 1919.

Mahadev Desai, *Day to Day with Gandhi* (cited as *Day to Day*), 2nd ed., 9 vols. (Varanasi 1968–73). The diary of Mahadev Desai, Gandhi's secretary from 1917 to 1942, translated from the Gujarati, with Gandhi's words in English.

Gopalkrishna Gandhi, ed., *The Oxford India Gandhi: Essential Writings* (cited as Gopalkrishna Gandhi, *Essential Writings*), New Delhi 2008.

R. Iyer, ed., *The Moral and Political Writings of Mahatma Gandhi*, 3 vols, (cited as Iyer, *Writings*) Oxford University Press 1986–87. This is the fullest collection of his philosophical writing.

R. Iyer, ed., *The Essential Writings of Mahatma Gandhi* (cited as Iyer, *Essential Writings*), a one-volume abridgement, Ahmedabad 1990, Delhi 1993.

Nilam Parikh, *Gandhi Wrote to His Sons and Daughters-in-Law "Be Fragrant Wherever You Be."* Delhi 2008.

D. G. Tendulkar, *Mahatma*, 8 vols., Delhi 1951–54.

Modern Writers in the Christian Tradition

Ruskin, *Unto This Last*, 1862.

Thoreau, *Civil Disobedience*, 1848.

Thoreau, *Walden*, 1854.

Tolstoy, *The Kingdom of God Is Within You*, 1893, translated by Constance Garnett, New York 1894 (citations from the Dover Books reprint of 2006) and by Aylmer Maude, Oxford University Press, London, 1935.

Tolstoy, *The Kreutzer Sonata and Other Stories*, Oxford 1998, including afterword.

Tolstoy, *Letter to a Hindoo*, 1908.

Tolstoy, *Slavery of Our Times*, 1890.

GANDHI: SECONDARY SOURCES

Aditya Adankar, "Karna's choice: courage and character in the face of an ethical dilemma," in T. S. Rukmani, ed., *The Mahabharata: Whatever Is Not Here Is Nowhere Else*, New Delhi 2005, ch. 9.

Akeel Bilgrami, "Gandhi the philosopher," on his website and in *Economic and Political Weekly*, 38, 2003, 4159–65.

Margaret Bourke-White, *Interview with Gandhi*, Travel Book Club, London 1951.

Judith Brown, "Gandhi and civil resistance in India 1917–47: key issues," in Adam Roberts and Timothy Garton Ash, eds., *Civil Resistance and Power Politics*, 2009, ch. 3, pp. 43–57.

Judith Brown, "Gandhi and human rights: in search of true humanity," in Anthony J. Parel, ed., *Gandhi, Freedom and Self-Rule*, Lanham, Md. 2000.

Margaret Chatterjee, *Gandhi's Diagnostic Approach Rethought*, Delhi 2007.

Margaret Chatterjee, *Gandhi's Religious Thought* (cited as Chatterjee, *Religious Thought*), Notre Dame 1983.

Candulal Bhagubhai Dalal, *Harilal Gandhi*, translated into English by Tridip Suhrud, Orient Longman, Hyderabad, 2007.

Faisal Devji, *The Terrorist in Search of Humanity*, London 2008.

Rajmohan Gandhi, *Mohandas: A True Story of a Man, His People and an Empire*, Delhi 2006.

Ashoka Gupta, *In the Path of Service*, Kolkata 2008.

Vinit Haksar, *Rights, Communities and Disobedience*, 2nd ed., Delhi 2001.

R. Iyer, *The Moral and Political Thought of Mahatma Gandhi* (cited as Iyer, *Thought*), Delhi 1973.

Martin Luther King, *Stride Toward Freedom*, New York 1958.

Carl Olsen, *Celibacy and Religious Traditions*, Oxford 2008.

Bhikhu Parekh, *Colonialism, Tradition and Reform*, rev. ed., New Delhi 1999.

Bhikhu Parekh, *Gandhi's Political Philosophy* (cited as Parekh, *Political Philosophy*), Notre Dame 1989.

Anthony J. Parel, ed., *Gandhi, Freedom and Self-Rule*, Lanham, Md. 2000.

Anthony J. Parel, *Gandhi's Philosophy and the Quest for Harmony*, Cambridge 2006.

Adam Roberts and Timothy Garton Ash, eds., *Civil Resistance and Power Politics*, Oxford 2009.

Gene Sharp, *The Politics of Nonviolent Action*, Boston 1973, later published as 3 volumes (*Power and Struggle, The Methods of Nonviolent Action, The Dynamics of Nonviolent Action*) and *Waging Nonviolent Struggle*, Boston 2005.

Cornelia Sorabji, interview with Gandhi, *Atlantic Monthly* April 1932, pp. 453–58, narrated in Richard Sorabji, *Opening Doors*, London and New Delhi 2010, pp. 343–47.

Richard Sorabji, *Opening Doors: The Untold Story of Cornelia Sorabji, Reformer, Lawyer and Champion of Women's Rights in India*, London and New Delhi 2010, chs. 20 and 21.

Usha Thakkar and Jayshree Mehta, eds., *Understanding Gandhi: Gandhians in Conversation with Fred J. Blum*, Delhi 2011.

THE STOICS: SECONDARY SOURCES

Mark Alfano, "A genealogy of the conscience of the consequentialists," M.A. dissertation, CUNY Graduate Center, 2009.

Mark Alfano, "Gyges in the Panopticon: an empirical investigation of social distance heuristics," submitted for publication, 2010.

Julia Annas, *The Morality of Happiness*, Oxford 1993.

Shadi Bartsch, *The Mirror of the Self*, Chicago 2006.

Isaiah Berlin, "The birth of Greek individualism," in Isaiah Berlin, *Liberty*, ed. Henry Hardy, Oxford 2002, pp. 287–321 (the first of three Storrs lectures given at Yale in 1962 as "Three turning-points in political thought," and originally called, "the Greeks," first published by Henry Hardy in *Common Knowledge* 7, 1998, 187–214, as "A turning-point in political thought," and reprinted in *Liberty*).

Edwyn Bevan, *Stoics and Sceptics*, Oxford 1913.

Tad Brennan, "Reservation in Stoic ethics," *Archiv für Geschichte der Philosophie* 82, 2000, 149–77.

Charles Brittain, "Rationality, rules and rights," *Apeiron* 34, 2001, 247–66.

Jacques Brunschwig, "Sur deux notions de l'éthique stoïcienne: de la 'réserve' au 'renversement,'" in G. Rhomeyer-Dherbey and J-B. Gourinet, *Les Stoïciens*, Paris 2005, pp. 149–77.

Peter Brunt, "Stoicism and the Principate," *Papers of the British School at Rome*, 43, 1975, 7–35.

Myles Burnyeat, "Did the ancient Greeks have the concept of human rights?," *Polis* 13, 1994, 1–11

M. Colish, *The Stoic Tradition from Antiquity to the Early Middle Ages*, Leiden 1985.

M. H. Fisch, "Alexander and the Stoics," part 4, *American Journal of Philology*, 58, 1937, 129–44.

Christopher Gill, "Peace of mind and being yourself: Panaetius to Plutarch," in *Aufstieg und Niedergang der römischen Welt* part 2, vol. 36, no. 7, pp. 4599–4640.

Marie-Odile Goulet-Cazé, *Les Kynica du stoïcisme*, Stuttgart 2003.

Miriam Griffin, "Political thought in the age of Nero," *Neronia VI, Rome a l'époque néronienne*, Collection Latomus 268, 2002, pp. 325–37.

Miriam Griffin, *Seneca: A Philosopher in Politics*, Oxford 1976, 2nd ed. 1991.

Miriam Griffin, "Seneca's pedagogic strategy: *Letters* and *de beneficiis*," in Richard Sorabji and Robert W. Sharples, eds., Greek and Roman Philosophy 100 BC–200 AD, *Supplement to the Bulletin of the Institute of Classical Studies*, 94, 2007, vol. 1, pp. 89–113.

Brad Inwood, "Rules and reasoning in Stoic ethics," in Katerina Ierodiakonou, ed., *Topics in Stoic Philosophy*, Oxford 1999, ch. 4, pp. 95–127.

Brad Inwood and Lloyd Gerson, trans., *The Stoics Reader*, Indianapolis 2008.

A. A. Long, "Stoic philosophers on persons, property ownership and community," in Richard Sorabji, ed., *Aristotle and After*, supplement 68 to the *Bulletin of the Institute of Classical Studies*, 1997, ch. 2, 13–32.

A. A. Long and D. N. Sedley, *The Hellenistic Philosophers*, vol. 1, chs. 26–67, Cambridge 1987.

Syed Mohamed Mehdi, "The Political Dimension of the Contemplative Life: Engagement and Disengagement in Plato, Seneca and Gandhi," Ph.D. dissertation, McGill University 2007.

Phillip Mitsis, "The early Stoic theory of natural law," in K. Boudouris, ed., *Hellenistic Philosophy*, Athens 1993–94, vol. 2, pp. 130–40.

Phillip Mitsis, "Moral rules and the aims of Stoic ethics," *Journal of Philosophy* 83, 1986, 556–58.

Phillip Mitsis, "Natural law and natural right in post-Aristotelian philosophy," in *Aufstieg und Niedergang der römischen Welt*, part 2, vol. 36, no. 7, Berlin 1994, 4812–50.

Phillip Mitsis, "Seneca on reason, rules and moral development," in Jacques Brunschwig, Martha Nussbaum, eds, *Passions and Perceptions*, Cambridge 1993, Ch 10, pp. 285–312.

Phillip Mitsis, "The Stoic origin of natural rights," in Katerina Ierodiakonou, ed., *Topics in Stoic Philosophy*, Oxford 1999, ch. 6, pp. 153–77.

Phillip Mitsis, "The Stoics and Aquinas on virtue and natural law," *Studia Philonica Annual*, 15, 2003, 35–53.

Phillip Mitsis, "The Stoics on property and politics," *Southern Journal of Philosophy*, 43, 2005, 230–49.

Phillip Mitsis and J. de Filippo, in Paul Vander Waerdt, ed., *The Socratic Movement*, Ithaca, N.Y. 1994, pp. 252–71.

Tapan Raychaudhuri, *The World in Our Time*, Noida, India 2011, ch. 8.

Malcolm Schofield, "Epictetus on Cynicism," in Theodore Scaltsas and Andrew Mason, eds., *The Philosophy of Epictetus*, Oxford 2007, pp. 71–86.

Malcolm Schofield, *Saving the City*, London 1999

Malcolm Schofield, *The Stoic Idea of the City*, Cambridge 1991.

Malcolm Schofield, "The syllogisms of Zeno of Citium," *Phronesis* 28, 1983, 31–58.

David Sedley, "The ethics of Brutus and Cassius," *Journal of Roman Studies* 87, 1997, 41–53.

David Sedley "The Stoic-Platonist debate on *kathêkonta*," in Katerina Ierodiakonou, ed., *Topics in Stoic Philosophy*, Oxford 1999, pp. 128–52.

John Sellars, *The Art of Living: The Stoics on the Nature and Function of Philosophy*, Aldershot 2003.

John Sellars, "Stoic cosmopolitanism and Zeno's *Republic*," *History of Political Thought* 28, 2007, 1–29.

Richard Sorabji, *Animal Minds and Human Morals*, London 1993.

Richard Sorabji, *Emotion and Peace of Mind: From Stoic Agitation to Christian Temptation*, Oxford 2000.

Richard Sorabji, "Graeco-Roman origins of the idea of moral conscience," *Studia Patristica*, 44, 2010, 361–83.

Richard Sorabji, "'Moral conscience': contributions to the idea in Plato and Platonism," in Vassilis Karasmanis and Arnold Hermann, eds., *The Presocratics and Plato: A Festschrift for Charles Kahn*, Las Vegas 2012.

Richard Sorabji, *Self: Ancient and Modern Insights about Individuality, Life, and Death*, Oxford and Chicago 2006.

Richard Sorabji, "Stoic reservation in wants and expectations: a footnote on its logic," in Katerina Ierodiakonou and Ben Morison, eds., *Epistêmê, etc*, Brill Leiden, 2011.

Richard Sorabji and David Rodin, eds., *The Ethics of War: Shared Problems in Different Traditions*, Aldershot 2006.

Richard Sorabji and R. W. Sharples, eds., *Greek and Roman Philosophy 100 BC–200 AD*, *Bulletin of the Institute of Classical Studies*, suppl. 94, 2007.

J. B. Stockdale, "Testing Epictetus' doctrines in a laboratory of human behaviour," *Bulletin of the Institute of Classical Studies*, 40, 1995, 1–13.

Gisela Striker, "Following nature: a study in Stoic ethics," *Oxford Studies in Ancient Philosophy* 9, 1991, 1–73

Paul Vander Waerdt, "The Stoic Theory of Natural Law," Ph.D. diss. Princeton 1989, esp. pp. 18–28, 270–83.

Paul Vander Waerdt, "Philosophical influence on Roman jurisprudence? The case of Stoicism and natural law," *Aufstieg und Niedergang der römischen Welt*, part 2, vol. 36, no. 7, Berlin 1994, pp. 4851–4895.

Katja Vogt, *Law, Reason and the Cosmic City*, Oxford 2008.

Peter Winch, "The universalisability of moral judgement," *Monist* 49, 1965, 196–214.

INDEX